The Real Peace Process

Religion and Violence

Series Editors
Lisa Isherwood, University of Winchester, and Rosemary Radford Ruether,
Graduate Theological Union, Berkeley, California

This interdisciplinary and multicultural series brings to light the ever increasing problem of religion and violence. The series will highlight how religions have a significant part to play in the creation of cultures that allow and even encourage the creation of violent conflict, domestic abuse and policies and state control that perpetuate violence to citizens.

The series will highlight the problems that are experienced by women during violent conflict and under restrictive civil policies. But not wishing to simply dwell on the problems the authors in this series will also re-examine the traditions and look for alternative and more empowering readings of doctrine and tradition. One aim of the series is to be a powerful voice against creeping fundamentalisms and their corrosive influence on the lives of women and children.

Published:

Reweaving the Relational Mat
A Christian Response to Violence against Women from Oceania
Joan Alleluia Filemoni-Tofaeono and Lydia Johnson

Weep Not for Your Children: Essays on Religion and Violence
Edited by Lisa Isherwood and Rosemary Radford Ruether

In Search of Solutions: The Problem of Religion and Conflict
Clinton Bennett

America, Amerikkka: Elect Nation and Imperial Violence
Rosemary Radford Ruether

Shalom/Salaam/Peace: A Liberation Theology of Hope in Israel/Palestine
Constance A. Hammond

Faith-Based War
From 9/11 to Catastrophic Success in Iraq
T. Walter Herbert

Forthcoming:

A Cry for Dignity
Religion, Violence and the Struggle of Dalit Women in India
Mary Grey

Edith Stein and Regina Jonas
Religious Visionaries in the Time of the Death Camps
Emily Leah Silverman

US War-Culture, Sacrifice and Salvation
Kelly Denton-Borhaug

The Real Peace Process
Worship, Politics and the End of Sectarianism

Siobhán Garrigan

LONDON   OAKVILLE

Published by Equinox Publishing Ltd.

UK: 1 Chelsea Manor Studios, Flood Street, London, SW3 5SR
USA: DBBC, 28 Main Street, Oakville, CT 06779

www.equinoxpub.com

First published 2010

British Library Cataloguing-in-Publication Data
A catalogue record for this book is available from the British Library.

ISBN-13   978 184553 693 0   (hardback)
          978 184553 694 7   (paperback)

Library of Congress Cataloging-in-Publication Data

Garrigan, Siobhán.
    The real peace process : worship, politics, and the end of sectarianism / Siobhán Garrigan.
      p. cm. — (Religion and violence)
    Includes bibliographical references (p.) and index.
      ISBN 978-1-84553-693-0 (hb) — ISBN 978-1-84553-694-7 (pbk.) 1.
Christian sociology — Ireland. 2. Public worship — Social aspects — Ireland. 3. Peace — Religious aspects — Christianity. 4. Catholic Church — Relations — Protestant churches. 5. Protestant churches — Relations — Catholic Church. 6. Ireland — Religious life and customs. I. Title.
BR793.G27 2010
264.009416'090511 — dc22
                         2009046769

Typeset by S.J.I. Services, New Delhi
Printed and bound in Great Britain by Lightning Source UK Ltd, Milton Keynes

For my parents,
Phil and Tony Garrigan

CONTENTS

ACKNOWLEDGEMENTS

According to Jeffrey Eugenides, 'No one is waiting for you to write your first book. No one cares if you finish it. But after your first, everyone seems to be waiting. You go from having nothing to lose to having everything to lose.' This is my second book. In the time between researching the first and publishing the second I have had the chance to become a theologian, something that has happened due only to a great deal of help. So I wholeheartedly thank those whose waiting for this second book was a burden to me, those who have encouraged me, bolstered me and cajoled me — they have confirmed in me a sense that there is, indeed, something at risk and, despite the concomitant panic, I am truly grateful.

To the students, staff and faculty of Yale University's Divinity School and Institute of Sacred Music, and to all who have worshipped in Marquand Chapel: thank you. Thank you also to the members of the critical theory seminar at the North American Academy of Liturgy who offered feedback on early drafts, particularly Bruce Morrill and Jim Farwell. And for inspiration on this theme over many years, thank you to Tim Gorringe, Nathan Mitchell, Colin Graham, Selina Guinness, Gary Hastings and Catríona Hastings.

My profound thanks go to those whose comments on this manuscript made it less flawed than it nonetheless remains and more interesting than it once was: particularly and especially to Sinéad Garrigan Mattar, Ludger Viefhues-Bailey and Phil Garrigan, but also and very much to Emilie Townes, Charbel Mattar, Christiana Peppard, Graham Ward, Scott Dolff, Melanie Ross, Ron Grimes, Dale Martin, Peter Heltzel, Jennifer Todd and Yvonne Naylor. I also give great thanks to those whose love, cooking or consolation were vital to this book's production: Patrick Evans especially, and Alice Lyons, Roz Meyer, Meike Blackwell, Montana

Peppard, Kevin Bailey, Ian Stevens, Molly Wheeler, and my family —
Tony, Phil, Owen, Catherine, Christine, Sinéad, Charlie, Orla, Ellie,
Paddy and Sasha.

My final thanks go to my parents, to whom this book is dedicated.
Being raised in their care has been the great blessing of my life.
It has also inspired the hope that ultimately lies at the heart of
this book: that we can love one another, even amid irreducible
differences.

PREFACE

'The Northern Ireland peace process has transformed a violent conflict into a cold peace.'[1]

My parents spent their honeymoon in Northern Ireland in August of 1968. It seemed a perfect recreational point between wedding celebrations with family in Corby, Liverpool and Cornamona (Co. Galway). In July of the following summer, I was born. In August of 1970 came my brother, Owen, and two years later we were joined by our sister, Sinéad. Finally, in May of 1974, Paddy arrived and, through the Spring of 1975, the family planned its first summer holiday. Our trajectory would be a lot like the honeymoon, starting with a trip to the Morans in Corby, followed by the Garrigans seeing us off at Liverpool docks before the long trip west in the Maxi, where we would eventually be stitched back together by the soft accents, brown bread and kind ways of the people in Cornamona. Never once did it seem that Northern Ireland would be a perfect recreational point en route. The honeymoon, such as it had been, was as over for the North as it was for my parents.[2]

In 1993, I headed up to Belfast on the bus from Dublin with my American Mennonite boyfriend. We were in Belfast to explore the possibility of setting up an Emmaus community, a multi-faith intentional community of formerly homeless people like the one

1. Jonathan Tonge, *The New Northern Irish Politics?* (New York, NY: Palgrave Macmillan, 2005), p. 1.
2. 'From August 1969 to the end of 1972, Northern Ireland experienced its worst period of violence since the 1920s. Those three years saw some of the most grisly killings of the conflict. ... Vigilantes on both sides were involved in an orgy of slaughter, and many innocent people who strayed into enemy territory were abducted, tortured and murdered.' Martin Dillon, *God and the Gun* (London: Orion, 1997), p. 23. Although it must be noted that from 1920–1968 could hardly be described as bucolic. See, M. Farrell, *Northern Ireland: The Orange State* (London: Pluto Press, 1976).

we ran in Coventry, England, and we soon realized that either this was just not the right time or we were just not the right people for the job. He was a Protestant. I was a Catholic. It was therefore hard to find accommodation, and harder to find food. We were told that pubs and chippers were either Protestant or Catholic, and we worried so much about which to go to that we ended up going to none. Fifteen years later, Belfast city is like almost any other European city: restaurants, hotels and entertainment spaces abound and in none of them are you at any more risk of being bombed to bits than anywhere else in the world. There are even multi-faith non-profit organizations.

Relief has come to many former sites of bitter civic conflict in this same period. The notorious Chilean torture chambers of Villa Grimaldi are now a peace park, Desmond Tutu's daughter now runs 'pilgrimages' to Robben Island and other sites of Black oppression in South Africa,[3] and my brother-in-law, giving a Lieder concert with his pianist sister, was welcomed back to his native Beirut after 35 years without any need for us to pray for his safety. Places that once witnessed some of the twentieth century's most atrocious violence now beckon calmly to lost children and tourist alike: welcome! Northern Ireland in general and Belfast in particular are just the same.[4] And so this book, which says, 'Hang on, we still have a problem and we need to address it' might seem like Cassandra in the midst of the spoils, or a begrudger among the boosters, as Roy Foster might have it.[5]

Let me say from the outset, therefore, that I rejoice wholeheartedly that paramilitary (and state-sanctioned) violence in Northern Ireland is effectively consigned to history, and I give thanks daily not just for the ceasefires, but also for the unprecedented and productive levels of civic co-operation. These are things most people around me believed they would never see in their lifetimes, even as they also prayed for them fervently, and it is a great mercy and a sheer delight to see them. That we can begin to think about a 'real peace' has been made possible by those who ended the armed conflict and created fairer civic structures.

3. See: www.tutuinstitute.org

4. The official tourism website for Belfast calls it: 'A young, lively city with a vibrant nightlife.' See: www.gotobelfast.com

5. R.F. Foster, *Luck and the Irish: A Brief History of Social Change c.1970–2000* (London: Penguin, 2007).

My concern is simply that we not pretend that the peace that we have is all the peace that we need. Implementation of the *Good Friday Agreement* (GFA)[6] has stopped the war on Northern Irish and British streets; but inevitably, in its mandate to deal with political processes and decommissioning, it has not addressed one of the most important ingredients of the conflict: religion. On this island in which religion and politics have been negatively mixed for centuries, the politics are now at last being fixed, but religion is not. Contrary to popular perception, the two are not separable: in an Irish context, religion and politics are the warp and weft of the same piece of cloth. So to be renovating one while leaving the other unexamined not only limits us to a 'cold' peace, but presages the inevitable deterioration of the fabric within the foreseeable future.

Imagining the situation analogically, the signing of the GFA was to life beyond its implementation as a wedding is to marriage. The planning for, and the work involved in sustaining a marriage is quite different from the sorts of activities involved in planning a wedding; moreover, the marriage brings all sorts of challenges no one could possibly have foreseen at the wedding. By extension, then, the GFA required all sorts of plans and arrangements, but the peace (how we live, now) requires a new set of attitudes and behaviours. This is where religious practices take on a new relevance because if only politics and not religion have been 'peace–processed', then religion might, not too long from now, sabotage this precious peace unless we submit it, too, to a peace-process.

In a recent argument about the religious identity of schools, the chief executive of Northern Ireland Integrated Schools put it like this:

> No matter how awe-inspiring the edifice we construct, when the seismic wave of underlying sectarianism and bigotry comes again, it will collapse. It seems we are being asked to accept a form of co-existence which, at best, is tenuous and at worst, will inevitably pursue the 'equal and separate' policies of America in the 1950s. Such policies will build on the default of division and could lead to the consolidation of difference.[7]

6. The Agreement (also known as the Good Friday Agreement or Belfast Agreement) was reached in Belfast on Friday, 10 April 1998. It is available online at www.nio.gov.uk/the-agreement
7. Michael Wardlaw, 'Building a new way of being together through integration', *The Irish Times*, Tuesday, 26 August 2008, p. 13.

In this book I explore some of the ways in which religion in Ireland and Northern Ireland contributes to 'the default of division', and how it is already implicated in 'the consolidation of difference'. I argue that there may have been a peace process, and there may now be a power-sharing government and a new police force in Northern Ireland, but there will not be genuine peace until religious life on this island desists from its sectarian attitudes and practices.

The book is based on fieldwork research I undertook in churches across Northern Ireland and the Republic of Ireland between 2001 and 2008, but it also builds on two remarkable recent studies of Irish society: Joe Liechty and Cecelia Clegg's *Moving Beyond Sectarianism*[8] in the civic realm and Norman Porter's *The Elusive Quest: Reconciliation in Northern Ireland*[9] in the political realm. It suggests that for their visions of co-operative communities to come about, it will be necessary to take far greater account of actual, current, religious practices on this island, because those practices have a power that no amount of cross-community dialogue or political/economic reform can undo.

Current levels of peace in Northern Ireland, and between England and Ireland, will be undermined if communities do not address these practically-powerful, symbolic and ritual ways by which profound sectarian attitudes are reinforced in churches through their words, interactions, art, gestures and sounds. This book, therefore, focuses not on religion as a phenomenon, nor on its representative texts, but, instead, on worship. How we imagine life beyond the peace process (i.e., living in peace with people of other traditions) has a great deal to do with how we worship, because ritualization plays a such a pivotal role in shaping not just our religious imaginations and communal/self-images, but also our very bodies and behaviours. By focusing particularly on worship, I also argue that if religious practices were re-oriented toward reconciliation, social-political peace would be greatly aided and I suggest ways in which congregations might change their worship habits in order to direct them away from sectarianism and toward reconciliation.

8. Joseph Liechty and Cecilia Clegg, *Moving Beyond Sectarianism: Religion, Conflict and Reconciliation in Northern Ireland* (Dublin: Columba Press, 2001).

9. Norman Porter, *The Elusive Quest: Reconciliation in Northern Ireland* (Belfast: Blackstaff, 2003).

The book is structured in three parts, each composed of a couplet of chapters. The first two chapters set out the problem theoretically and theologically and they describe the interdisciplinary method (based in ritual studies) that I use to tackle them. The second part (Chapters Three and Four) interprets a wide range of observations made during fieldwork, and offers a brief analysis of many aspects of Christian worship in Ireland and Northern Ireland, such as the phrasing of prayers, how anniversaries are treated, whether flags are used, and how people greet one another. The third part, then, takes two focused observations and examines them in greater depth: Chapter Five departs from the multi-denominational remit of the rest of the book in order to interrogate the specifically Roman Catholic practice of sharing only the element of bread and not of wine during Eucharist. And Chapter Six asks why Irish and Northern Irish people do not sing inside church like they sing outside of it. A short essay concludes the book by offering some practical suggestions for those who plan, lead and participate in worship in Northern Ireland and the Republic of Ireland today.

The research presented in these six chapters suggests, in three different, complementary ways, the possibility that Christian worship can both generate and resist sectarian attitudes and affirm or deny sectarian practices, even when many of the people gathered have prayer to and praise of God as their only conscious intention. It must be emphasized that in all my research I have never heard a sermon exhort anyone to hatred or violence against the 'other' community; I have never heard prayers that prayed for another person's downfall; and I have sometimes heard prayers for 'our brothers and sisters in faith', as well as sermons that advocated non-violent attitudes. So I am absolutely not saying that all is lost, or wrong, or hateful in Irish worship—far from it.

What I am saying is that sectarianism, like racism and sexism, works 'behind our backs' and we need to pay greater attention to the ways it is working against our current great hopes for peace by operating behind our backs in church. My hope is that by drawing attention to what we are doing in church, and to the ways it is sabotaging our peaceful goals, we can change it; because for Christians a cold peace is not a real peace.

Chapter One

WORSHIP AND SECTARIANISM

'One's own sectarianism is the only kind one can necessarily do anything about.'[1]

It would be naïve to think that everyone who goes to church does so with the sole intention of praying for their enemies. However, most people walking through a church door in Ireland think that they are doing a good thing, and they are certainly not doing so out of a conscious desire to do anyone else harm. My argument in this book is not that people going to church or leading worship are consciously engaging in sectarian activities by doing so. On the contrary, people from a wide range of religious backgrounds pray for peace in their worship and go to church as a community-building activity with positive effects beyond their own small community.

My argument is, rather, that the worship practices of many communities, contrary to the conscious peace-commitments of their members, allow congregations to engage in a series of verbal and non-verbal interactions which play out (and thereby reinforce) division and express biases and stereotypes, which produce prejudice. A striking example of this gap between what congregants understand faith to be about and what worship is actually accomplishing in the world arose in several of the churches I visited: the sermon preached peace but no peace gesture was made when the conventional time for peace-passing came. This book will present many more examples; it will demonstrate how they are in fact related to the perpetuation of sectarian devices in social life; it will suggest what might be done instead (e.g., pass the peace!); and it will imagine what the effects of such actions might be.

This chapter will introduce the foundational aspects of the study, explaining why it examines the whole island of Ireland and not just

1. Joseph Liechty and Cecilia Clegg, *Moving Beyond Sectarianism: Religion, Conflict and Reconciliation in Northern Ireland* (Dublin: Columba Press, 2001), p. 18.

Northern Ireland; how sectarianism and its effects should be understood in this context; the extent to which religion is a factor in the Irish–British conflict; and the methodological and theoretical underpinnings of the research that forms the basis of this book. By the end of this chapter I hope it will be apparent why it is vital at this time to take full account of the role of religious practices, especially worship, in addressing sectarianism in Ireland. It should also be apparent why sectarianism is here treated as an all-island problem (and not one confined to 'the North'[2]), as well as why the study of religious habits can both shed light upon and offer a route beyond sectarian attitudes and practices.

The Geography of Irish Theology

I set as the scope of this book all of Ireland—Northern Ireland and the Republic of Ireland—because the four major churches on the island (Roman Catholic, Presbyterian Church in Ireland, Church of Ireland, and Methodist Church) are all-Ireland in their structures of governance, theological education and self-description. To delineate the study in this way is not to affirm implicitly a nationalist or Republican view of Irish identity, but rather to promote a view that can otherwise be denied in the Republic: that religion in the South has a direct relationship to the situation in the North and, furthermore, that its lines of responsibility and implication stretch to, and beyond, those borders. There is a tendency among residents of the Republic to perceive 'the Troubles' as having belonged to Northern Ireland alone, and for but a short period in the twentieth century, ignoring the view that they were the product of whole-country conflicts spanning several decades.[3] Confounding this perception is the psychological and attitudinal legacy of these conflicts (animosity, tribalism, segregation, sectarianism, ethnic

---

2. All language in Ireland is potentially implicated in nationalist/colonialist debates, and how one refers to the geography is a prime example. 'Northern Ireland' is the legally and internationally recognized name for the territory currently most commonly referred to in the Republic as 'the North' and occasionally as 'the six counties'. Throughout the rest of this book, except for particular reasons, I refer to it as 'Northern Ireland', because that is its name in international law. It is an imperfect solution to a complicated problem.

3. See, for example, Peter Hart, *The IRA and Its Enemies: Violence and Community in Cork, 1916–1923* (Oxford: Clarendon Press, 1998).

and religious hatred, etc.), which continue to be evident not just in Northern Ireland, but in the Republic too, albeit in sometimes subtle forms. One example would be how English-sounding accents are treated on the public service broadcaster Radio Telefís Éireann (RTÉ) — they are frequently ridiculed or stereotyped, and it is not usually seen as discriminatory.[4]

This study also takes an all-Ireland stance because although residents of the Republic have generally grown used to thinking of the violence as confined to Ulster, and to thinking of sectarianism as a Northern problem, the media has recently begun to confront the inaccuracy of such a worldview.[5] Several key studies have brought to light the ways in which Irish people in the Republic as well as in Northern Ireland habitually harbour sectarian thoughts as a fundamental part of their world-view, and have challenged the country to develop awareness of these attitudes, exploring both their histories and their consequences. For example, Geraldine Smyth (the long-serving and pioneering former Director of the Irish School of Ecumenics) insists that *all* of Ireland is implicated in both the problem *and* the task of recovery that lies ahead. Speaking about the novel *The God of Small Things*, she says that Arundhati Roy's description of post-colonial India,

> speaks to our condition in Ireland, North and South, as we experience the conflicting reactions to the dismantling of our own "History House" with all its embattled history, its mythic fascination and its restless train of never-satisfied ghosts. For those with a neurotic craving for order and security, resting inside the "History House", warmed by the influence of totalitarian

4. For example, serving as a judge for the *All Ireland Talent Show* on 25 January 2009, long-time RTÉ broadcaster Blathnaid Ní Chofaigh, stated that, 'Irish people find English accents irritating.' A complaint of discrimination made against RTÉ One was denied, and the remark was adjudicated to have been, 'off-the-cuff...good humoured and moderate', merely an 'expression of her own view', even if also 'inappropriate'. See: 'Complaints Decisions', Broadcasting Complaints Commission (Dublin, March 2009), Ref 39:09, p. 96.

5. For example, in the first two weeks of December 2006, RTÉ collaborated with some of Ireland's most respected academics to produce television programmes on sectarianism for its 'Hidden History' series. Reviewing the series, Eoghan Harris remarked that, 'RTÉ's Hidden History series has helped us face a hard fact... [it has] forced us to face the tribal roots of the Irish Republic. Contrary to some smug Southern assumptions...sectarianism was not confined to Northern Ireland.' *The Irish Independent* (Sunday 17 December 2006).

politics, "communalist" culture, or fundamentalist religious constructions can feel normal.[6]

Sectarian hatred is very much alive in the South, and it is the sibling, not the distant cousin, of that which is so much more apparent in the North. At the height of the hunger strike crisis (August 1981), the then *Toaiseach*,[7] Dr. Garret Fitzgerald, received substantial criticism for saying that the Irish state at that time, 'was not the non-sectarian state that the national movement for independence had sought to establish, one in which Catholic, Protestant and Dissenter would feel equally at home; it had rather become a state imbued with the ethos of the majority in our part of the island' (by which he meant the religious ethos of Roman Catholics). Considering the possibility of an all-Ireland republic of the sort for which successive historical figures in those movements for independence had fought, he lamented its unlikelihood under present circumstances, commenting that, 'If I were a Northern Protestant today, I cannot see how I could be attracted to getting involved with a state that is itself sectarian … [in] our laws and our constitution, our practices, our attitudes'.[8]

Some might think that the generation since the hunger strikes has seen an end to all that Fitzgerald was talking about, what with the changes to the constitution brought about by the removal of the bans on the availability of contraception and divorce in the 1990s, the crises of faith caused by the many scandals within the church, and the changing shape of religious identity in the Republic due to the demographics of new immigration.[9] For example, Roy Foster's

6. Geraldine T. Smyth, 'Envisaging a New Identity and a Common Home: Seeking Peace on Our Borders', *Milltown Studies* (Winter, 2000), pp. 58–84; 59.

7. Literally 'the Chief', the *Toaiseach* in Ireland is comparable to the Prime Minister in other democratic states.

8. Garret Fitzgerald, quoted in Enda McDonagh, 'Church–State Relations in Independent Ireland' in J.P. Mackey and E. McDonagh (eds.), *Religion and Politics in Ireland and the Turn of the Millennium* (Dublin: Columba Press, 2003), pp. 41–63; 51.

9. Tom Inglis argues that nowadays, 'Irish Catholics can attain status, honour and respect, and they can attain political, economic and social power, without having to have Catholic religious capital or to have their forms of capital symbolically legitimized by the Church.' *Moral Monopoly: The Catholic Church in Modern Irish Society* (Dublin: University College Dublin Press, 1998), p. 206. My question is, however, not so much whether Catholics have become 'more Protestant', as Inglis suggests, but whether Protestants (or others who

satirical synopsis of Ireland's embrace of modernity between 1970 and 2000 begins with this assessment: 'as Irish people turned away from the Church, they looked to another kind of miraculous intercession: the economy.'[10] However, even after many people have turned away from the church and toward other gods, the preamble to the constitution retains its Catholic-nationalist rhetoric,[11] the language of the constitution is still imbued with a Catholic 'ethos',[12] and, of direct relevance to this present study, the other things that Fitzgerald flagged — 'our practices, our attitudes' — remain even less reformed than the constitution. Many Catholics in the Republic continue to see Catholicism as the normative religion of the State, Protestants as merely tolerated guests, and 'the North' as someone else's problem altogether.

This set of attitudes arose in the aftermath of the creation of the State, and has been remarkably resistant to change, despite the challenges to it presented by the recent arrival of immigrants and returning emigrants with their different faith traditions (or different understandings of the same faith tradition). In their acclaimed study, Ruane and Todd track the attitudes of Southern Catholics over the past 100 years and comment that: 'The South rejected partition but was required to accommodate itself to it. ... The solution the South chose was to distance itself from the North and to resist attempts

are not Catholic) have anything like the same access to status, honour and respect in the Republic even after its Catholic inhabitants have stopped going to Mass en masse.

10. R.F. Foster, *Luck and the Irish: A Brief History of Social Change c.1970–2000* (London: Penguin, 2007), p. 7.

11. 'In the Name of the Most Holy Trinity, from Whom is all authority and to Whom, as our final end, all actions both of men and States must be referred,/We, the people of Éire,/Humbly acknowledging all our obligations to our Divine Lord, Jesus Christ, Who sustained our fathers through centuries of trial,/Gratefully remembering their heroic and unremitting struggle to regain the rightful independence of our Nation,/And seeking to promote the common good, with due observance of Prudence, Justice and Charity, so that the dignity and freedom of the individual may be assured, true social order attained, the unity of our country restored, and concord established with other nations,/Do hereby adopt, enact, and give to ourselves this Constitution.'

12. Which is taken as foundational for many schools and some hospitals, and which has consistently been contested on legal grounds (usually to do with employment rights vis-à-vis gender and sexuality). One recent example is Mark Coen, 'Religious Ethos and Employment Equality: A Comparative Irish Perspective' in *Legal Studies* 28:3 (July 2008), pp. 452–74.

by Northern nationalists to involve it. The two societies went their separate ways and Southerners recognised less and less of their own experience in that of Northern Catholics.'[13] Political and economic factors played a large part in creating this divorce, what with the feeling of impotence in the face of achieving independence for all 32 counties, the impossibility of continuing Michael Collins's strategy of destabilization while running an effective government, and the sense that Ireland's pocket of viable industrial activity had been taken away. However, religious factors were combined with politics and economics in such a way that religion became polarized through these after-effects of partition. Prior to partition, the nationalist cause was and had long been something for which Protestants as well as Catholics fought. After it, with the Southern Catholics 'going their separate ways', the landscape of 'nationalism' subtly changed and was presented increasingly as a Catholic (and an anti-Protestant) concern.[14]

Within this polarized landscape, the things that marked a person as 'Catholic' became the things that legitimated them as 'Irish'. As one of my relations in the west of Ireland remarked in 2006 of the recent influx of immigrants: 'At least these Poles and Darkies go to Mass'; meaning, the new immigrants' participation in the core practice of Roman Catholicism (Mass) indicates they have a minimal qualification for citizenship in Irish society. Or, roughly translated: these newcomers are not fully welcome here, but they're better than Protestants, Catholicism being the constituent marker of Irishness. His assessment is shot through with ethnic and racial prejudice, but its fundamental prejudice (the one against which the others are tested and found to be relative) is an anti-Protestant one, and he is far from alone in measuring the world by this standard.

Another example is the discussion around the creation of a *gaelscoil*[15] in Westport, Co. Mayo in the mid-1990s. A group of local

13. Joseph Ruane and Jennifer Todd, *Dynamics of Conflict in Northern Ireland: Power, Conflict and Emancipation* (Cambridge: Cambridge University Press, 1996), p. 251.

14. Ruane and Todd, *Dynamics of Conflict in Northern Ireland*, pp. 49–57.

15. A school for 5–13 year-old children where all classes are taught in the Irish language. *Gaelscoil Na Cruaich* took its first 7 students in September 1995, but was not approved by the Department of Education until August 1996. The public meetings were held in the intervening months, and resulted in two applications to the Government. (One from the multi-denominationals, one

residents (the majority of them 'blow ins'[16]) who had campaigned for the establishment of a *gaelscoil* argued that the school should be multi-denominational. At a series of public meetings, with local TDs[17] present, a larger group (the majority of whom had been born in the town) resisted vehemently, with individuals arguing that if the school were multi-denominational and not purely Catholic, 'it would make us secular', 'they would be teaching homosexuality' and their children 'would not get a proper education'. But the premise that underpinned the argument that eventually won was that: the Irish language is the symbol of Irish identity, and Irish identity is necessarily Roman Catholic: how can you have an Irish-language school, therefore, which is not normatively Roman Catholic? The fact that the *gaelscoil* was so recently founded on this premise, and that a new generation is now being taught there, is further evidence that sectarian thinking is an all-Ireland problem.[18]

Furthermore, as post-colonial commentators increasingly note, the problem of sectarianism, which one finds played out in one form or another in former imperial territories all over the world and not just in the Irish Republic, far from being generated by indigenous mismanagement or latent tribalism (as classic imperial analyses would have it),[19] is directly related to, and possibly even

from the Catholic-onlys; the latter was approved by the Minister for Education on the basis — which some saw as a technicality masking the ideological issues at stake — that they could guarantee enrolment of 20 children in the new intake).

16. The name given to people who come to live in the town who were not born in the area.

17. Elected representatives to *Dáil Éireann*, the national Parliament; like Members of Parliament (MPs) in the UK or Senators in the USA.

18. Although it should be noted that there have been other *gaelscoileanna* established in other parts of the country as inter-denominational and even multi-faith during this same period.

19. For example, Robert W. White, 'Social and Role Identities and Political Violence: Identity as a Window on Violence in Northern Ireland' in Richard D. Ashmore, Lee Jussim and David Wilder (eds), *Social Identity, Intergroup Conflict and Conflict Resolution* (New York: Oxford University Press, 2001), pp. 133–58. Moreover, White points out how imperial analyses ultimately backfire, observing that, 'viewing the conflict as external "them versus them" [rather than "us versus them"] contributes to policy mistakes on the part of the British government.' (p. 151). To illustrate the point, Prime Minister Tony Blair's chief aide referred to the Northern Irish conflict as having presented to their government as: a 'dreary and incomprehensible dispute between

manufactured by, the original colonial power and the aftermath of its withdrawal. 'Lest we forget,' remark Peter Shirlow and Brendan Murtagh, 'the sectarianism of society in the UK is encouraged by a government intent upon the promotion of faith schools and legislation centred upon religious hatred. The same government that subjects the British labour market to the unfettered forces of globalisation but fails to acknowledge the causal link between that process of economic change and the ghettoisation of life along racial lines.'[20] Ireland's status is (as the next chapter will suggest), far from straightforwardly 'post-colonial', and the UK's habilitation of religion in civic policies is far from straightforwardly divisive; but it cannot be denied that the 'racialization of religion'[21] has been a notable feature of the historically complicated relations between British and Irish management of Ireland. Increasing awareness of the place of religion (in the form of attitudes and practices) is therefore vital to the task of first noticing and then dismantling sectarianism in this yet-young State.

Now, while I am arguing that there are grounds for taking seriously what Fitzgerald identified as the problem in the Republic (the sectarianism of our attitudes and practices), I am not suggesting for an instant that there is parity in either nature or degree of sectarian manifestations between Northern Ireland and the Republic of Ireland. The strain under which everyone in Northern Ireland has lived, the immediate history of juridical injustice, the threat and the reality of horrific violence, and the peculiar pain that so very many Northern Irish families have experienced as a result of violence or the threat of violence, is unknown by most people in the Republic. Nevertheless, this study insists on two things: first, that sectarianism is an all-Ireland problem, North and South and, second, that the problem remains an implicitly violent one in the

two tribes somewhere on the periphery of the country.' See, Jonathan Powell, *Great Hatred, Little Room: Making Peace in Northern Ireland* (London: Bodley Head, 2008).

20. Peter Shirlow and Brendan Murtagh, *Belfast: Segregation, Violence and the City* (London: Pluto Press, 2006), p. 3.

21. 'In the aftermath of *The Satanic Verses* affair in Great Britain, Black and Irish feminists, despite their different constituencies, have made common cause against the "racialization of religion" as the dominant discourse through which the State represents their conflicts and struggles, however secular or even "sexual" they may be.' Homi Bhabha, *The Location of Culture* (New York: Routledge, 1994), p. 3.

South. Just because relatively few people have died due to violence in the South in these past 40 years does not mean that the problem of violence is absent: the violence inflicted by the sorts of remarks made by my relative, or by the locals about the *gaelscoil*, reflect and contribute to a body of attitudes that wrecks lives, individual and communal.

The Killing Power of Faith-Based Claims: Defining Sectarianism

Such seemingly small remarks as those in the above illustrations may hardly seem to convey any 'life-wrecking' power. However, my primary concern as a theologian is the fact that historically Christians kill other people of faith (whether fellow Christians, or Jews, Muslims, Buddhists, non-believers or others) on the grounds of a faith-contest. Through studying acts of violence by Christians in political life, I have come to recognize that people of faith take one another's lives ontologically and morally as well as physically. Only the last is usually considered 'life-wrecking', but ontologically, Christians kill one another by the ways they *think*, denying one another's standing in the eyes of God. For example, Catholics are seen by many Protestants as being ultimately answerable to the Pope and not to God, or as never having had a personal conversion and, either way, therefore, not Christians. Conversely, Protestant worship assemblies are seen by the Catholic magisterium as not even worthy of the name 'churches'. By such claims, Christians kill other people's status as equally created — by and beloved — of God. Like Cain and Abel, they dismiss the sibling.

Morally, Christians also kill one another by the things they say and do. They deny one another through all manner of pronouncements and actions that constitute the denial of political community — and the denying of another person's being and right to the same rights as other human beings is a form of killing. From attitudes like this arise such effects as the legacy of African American people in the South of what is now the USA, who were not allowed to worship in the same pews as white people. From them also spring sermons condemning homosexual people that lead to the most extraordinarily painful splits in families, communities and within individual persons. And last but by no means least, Christians kill fellow people of faith bodily, as they have for years in Ireland and England, and elsewhere in the world, such as Bosnia.

The particular ways in which lives are wrecked in Ireland, the ways that comprise Fitzgerald's 'attitudes and practices' are interpreted in contemporary discussions under the umbrella term of 'sectarianism'.[22] The fact that Irish media reports tend to take seriously only the physical sort of killing and avoid naming as 'violent' the rounds of daily social hatreds, fears and prejudices that constitute sectarianism reveals a lot about Irish attitudes to it. There has been for some time, particularly in reference to 'The Troubles' by the general population in the Republic, a habit of using the word 'sectarianism' to refer to paramilitary violence in Northern Ireland.[23] However, the implication that 'sectarianism' is synonymous with 'paramilitary violence' is a potentially powerful mechanism for permitting people to persist in prejudices and discriminations, embedding everyday hateful notions about one's neighbours ever deeper into the structure of social life, while simultaneously seeing such notions as 'harmless' because they do not erupt into the sorts of violence one has first set up as defining of sectarianism.

The dictionary is clear, however, that the key expression of sectarianism is attitudinal; indeed its definition of sectarianism mentions *only* attitudes and not violent crime: 'Sectarianism: The sectarian spirit; adherence or excessive attachment to a particular sect or party, esp. in religion; hence often, adherence or

22. As Jonathan Tonge notes, 'The GFA said very little on the problem of sectarianism in Northern Ireland. Although it established a variety of commissions to deal with inequality and perceived injustice, its primary focus was on the constitutional accommodation of political elites. The unstated assumption was that resolution of the constitutional conflict would result in the normalization of society and the eventual eradication of societal sectarianism. This was ambitious, given that 23 per cent of the population claimed to have family or close friends who had been injured in a sectarian incident' Jonathan Tonge, *The New Northern Irish Politics?* (New York: Palgrave Macmillan, 2005), p. 188.

23. However, not only in the Republic, and not only in common parlance. Neil Jarman notes that the UK Government's *The Community Attitudes Survey* taken in Northern Ireland each year since 1992 (www.csu.nisra.gov.uk) gives the same impression: 'In fact the only reference to sectarian violence is in the later section of the questionnaires where it is coupled with references to "terrorist activity", suggesting that sectarian violence is seen as very close to if not synonymous with paramilitary activity', pp. 28–29. Neil Jarman, 'No Longer a Problem: Sectarian Violence in Northern Ireland' in *Institute for Conflict Research: Papers* (March 2005), pp. 1–64.

excessive attachment to, or undue favouring of, a particular "denomination"'.[24] This transnational definition has been substantially expanded by those scholars who recognize that while sectarianism may be the best word for describing Catholic–Protestant division within Irish–British relations, especially as they play out in Northern Ireland, it is nevertheless a more complicated and far-reaching condition than that for which the dictionary accounts. For example, John Brewer defines it as: 'the use of denominational boundaries in a social project to enforce social exclusion by one religious group against others',[25] drawing attention to the fact that what ends up being the oppressive factor may not look like a 'religious' thing. An awareness of the fact that a sectarian landscape is caused by the ways in which religious boundaries condition *other* factors thus furnishes an essential supplement to dictionary definitions.

Religious denominations do not exist in isolation but in a network of social relations and, therefore, any living out of the dictionary's focus on denominational self-understanding, especially over generations, is going to affect most if not all not-specifically-denominational aspects of civic life, from government to gardening. Sectarianism may refer primarily to the religious content of attitudinal bias,[26] but such bias, like religious feeling or belief itself, is invariably co-produced with other attitudinal and emotional factors (such as political persuasion or social affiliation and self-perception); hence the religious component cannot be completely 'separated out' from the attitudinal matrix. As Joe Liechty and Cecilia Clegg remark, 'Sectarianism is so complex a problem because it involves religion and politics and economics and a host of other factors. Only approaches that can take in this whole range stand a chance of understanding sectarianism'.[27]

Liechty and Clegg's work on sectarianism gives a profound and comprehensive account of the nature of sectarianism, but also of

24. Oxford English Dictionary.

25. John D. Brewer, 'Northern Ireland: Peacemaking among Protestants and Catholics' in Mary Ann Cejka and Thomas Barmat (eds), *Artisans of Peace: Grassroots Peacemaking among Christian Communities* (Maryknoll, NY: Orbis Books, 2003), pp. 67–95; 86.

26. For a definition of sectarianism as essentially 'religious bigotry', see, Tonge, *New Northern Irish Politics?*, p. 194.

27. Liechty and Clegg, *Moving Beyond Sectarianism*, p. 62.

the problem of moving beyond it. Their book is the product of the Irish School of Ecumenics' *Moving Beyond Sectarianism* (*MBS*) project, for which they were the principal investigators from 1995–2001. After conducting interviews with hundreds of individuals and community groups in (mostly) Northern Ireland, and hosting dozens of intra- and inter-denominational workshops, they emphasize the point that sectarianism is not best defined as its visibly violent events, but rather as 'the destructive patterns of relating'[28] that create and reinforce divisions between groups. They insist upon the primacy of small, interpersonal interactions and judgements in the creation and maintenance of the sectarian system, saying that, 'Sectarianism is a *complex* of problems—including dividing, demonising, and dominating.'[29] That person whom you think must be backward because of his/her accent, or unenlightened because she/he comes from a certain location, the group that you do not want to move into your neighbourhood for fear of property prices dropping, that couple whom you just cannot stand with their worthy bumper-stickers, sandals and vegetarian kids. *MBS* demonstrates that petty hatreds like these are judged as innocuous at one's peril: they are the result of habits of prejudice, objectification and hatred, and they conspire to prevent free and fair relations at all levels of society.

When people are confronted not with violent stories of explicit hate-acts (which allow them to remain in the objectifying mode, blaming sectarianism on someone worse than they) but with small church stories about implicit hate-thoughts, they have the opportunity to view these petty hatreds, and the ways they play-out in church, in a new way. As such, they are challenged to consider the ways in which 'sectarianism' refers not only to paramilitary violence, not only to segregation, but also (and mostly) to their everyday thoughts and habits, and every mundane fibre of their daily material lives. By considering the full reach of the phenomenon, people are presented with the option to re-frame their world in ways that are no longer ultimately self-defeating.

Yet the most important contribution of *MBS* is the authors' depth of understanding about why people usually opt *not* to re-frame their world or to live in less self-defeating ways. They express this

28. Liechty and Clegg, p. 104.
29. Liechty and Clegg, *Moving Beyond Sectarianism*, (Italics mine) p. 37. For a fuller discussion of the everyday interactions that comprise sectarianism's 'destructive patterns of relating', see *MBS*, pp. 103–106.

by providing an account of sectarianism's attractions, explaining how it, 'has become a system so efficient that it can take our sane and rational responses to a situation which it has generated and use them to further deepen sectarianism.'[30] They thus account for why sectarianism appeals to ordinarily good people, and how it feels as if it helps rather than hinders them in their efforts at peaceful living:

> The sectarian system can sometimes use even our best efforts to build itself up. ... We choose to worship, educate, and marry almost exclusively among our own. Our motivation is not to be sectarian, it is to build strong communities, but because our efforts fall within the boundaries set by sectarianism, our best pastoral efforts can end up strengthening the sectarian divide. ... So it is that the sectarian system, born from gross violence and what most people would now see as unapologetic injustice, can now maintain itself on a diet consisting largely of our rational responses, understandable comparisons, good intentions and positive actions.[31]

This insight—that sectarianism, although rationally perceived as an evil by church folk, is nevertheless performed by them because of community-building perceptions and constructive intentions—will be vital to the remainder of this book.

The Effects of Sectarianism

It would be a mistake to think I am simply warning that the sectarianism that is harboured in the aftermath of the Good Friday Agreement (GFA) exists mostly underground, in unexpressed thoughts, with the potential to fester and one day, far from now, erupt. Rather, the actual effects of sectarian thinking are discernible now. Hatred, animosity and fear are expressed in things like acceptable 'inappropriate' speech on television, graffiti on street walls and road curbs,[32] and vandalism specifically directed at the

30. For example, as will be discussed below, the way people choose to live among their own, for safety, withdrawing from mixed situations in which they might get hurt, now results in far greater segregation, far less mixing, in housing and other civic groupings than ever before in Northern Irish history.

31. Liechty and Clegg, *Moving Beyond Sectarianism*, pp. 13–14.

32. For an account of the sectarian nature of graffiti see: Shane Alcobia-Murphy, *Governing the Tongue: The Place of Art/The Art of Place* (Newcastle: Cambridge Scholars Press, 2005), e.g., pp. 105–106.

'other' community.[33] Segregation in housing, schooling and workplaces remains an issue (as the next section will demonstrate) and, furthermore, contrary to the strong impression of an established 'peace' as presented by British and Irish governments, violence has not stopped in Northern Ireland. Merely the *nature* of violence has changed: there are fewer deaths (due to fewer murders/acts of war), but far more incidences of intimidation.[34]

Rupert Taylor argues that sectarianism has in fact grown worse since (and in part due to) the GFA and one of his key pieces of evidence is his account of 'increased paramilitary violence in the form of shootings, beatings and injuries.'[35] Along similar lines, Colin Knox reports that, 'Paramilitaries have become the law-enforcers within communities' adding his assessment that while a certain amount of violence is inevitable, it is the *sectarian* nature of the current violence (it is not just ordinary crime) — combined with the government's toleration of it — that is cause for alarm: 'Mutilations, torture and exiling cannot come within the purview of an "acceptable level of violence" or be seen as part of the imperfections of peace.'[36] Furthermore, the targets of violence are increasingly what might be considered *liturgical* spaces: Shirlow and Murtagh report that, 'The nature of violence has shifted away from paramilitary and state assaults towards a more sectarianised and repetitive violence of interface rioting and attacks upon the symbols of tradition such as Orange Halls, GAA property and churches.'[37] My concern is not to judge whether sectarianism has become worse since the GFA or

33. Such as attacks on Orange Halls and Churches, the writing of paramilitary names and slogans on other people's property and the damaging or destruction of cars in a certain specific area — all of which are reported in the newspapers daily at the time of writing.

34. See: Peter Shirlow and Brendan Murtagh, *Belfast: Segregation, Violence and the City* (London: Macmillan, 2006), pp. 52–56.

35. Rupert Taylor, *Consociational Theory: McGarry and O'Leary and the Northern Ireland Conflict* (Oxon: Routledge, 2009), p. 325. Although, in the same volume, John Mc Garry and Brendan O'Leary disagree. See: 'Under Friendly and Less-Friendly Fire' (pp. 333–88), 385. And, in another assessment, Jonathan Tonge sees evidence of developing sectarian activity but does not see the GFA as necessarily having anything to do with it: *The New Northern Irish Politics*, p. 218.

36. Colin Knox, 'See No Evil, Hear No Evil: Insidious Paramilitary Violence in Northern Ireland', *British Journal of Criminology* 42 (2002), pp. 164–85, 180.

37. Shirlow and Murtagh, *Belfast*: see especially p. 3.

not; it is simply to establish that it exists, persists and has symbolic power.

Segregation is perhaps sectarianism's most visible expression and Belfast's housing is currently more segregated than at any previous point in its history.[38] Moreover, the effects of segregated housing guarantee that sectarianism will persist (and perhaps worsen) in future generations because when people live with their own group alone they do not cultivate knowledge of the other group. As Shirlow and Murtagh remark, 'Segregation and related mobility issues mean that whole swathes of the city are [now] virtually unknown to citizens living within Belfast.'[39] The lack of knowledge of the 'other community' that results from strictly demarcated neighbourhood boundaries fosters even greater ignorance than used to exist. Knowledge of areas inhabited by the other community (and therefore of their cultures and sensibilities) which was common in the recent past, is rare today, and studies show that with that older knowledge came greater tolerance of, and even fondness for, the other community than is currently in evidence.[40]

In Belfast city after the GFA, there are more shared commercial spaces, such as shopping areas and restaurant developments, but, as Claire Mitchell notes, these are available only to those of a certain income[41] and might in fact serve to reinforce sectarian resentment at the majority (working-class) level. Moreover, even among the middle classes, the appearance of mixing may mask the reality of intimidation. As an illustration of the evidence of increased and

38. In 1999 The Northern Ireland Housing Executive (NIHE) classed 71 percent of housing estates in Northern Ireland as segregated; by 2006 the figure was 95 percent (www.nihe.gov.uk). Belfast city is more segregated than the rest of Northern Ireland, and, since the Good Friday Agreement has become increasingly so. Shirlow and Murtagh assess that, unlike any previous point in the city's history, now 'the majority of persons from a Catholic or Protestant community background live in places that are at least 81 per cent Catholic or Protestant.' *Belfast*, p. 59.

39. Shirlow and Murtagh, *Belfast*, p. 66.

40. See the results of their cross-generational interviews. Shirlow and Murtagh, *Belfast*, pp. 57--80.

41. 'for those who can afford it, there are more social spaces, cosmopolitan activities and meeting places opening up in "neutral territory", but the effects of segregation are undeniable, and in areas like housing and education, they are being reinforced rather than dismantled.' Claire Mitchell, *Religion, Identity and Politics in Northern Ireland: Boundaries of Belonging and Belief* (Abingdon: Ashgate, 2006), p. 63.

more varied intimidation as provided in Shirlow and Murtagh's study, in the Spring of 2008 two friends of mine were waiting for a table in a restaurant in the only remaining (and decreasingly) mixed neighbourhood of Belfast. The man from a couple at a neighbouring table got up and came over to my male friend, his wife smiling all the time at his female companion. 'Just watch it', said the man, 'we do not want your type round here. So if you know what's good for you, you'll leave. I mean it: leave, now.' My friend, a quiet, bland-looking artist with no ties to anyone in the city, surmised that he must have simply 'looked' Catholic. Sectarian intimidation persists, no matter how 'neutral' the new civic spaces, such as restaurants, have been designed to be.

Perhaps the most significant, and divisive site of increasing segregation is in education. Education policy is a supremely contentious aspect of public life on both sides of the border. In Northern Ireland, fewer than 5 percent of children attend multi-denominational ('integrated') schools despite the number of such schools having increased[42] (implying that, where the choice exists, parents are actually choosing to send their children to schools which are entirely either Protestant or Catholic in demographic).[43] And the *gaelscoil* discussion above is an example of a common matter in the Republic's civic life: in a country in which schooling is already quite rigidly demarcated along denominational lines,[44] the instances of new schools being established as non-denominational or multi-denominational has only increased with the arrival of a critical mass of immigrants in the past five years.

42. However, it is important not to read this 'increase' as implying a positive policy toward integrated schools in the Department of Education, as the recent discussion in the House of Lords makes clear. See the debate of Monday, 17 July 2006, transcribed at: www.theyworkforyou.com/lords/?id=2006-07-17b.993.217

43. See: T. Gallagher, A. Smith and A. Montgomery, *Integrated Education in Northern Ireland: Participation, Profile and Performance* (University of Ulster: UNESCO Centre, 2003).

44. From as recently as March 2008: 'Two characteristics define and structure the primary education system in the Republic of Ireland. First, there are no state-run primary schools. All primary schools are run by private bodies to which the state contributes financial support. Secondly, 98 per cent of these private organisations are religious. ...Out of more than 3,170 primary schools in the country, only 44 are privately initiated multi-denominational schools.' Alison Mawhinney, *Submission to the Human Rights Committee with Respect to the Third Periodic Report of Ireland*, p. 11.

Strong arguments have been made in recent years for viewing separate schooling as *not* segregation, and nothing to do with sectarianism.[45] Against this, other studies have argued that separate schooling increases misunderstanding of the 'other religion'[46] and, despite a national curriculum, teaches all manner of religious-political positions as normative through what is often called the 'ethos' or the 'hidden curriculum' of the school.[47] The debate about what is 'cultural' and what is 'sectarian' is at the heart of both sets of arguments,[48] and it has implications for Christian worship. That the raising of the (British) flag during a prayer service in a Protestant school, or the celebration of Mass for St. Patrick's day in a Catholic school (or any number of other liturgical actions) are expressions of cultural identity is without doubt, and, in the vast majority of cases, performed with no sectarian intent.

The *effects* of such performances though, cumulative as they are, and in a context where identities and other social normativities are being co-created daily, is more complicated. For a start, they are not just cultural markers, they are theological: who God is thought to be is simultaneously expressed in and derived from all acts of worship. Consequently, when one makes a decision later in life, and thinks about how it relates to one's faith, to what God would

45. John Coolahan describes multi- or non-denominational schools as 'accommodations', simply a necessary response to immigration in his essay 'Church–State Relations in Primary and Secondary Education' in James P. Mackey and Enda McDonagh (eds), *Religion and Politics in Ireland at the Turn of the Millennium* (Dublin: Columba Press, 2003), pp. 132–51.

46. Sometimes to a quite extraordinary degree of mis-representation. See: D. Murray, *Worlds Apart: Segregated Schools in Northern Ireland* (Belfast: Appletree Press, 1985).

47. See: J. Darby and S. Dunn, 'Segregated Schools' in R.D. Osborne, R.J. Cormack and R.L. Miller (eds), *Education and Policy in Northern Ireland* (Belfast: Queens University and The University of Ulster, Policy Research Institute, 1987), pp. 85–98.

48. Regarding life after the *GFA*, 'A crucial feature of an expected political transformation was the pluralist notion that the right to promote Irish and British cultural traditions had been enforced constitutionally. However, such arguments failed to remember that the most passionate renditions of identity in Northern Ireland are not merely cognitive, nor are they heavily influenced by the "holding operation" of constitutional change that has taken place, These atavistic renditions are based upon material realities such as segregation, notions of territorial loss, an inability to share space within a host of urban and rural arenas and the experience of harm.' (And everything that happens in church, I would add.) Shirlow and Murtagh, *Belfast*, p. 40.

expect, these early actions (such as flag-raising and hymn-singing) have a profoundly formative effect. Theologies are never just ideas about God, they are blueprints for living, because how one thinks of God conditions what one expects of oneself in the world. Separate schooling in Ireland and Northern Ireland is then perhaps the prime example of what *MBS* lays bare: sectarianism usually happens not through any will to hate, but through our best intentions and our efforts to live good, ethical lives — in a profoundly divided cultural system.

At a minimum (setting aside arguments of cultural versus sectarian performance), the *effects* of separate schooling inevitably bolster separate arrangements in the wider life of any given community through the limits placed on the relationships thus formed — for children, parents and staff alike. These relationships become the anchor of community life through the mere fact of association, and if the daily encounters in the classroom or at the school gate are reinforced by meeting in church on Sunday (as they often are) then the inadvertent result is a ghetto of sorts. People are going about the main business of their day, forming social bonds, making allegiances that last the rest of their lives, all within a homogenous religious community. Contrast this with communities wherein people form denomination-based relationships through Sunday worship, but then engage in a whole host of non-denomination-based relationships with people met through schools (as children and as parents); in such cases, when situations demand that one call upon a neighbour for help, the circle of possible contacts is much more diverse.

Furthermore, as Claire Mitchell has demonstrated, 'separate education is significant because it is connected to other forms of social segregation,'[49] such as marriage, class-boundary maintenance, and community-formation, as visible in such things as workplace practices. She reports that, '94 per cent of Catholics and 88 per cent of Protestants have a partner of the same religion,' and comments that, 'Although a growing percentage of people now say that they would not mind if one of their very close relatives were to marry a partner of the other religion, high rates of endogamy persist.'[50] As such she brings to light a salient aspect of the current climate across

49. Mitchell, *Religion, Identity and Politics*, p. 61.
50. Mitchell, *Religion, Identity and Politics*.

the whole island: people are saying that attitudes are open even as practices point not only to the maintenance of the sectarian *status quo*, but to its aggravation. The resignation of the only Protestant member of a GAA[51] club in Fermanagh in 2009 provides a striking illustration. This is the report from the front page of *The Irish Independent* newspaper:

> A PROTESTANT *GAA* player has quit the game over sectarian abuse by rival players, he claimed yesterday. *Darren Graham* (25) from Lisnaskea, *Co Fermanagh*, whose soldier father and two uncles were shot dead by the *IRA*, said he was hounded out because of his religion. ...Darren was just three weeks old when his father Cecil, who was a member of the UDR, was shot and fatally wounded by the IRA. Two of Darren's uncles, Ronnie and Jimmy Graham, who both served in the UDR as well, were also shot dead by the IRA in 1981 and 1985. He said he was giving up the sport altogether because of persistent sectarian abuse from certain players in three clubs in particular. Darren, who works as a joiner with local firm the Clarke Group, stressed he got on well with those within his own club and with people in his local community.[52]

The interplay of rhetorics regarding religious and political identity markers (as well as gender expectations) in this short extract is an acute example of the everyday negotiations of anyone in Ireland who transgresses the boundary so avidly patrolled by Catholic and Protestant communities alike. Also, any Irish or Northern Irish person reading the story will note the detail of his workplace (the company has a Protestant name) and register it, alongside his family's status as contributors to the UDR and victims of IRA violence, as legitimating him as truly part of the Protestant community (meaning he has not lost his connections with it altogether because raising a Catholic daughter is a sure sign he is one of the minority of Protestants who have 'intermarried' with a Catholic, and playing in a GAA club is a sign he is unusually tolerant, if not sympathetic, to a normatively Catholic way of spending his leisure

---

51. 'Gaelic Athletic Association' (GAA) is the professional body for the sport of Gaelic football (a uniquely Irish cross between rugby and football). There is a GAA branch in almost every town in Ireland, and it is usually seen as a mainstay of Irish (read: Catholic) culture, not just sport. Although officially open to any who wish to play, Protestants comprise a distinct minority of GAA members.

52. *The Irish Independent* (Dublin) 2 August 2007.

time: both things that would mark him as 'not sufficiently Protestant' in many quarters). Workplace identification is vital in sustaining (and proving, if need be) one's marks of belonging in one's own community.

As with housing and education, attitudes about workplace-belonging are changing: 83 percent of Northern Irish people now say they prefer a religiously-mixed workplace, and this is a big change from previous surveys in the 1960s and 1980s.[53] Practices, however, while changing, are doing so only slowly. During my visit to a Church of Ireland parish in Co. Mayo in 2008, the lay minister told me about a member of the parish who had worked for the main employers in the town for 15 years but had not told any of his workmates he was a Protestant. He had heard anti-Protestant slurs, but he wanted to be able to socialize and join in the banter, and he wanted to fit in; so, while not actively claiming to be Catholic, he was careful never to 'come out' as a Protestant. Occasionally it really bothered him, but the alternative was too painful to act upon: he felt that if people knew he was Protestant they would withdraw from him, not invite him to things they currently invited him to, and not treat him as part of the group in work (and the lay minister thought he was right). Furthermore, despite reported shifts in attitude, and despite the unemployment rate in Northern Ireland having gone from one of the highest to one of the lowest in Europe in the past ten years, as Jonathan Tonge points out, 'One stubborn differential persists: the rate of unemployment among Catholics is over twice that among Protestants.'[54]

Finally, of course, worship is segregated. It might seem strange to frame it that way, because worshipping along denominational lines is just the normal way of things not only in Ireland but in most of the world. However, on an island on which social life is organized along a strict Catholic–Protestant line of demarcation, worshipping as Catholic or as Protestant takes on a peculiar character, and one

53. Northern Ireland Life and Times Survey, 2003. However, this statistic is the product of others that complicate the given impression: 'Although three-quarters of the population claim to prefer a mixed-religion workplace, one in five Protestants would prefer a single-religion work environment, as would one in seven Catholics (NILTS, 2001).' Tonge, *New Northern Irish Politics?*, p. 202.

54. Tonge, *New Northern Irish Politics?*, p. 201.

very different from other countries in which people simply 'choose' to attend one place of worship or another. Evidence of this is plainest in the fact that in popular speech, most large towns in the Republic do not have a 'Methodist' or a 'Presbyterian' or an 'Anglican' church; they have a 'Protestant' Church. That a Protestant church is, in fact, affiliated with a single denomination is often understood thinly, if at all, by the residents of the town.[55]

Segregation is not the same as differentiated arrangements, simply getting along while doing one's own thing. Segregation enmeshes people in polarized, antagonistic relationships, separated for mutual safety against the perceived threat of the other, and embedding whole generations in little-understood but deeply felt separateness. It is therefore the *symbolic* quality of segregation as much as its quotidian consequences that is at issue, because 'the meaning of segregation undermines the capacity to shift society onwards.'[56]

The Role of Religion in the Irish–British Conflict

We do not need bombs to take seriously the fact that this level of division and misunderstanding is not just fuel for future conflict but actual current attitudinal aversion, separation, and contempt. The GFA has brought enough peace to end the physical killing, but it was never designed to bring the sort of peace that would end the sorts of attitudes and practices described above. Because Irish–British sectarianism is manufactured in no small way by religious language and religious social structures, and because religion is manufactured largely by going to church (that is, by what happens in worship), this book will engage with religion in general and worship in particular to figure out how 'faith' can help to dismantle this hatred. The first step is acknowledging that religion is part of the problem.

The role of religion in the Irish–British conflict has been repeatedly under-described in government, media and academic studies from

55. For a good discussion of the term 'Protestant' as it is and has been used in Ireland and Northern Ireland see Kenneth Milne, 'The Protestant Churches in Independent Ireland' in Mackey and McDonagh, *Religion and Politics*, pp. 78–79.
56. Shirlow and Murtagh, *Belfast*, p. 1.

the 1960s until the 2000s.[57] By the time of the GFA, the generally-accepted position was that there was no particularly privileged 'cause' of the Northern Irish conflict[58] but, rather, a set of mutually-constituting causes.[59] Most studies emphasized that the conflict was co-produced (by ethnic, political, economic, and geographical factors) and some included religion in this mix,[60] but the majority of studies downplayed the role of religion, tending instead to a sort of sociological reductionism. As Claire Mitchell observed after completing her survey of studies in print by 2006: 'Something of an academic consensus now hangs around the idea that the conflict is essentially ethno-national, and that other factors merely reinforce rather than constitute ethnic division.'[61]

There were exceptions, of course, such as Steve Bruce, John Fulton and John Hickey, all of whom argued for the need for attention to religious as well as political and economic indicators in sociological studies of Northern Ireland. Hickey, as his critics contend, may

57. For example, 'Explanations that emphasize the primacy of religion... need to be exposed to strong light. When that happens, they evaporate, leaving little residue.' John McGarry and Brendan O'Leary, *Explaining Northern Ireland: Broken Images* (Oxford: Blackwell, 1995), p. 213.

58. I say 'Northern Irish conflict' rather than the more common 'conflict in Northern Ireland' in recognition that the conflict was not played out only in Northern Ireland. Bombings and other acts of war by Northern Irish paramilitary factions were frequently enacted in England and occasionally in the Republic of Ireland and, some have suggested, also by the British military: see for example Paul Larkin, *A Very British Jihad: Collusion, Conspiracy and Cover-Up in Northern Ireland* (Belfast: BTP Publications, 2004).

59. One significant exception was B.K. Lambkin, who, while wanting to agree with those who resist overly reductionistic or simplistic assessments of the situation (i.e., the need for a single cause; or the idea, common at the start of the 'troubles' that it's just due to intolerance between Roman Catholics and Protestants) argued that, while interwoven with a great many factors, there is, in fact, a single common thread to the conflict, and it is religion. See B.K. Lambkin, *Opposite Religions Still? Interpreting Northern Ireland after the Conflict* (Aldershot: Avebury, 1996). Lambkin, a former headteacher of one of the very few multi-denominational schools in Northern Ireland, was also very concerned to address what he perfectly calls 'the conflict about the conflict' (p. 5), that is, the debate about whether religion played any significant part as a determinative factor in the 'troubles'.

60. Joseph Ruane and Jennifer Todd's excellent account, *Dynamics of Conflict in Northern Ireland: Power, Conflict and Emancipation* (Cambridge: Cambridge University Press, 1996), being one of very few such works to take seriously religion as a factor (but only one of many mutually constituting factors) in the co-production of the conflict.

61. Mitchell, *Religion, Identity and Politics*, p. 1.

well have underestimated the co-producing nature of the interplay between religion and other factors, focusing too simplistically on religion alone, but some of the things he identified in 1984 have only come more into the light in the 25 years since; for example: 'while differences in the social structure between Protestants and Catholics are being slowly eliminated, the importance of the other difference—religion—is being increasingly emphasized. Conflict now centres upon the distinction of religious belief and the world view based upon it.'[62] As life after the combination of the Celtic Tiger and the GFA has revealed, even when there are profound improvements in economics and politics, segregation, intimidation and numerous forms of specifically sectarian social hostility and crime remain.

Another important exception was the Opsahl Commission, the product of many years of research by people from a wide range of disciplines and backgrounds in the form of a 'Citizens' Inquiry'. The authors concluded that, 'It simply comes to this: the Northern Ireland conflict is in part economic and social, in part political and constitutional, and also in part religious, and damagingly so.'[63] It is that last phrase that is the significant remark for this current study, because it draws attention to the possibility that all the other factors combined might not have such a devastating impact were it not for their combination with the factor that is religion. One final exception, and one that has been influential in reorienting recent social scientific approaches to the study of Northern Ireland, was Ruane and Todd's mapping of identity-formation. While not claiming too much for religion, they nevertheless insisted that:

> Religion more than ethnic or historical origin or politics or identity is the mark of community membership. It is religion which sorts into communities, even though the overt communal conflict is much more about economics, politics or identity than theology. That is why, when two people meet in Northern Ireland, the first priority is to establish each other's religion, and why it is important not simply to know whether a person is nationalist or unionist but whether he of she is a Catholic or a Protestant nationalist or unionist. In each case, the difference is profound.[64]

62. John Hickey, *Religion and the Northern Ireland Problem* (London: Gil and McMillan, 1984), p. 105.
63. Andy Pollak (ed.), *A Citizens' Inquiry: The Opsahl Report on Northern Ireland* (Dublin: The Lilliput Press, 1993), p. 101.
64. Ruane and Todd, *Dynamics of Conflict*, p. xiv.

Instantly identifying one another along religious lines is something most Irish people are conditioned to do from infancy, because of the role it plays in permitting interaction (and the next chapter will examine in more depth how this plays out specifically in worship). But when Ruane and Todd proceed to remark that the 'conflict is much more about economics, politics or identity than theology' they are understandably assuming a definition of 'theology' as doctrine or discursive statements of belief rather than the sort of theology that is at play in, for example, a person's first instinct being to figure out the religion of the person whom they are greeting.[65] Yet habitual interactions such as these constitute the places in everyday life in which theology is concretized, negotiated and expressed in the world and the content of this 'lived theology' recasts the notion of the relationship between theology and politics. Who God is, how God is known, and where God's people define themselves as being are all subtly but assuredly understood and communicated through such interactions. 'Theology', as some of its disciplines have recently rediscovered (and others, such as liturgical studies, never forgot), is composed of and expressed in *practices* as well as doctrines; indeed, some would argue, it is *mostly* a matter of practices.

Why Focus on Worship?

This book, then, starts to account for the role of ordinary and seemingly benign religious practices in sectarianism in Ireland and Northern Ireland. Other studies have begun to establish the role of religion through assessing the contribution of cross-community dialogue in identifiably religious contexts.[66] Instead of dialogues,

65. Liechty and Clegg's extensive study also resulted in the conclusion that religion must be of prime importance in the landscape of Irish life because of all the things that people could try to find out when first meeting another (such as their politics, or national-affiliation), what they in fact always seek is to know one another's religion. For a full discussion of the place of religion in sectarianism, see, *Moving Beyond Sectarianism* (pp. 28–62).

66. For example, *Moving Beyond Sectarianism*, which the authors decided, in addition to doctrinal definitions, must 'also take seriously religion as a shaper of individual and communal worldview, religion as church institutions, religion as a community-building dynamic and as communities, religion as social institution and agent of socialization, religion as a source of moral formation' (p. 31).

interviews or surveys, however, this book assesses the situation primarily via identifiably religious things that people do together. It is based on the belief that such practices (i.e., worship norms and habits) are a part of what shapes the imaginations and actions that form sectarian attitudes and fuel sectarian violence. It is also based on the belief that these practices, when directed towards reconciliation, can contribute greatly to the generation of positive change and genuinely peaceful cohabitation.[67] However, it is important to note that while I am investigating the role of religion, I am not suggesting that it is the 'primary' cause of the strife; nor am I suggesting that it is a discrete factor, because this thing we call 'religion' is itself both a construct and an agent with political, economic and ethno-national constituents and effects.

Why focus on religious *ritual* practices? Because what human beings do with their bodies sometimes betrays what they do with their thoughts. What people actually do and say in worship (which is often different—slightly, but significantly—from what they are prescribed to do, and from what they say they do[68]) reveals a great deal about the symbolic-cognitive-embodied world in which they live. Many, if not most, Christians will find it hard to tell you in detail what, exactly, they believe in doctrinal terms, but they will not find it hard to go to church on Sunday and do what they do in worship. There seems to be an opportunity, then, to observe what people do and thus reflect upon their embodied expression of 'religion'.

Indeed, I suspect the reason that so few studies have tackled the religious component of the Irish conflict is that attempts to do so

67. I am encouraged in this line of reasoning by Gladys Ganiel's studies of Evan-gelicals in Northern Ireland and her insistence that we move 'beyond the unimportant-dangerous dichotomy that has been imposed on religion' to a position that recognizes religion's potential in constructive community relations, including reconciliation. See, Gladys Ganiel, 'A Framework for Understanding Religion in Northern Irish Civil Society' in Christopher Farrington (ed.), *Global Change, Civil Society and the Northern Ireland Peace Process: Implementing the Political Settlement* (Basingstoke: Palgrave Macmillan, 2008), pp. 159–82; especially p. 159.

68. See Martin Stringer, *On the Perception of Worship* (New York: Continuum, 1999). For example: 'Practically all discussion of worship, liturgy or ritual attempt to provide a discussion of the rite from within the context of the rite itself... This raises a problem for [social-scientific studies] because it is impossible to question or interview people while they are actually involved in the process of worship', (p. 72).

have been downright contradictory: the beliefs most Christians describe when they talk about religion speak directly against sectarian thoughts and actions, so how come those same Christians are engaged in such a web of sectarian habits and attitudes in their daily lives? The reason (researchers understandably conclude) must lie mostly elsewhere than in religion. My contention is that the things most Christians *do* when they practice their religious rites do in fact have recognizable associations with the web of sectarian thoughts and actions in which the culture as a whole is engaged. And, moreover, researching what they *do* can surface some unarticulated (and under-acknowledged) aspects of what they *believe*.

Now, this is not to say that worship is responsible for sectarianism in general or the Northern Irish conflict in particular. Not at all. Like most other commentators, I understand the conflict to have been generated by a complex set of mutually-constituting factors, of which religion is but one among many. However, I believe it to be a uniquely significant one. And my worry about it is that while we have figured out so much of what was wrong with the other constitutive factors of 'the Troubles' (paramilitary violence and intimidation, direct rule, discrimination, unjust policing, lack of access to basic services and legal process), and at least begun to set in places mechanisms and institutions to fix them (decommissioning, devolved government, power-sharing leadership, new police force, fair processes for the Ombudsperson), we have not yet figured out, much less begun to correct, the ways in which religion and religious practices are a factor in this sectarian conflict.[69]

I use observation of what is happening in worship in Ireland as the basis of this book because worship is commonly agreed to be an identifiable 'religious' practice, whereas many potentially important activities in a person's life are not. Take, for example, the question of ethical motivations. Some non-church-going people say that the reason they give to charity is 'religious', and yet other very pious people give to charity but say it has nothing to do with religion. Verifying what is, and is not, understood as a 'religious practice' by the practitioner or the community in which she/he lives

69. Excepting my strong focus on practices in general and on worship in particular, such a theoretical approach finds a precedent in that of L. Philip Barnes, 'Was the Northern Irish Conflict Religious?', *Journal of Contemporary Religion* 20:1 (January 2005), pp. 55–69.

is an ultimately impossible endeavour for any scholar, such practices being complex and beyond such simplistic characterization. Furthermore, while many people identify a whole host of the thoughts, actions and interactions that make up daily life as 'religious', it is hard for the person wishing to study these to access them. For example, even if the way a person arranges small items at home (such as holy water containers by the front door or a Bible by the bed) could be identified as 'religious practices', they are nevertheless very hard to observe because they are, by nature, relatively private. What goes on in church on Sunday morning is no less complicated, no less the object of subjective perception. It is, however, observable on the one hand (i.e., it is *public* discourse) and collective on the other, meaning that people assent to be part of a particular activity that is not idiosyncratic.[70]

There are mechanisms associated with Christian worship that are designed to prevent it tending to the service of sectarianism. Sometimes these mechanisms dwell within the tradition itself, particularly in text-based traditions: for example, the significance of those little rubrics which it might seem there are good reasons to omit (like 'invite the people to pass the peace'). But, oftentimes, given that the nature of worship is that we make it up as we go along (even as it is ever, of course, believed to be subject to the Holy Spirit's inspiration), a significant level of conscientization is required to ensure that one's ritual is not tending in the service of hate-making.

A Few Notes about the Method of this Study

It is this conscientization that this book is about. It aims to develop a liturgical critical theory that can be done by any worshipper or worship leader. I am using the phrase 'liturgical critical theory' in at least two senses: first, as a way of fore-fronting the experiential (some may say 'performed' or 'practised') aspects of faith (as opposed to the written). So, the theory itself is 'liturgical', meaning

---

70. I am not going to look at Orange marches, GAA gatherings, gable-wall murals, etc, although I do see them as 'liturgical' in a broad sense. Instead, for reasons given at the end of this Chapter, I focus more narrowly, on what can be observed in church buildings on a Sunday morning.

it is practical in both its object and its subject.[71] Second, it is a critical theory of liturgy, meaning that it is trying to create a critical theory of worship practices that can enable ordinary worship-goers (including clergy and other ministers) to achieve the double objective of loving their tradition and yet doing so in an inherently self-aware way and with love for people who are not of their own tradition.

Critical theory is characterized by a set of methodologies that are always interdisciplinary, dialectical, reflexive, and critical. James Finlayson expands on how these four essential qualities play out:

> Together with interdisciplinarity, the reflectiveness of critical theory was supposed to unmask what the Frankfurt School theorists considered to be the "positivist" illusion afflicting traditional theories (such as the natural sciences), namely that the theory is just the correct mirroring of an independent realm of facts. That dualist picture of knowledge encouraged the belief that facts were fixed, given, and unalterable, and independent of theory. Critical theorists rejected that picture in favour of a more Hegelian, dialectical conception of knowledge, according to which the facts and our theories are part of an ongoing dynamic historical process in which the way we view the world (theoretically or otherwise) and the way the world is reciprocally determine one another.[72]

By using the ethos of critical theory, I am first of all placing this project in a lineage that goes back at least to Horkheimer and Adorno, who insisted on the need to develop philosophical bases of thought that can assess a situation from within itself. The Frankfurt School's mature project was in considerable part motivated by the question: how did the Holocaust happen and how can we make sure nothing like it ever happens again? As the full awfulness of what has been happening in Northern Ireland since 1968, and between Britain and Ireland for centuries, begins to dawn on the wider world, the mercy of an emerging past tense permits a not dissimilar question to arise.

---

71. Writing about Horkeimer and Adorno's vision, James Finlayson highlights this practical component: 'the task of theory was practical, not just theoretical: that is, it should aim not just to bring about correct understanding, but to create social and political conditions more conducive to human flourishing than the present ones.' James Gordon Finlayson, *Habermas: A Very Short Introduction* (Oxford: Oxford University Press, 2005), p. 4.

72. Finlayson, *Habermas*, p. 3.

It seems sensible, therefore, to house the current investigation in a philosophical project that was founded in response to sectarian atrocities, and has discerned the vital necessity of a self-analytical method and articulated its parameters, even as its interpretative manifestations are still being tested in the world. Perhaps the distinctive marker of this approach is that it does not simply describe how a situation is flawed but also tries, 'by identifying progressive aspects and tendencies within it, to help transform society for the better.'[73] Critical theory can therefore be characterized as having 'two different kinds of normative aim: diagnostic and remedial.'[74] As such, it is widely viewed as a 'practical' philosophy, and, therefore, I consider it to be well-suited to the theological study of worship (composed, as it is, of bodily practices).

It has often been remarked that theologians and other scholars of religion have been notoriously quiet on the Irish–British conflict.[75] Indeed, Christian theology could be pointed to as proof that what was happening in Northern Ireland was *not* religious: its books are everywhere full of condemnation of inter-Christian aggression and justifications for non-violence in every aspect of living with all peoples, and its ministers were (almost) everywhere preaching that the violence was wrong and must stop. It is not therefore terribly surprising that looking to Christian theology could not provide insight into either why this conflict started, or why it persisted.

However, with the recent (re-)turn to studying practices and not only beliefs in theology, a vista has opened which has particular possibilities for situations of conflict involving Christians. While Christians' theological beliefs offer little insight about the violence in which they are involved, their practices may. Indeed, a theological interpretation of ordinary Christians' ritualizing performances might hold the key to unlocking deep attachments to ultimately self-

---

73. Finlayson, *Habermas*, p. 4.
74. Finlayson, *Habermas*, p. 4. Punctuation altered.
75. Notable exceptions include the remarkable faculty of the Irish School of Ecumenics, including Geraldine Smyth, Linda Hogan and David Tombs, as well as Terence McCaughey's *Memory and Redemption: Church, Politics and Prophetic Theology in Ireland* (Dublin: Gill and Macmillan, 1993) and Mary Condren's outstanding work on mercy. See, for example: 'Mercy Not Sacrifice: Toward a Celtic Theology', *Feminist Theology* 15 (May 1997). Also, 'Gender, Religion, and War,' in Linda Hogan and Dylan Lee Lehrke (eds), *Religion and the Politics of Peace and Conflict*, Princeton Theological Monograph Series (Eugene, OR: Wipf and Stock, 2009), pp. 125-58.

defeating ways of living. A significant example is offered in the next chapter, which considers the subject of reconciliation. It will be suggested that while Christian theologies of reconciliation can acquire a high degree of cross-community assent at the level of textual scholarship, Christian practices of reconciliation reveal variations in the conception of relationship (between God and people, and people with other people) that are so extreme as to be able to offer insight into why reconciliation in Ireland has so far proven an 'elusive quest'.

Second, I follow Jürgen Habermas, who wrote that his method was to retain his German traditions, even as they had included the Naziism of his youth, which he later deplored, but to do so 'in a self-critical spirit with the skepticism and the clear-sightedness of the man who has already once been fooled.'[76] By this, I seek to affirm that the sorts of diagnoses and remedies presented here are offered from nowhere else than from within a tradition that has sheltered great evil. Remaining within one's own context in order to dismantle its destructive ways is why this sort of critical theoretical method is called 'immanent criticism'. Immanent criticism is so named to convey the fact that, 'critical theorists aim to criticise an object—a conception of society or a work of philosophy—on its own terms, and not on the basis of values or standards that transcend it, in order to bring its untruth to light.'[77] Thus, when I assess certain Irish worship practices in the central chapters of this book, I will not be doing so using any criteria other than those that govern Christian worship in Ireland. In some cases those criteria are derived from texts—authorized texts with rubrics for worship (such as the Church of Ireland follows) or teachings about worship (as Roman Catholics possess), but in others those criteria come from oral traditions of practice that are just as normative, but largely unwritten (for example, multiple Evangelical and Pentecostal practices within otherwise text-based denominations as well as outside them).

Third, I am seeking a mechanism for critiquing worship practices that takes liturgical studies out of the realms of either taste or partisan politics. A liturgical critical theory is not conditioned by such things, even as a pastoral liturgical theology rightly is; instead,

76. P. Dews (ed.), *Autonomy and Solidarity: Interviews with Jürgen Habermas* (London: Verso, 1992), p. 46.
77. Finlayson, *Habermas*, p. 9.

its eye is on the socio-political prize of not living with fear or hatred or contempt (neither one's own, nor another's). It has no truck with the notion of 'best' practice, or 'best' forms, or 'best' music. It does not even care about 'the right way' of doing something (in the sense of commentaries upon a particular issue, such as: you should not have individual bulletins; you should not use poetry), the 'right way' in this study being conceived instead as a complex combination of tradition-plus-local-context in response to contingent realities and sensibilities, changing over time and with the assent of the community. As with much in practical theology, its concern is not so much to prescribe all possible 'right' ways as it is to identify 'wrong' ones.

Fourth, I am seeking a theoretical model that is capable of reinforcing the efforts of the grassroots community organizers, whose diligent efforts through adult education workshops, mutual support groups, local campaigns and schools interventions have been making similar points, over many years.[78]

What happens in worship in Ireland has lessons for how worship is planned, led and studied all over the world. Which is not to claim the lessons are universally applicable; it is just to say that the study of worship habits in this local context can highlight some of the ways in which both specific local practices and Christian worship *per se* walk a line between peace-making and evil-tending every time they are performed. Liturgy is a far more fragile animal than theology has tended to realize, for while it creates subjectivities, it is also simultaneously created by them; this has historically been masked by the perception of liturgy as a genre of human behaviour that suffers from the illusion of seeming fixity, 'normativity', and inherent-goodness. However, as Don Saliers has remarked, 'Liturgical theology suffers when it fails to acknowledge "hidden" power issues and the malformative histories of practice.'[79] Liturgy,

---

78. For a survey of grassroots organizers in the context of Irish sectarianism, see for example, John D. Brewer, 'Northern Ireland: Peacemaking among Protestants and Catholics' in Mary Ann Cejka and Thomas Barmat (eds), *Artisans of Peace: Grassroots Peacemaking among Christian Communities* (Maryknoll, NY: Orbis Books, 2003), pp. 67–95.

79. Don E. Saliers, 'Afterword' in E. Byron Anderson and Bruce T. Morrill, *Liturgy and the Moral Self: Humanity at Full Stretch: Essays in Honor of Don E. Saliers* (Collegeville, MN: Liturgical Press, 1998), p. 214.

then, when equipped with both the wisdom of the ages and an accurate awareness of the needs of the moment, can and must become proficient at constantly checking-in with itself about whether it is using its powers for good and not for evil.

To attain such a liturgical critical theory in a particular context, one needs first a liturgical anthropology, a way of observing and describing what people are actually doing as worship in a given locale: a gestalt of worship, if you like. Alongside others interested in the connection between theology and church life as-lived, my method is based in recent developments in ethnography, especially as they relate to the study of ritualization. I therefore owe a great methodological debt to the field of ritual studies,[80] but also to its theological interpreters,[81] because in showing the anatomy of sectarian liturgical subjectivity, I make my theological awareness a key part of the project. Like the work of Catherine Bell, therefore, this study notes, for example, that even ritualizations of resistance are based on the ways the body has already been atomized; but like the work of William T. Cavanaugh it sets such an observation in the service of ecclesiology, questioning whether and how the church can resist the destructive political realities within which it exists.

In preparation for writing this book, my most important research tool was my own body in the spaces being studied, because (following Bell) I took as my starting point the premise that one can only research ritualizations from within a body that is acted upon and configured in its subjectivity. I look at Christian worship, therefore, from my vantage point as a participant in the spaces and moments being studied. There is a vital difference between ethnographies that rely primarily on observer-participation and those that rely primarily on interviews, surveys or questionnaires, and this study is based on the former. As such, it also draws on the work of those late-twentieth century anthropologists who

80. In particular, the work of Ron Grimes. See, for example: Ronald L. Grimes, *Beginnings in Ritual Studies* (Washington DC: University Press of America, 1982); *Ritual Criticism: Case Studies in Its Practice, Essays on Its Theory* (Columbia, SC: University of South Carolina Press, 1990); and *Deeply into the Bone: Reinventing Rites of Passage* (Berkley, CA: University of California Press, 2000).

81. Notably Nathan D. Mitchell. See for example, *Liturgy and the Social Sciences* (Collegeville, MN: Liturgical Press, 2000).

reoriented the academic perception of verifiability in the study of human behaviour, such as Karen McCarthy Brown's celebrated *Moma Lola*,[82] and it seeks to converse with the work of theologians such as Mitchell, Cavanaugh and Nicholas Healy who have taken up the question of religious subject-formation (particularly via liturgy). As Healy notes, 'Contemporary postmodern ethnography has largely abandoned the earlier notion of an "impartial observer" whose description of a culture is understood to be definitive because it is objective and unprejudiced'.[83]

In its theological variant, as a 'postmodern ecclesiological ethnography', which relies on the self-aware subject reporting from a localized position rather than the theologian as one charged with the task of the creation of an 'epic', Healy sees the possibility of 'open[ing] up our constructed identity to ongoing reassessment,'[84] creating a 'practical and prophetic ecclesiology' which is 'ever-moving, always struggling along with the theodrama.'[85] However, he also warns strongly against the dangers of theologians restricting themselves too rigidly to any single social-scientific style in their forays into ethnography and praises as lay examples both David Lodge's novels and Thomas Days' popular book about why Catholic congregations in the USA do not sing for the theological insights produced by their first-person 'thick descriptions'.[86] Like Kathryn Tanner in *Theories of Culture*, Healy thus calls for theological use of those new forms of ethnography which are designed to perform an essentially self-critical function, 'by uncovering and giving sense to the internal contestations of a culture, by disputing the homogeneity

82. McCarthy Brown argues that the conventional academic notion of 'objectivity' is a charade on the basis not just of feminist objections, but also because scholarship cannot access the *performative* quality of events and cultures by such methods. 'Ethnographic research, whatever else it is, is a form of human relationship. When the lines long drawn in anthropology between participant-observer and informant break down, then the only truth is the one in between; and anthropology becomes something closer to a social art form, open to both aesthetic and moral judgment.' Karen McCarthy Brown: *Mama Lola: A Vodou Priestess in Brooklyn* (Berkeley, CA: University of California Press, 1991, 2001), p. 12.

83. Nicholas Healy, *Church, World and the Christian Life* (Cambridge: Cambridge University Press, 2000), p. 176.

84. Healy, *Church, World and the Christian Life*, p. 175.

85. Healy, *Church, World and the Christian Life*, p. 185.

86. Healy, *Church, World and the Christian Life*, pp. 183–85.

and consistency of a culture, by resisting the temptation to assume unified cultural totalities.'[87]

The insidious thing about sectarianism is that it is adept at defying either empirical investigation or theological analysis, and this apparent impossibility of accountability has greatly bolstered its success in passing as normalcy or, even, as benign. This study is, then, following Healy, developing an inductive, interdisciplinary theological method as a way of resisting sectarianism's habit of eluding any single discipline's systematic ability to 'nail it'. This is why ritual studies, with its insistence on naming what can be observed through the scholar's own participation has an edge when it comes to warning when and how worship is complicit in destructive attitudes or practices. And this is why theologies that take full account of postmodern ethnographies are capable of speaking to situations in the church that is, rather than the church as theologians would wish it to be.[88] The church in Ireland is an intrinsic part of a society so riven by sectarian hatred that it is one of its defining characteristics, and thus it is upon these self-consciously post-'objective' methods of study that I rely in order to uncover what so many other studies have found it elusive to identify: the anatomy of sectarian liturgical subjectivity.

Specifically, then, the method of this study relies initially on Grimes's interdisciplinary pragmatics: particularly, but not exclusively, his delineation of the role of the scholar as *participant*, his emphasis on *performance* and the methods needed for its study, his alertness to the possibility of ritual *failure* and his constant attention to *power* dynamics in ritualizing. It then takes its hermeneutical lead from Catherine Bell's positioning of the body of the scholar in the corpus of the ritual action being studied. Refusing the conceptual existence of a thing called 'ritual' and discerning instead only the fact of ritual-making/doing, Bell turns the scholarly focus to 'ritualization', a term she uses to insist upon the inevitably specific, in-situ nature of any and every ritual-action. Such a focus highlights issues of agency, for the scholar as for the

---

87. Kathryn Tanner, *Theories of Culture: A New Agenda for Theology* (Minneapolis, MN: Fortress Press, 1997), p. 58.

88. Two excellent examples are Mary McClintock Fulkerson's *Places of Redemption: Theology for a Worldly World* (New York: Oxford University Press, 2007), and Martha Moore Keish, *Do This in Remembrance of Me: A Performed Approach to Eucharistic Theology* (Grand Rapids, MI: Eerdmans, 2008).

people studied, and, thus, permits a conceptualization of subjectivity and its ongoing-creation *vis-à-vis* ritual practices.

Crucially, in Bell's theorizing, this focus is always on the body — the body of the ritualizing agent, and the body of the scholar who is, inevitably, part of and not 'above' the ritual practices. Following Bourdieu, Bell's primary interest is in the ways in which this body is cultivated by its encounters, not as a fixed entity — 'The Body' — but, rather, as a (permanently evolving) set of dispositions. Moreover, she analyses how ritualization mediates the cultivation of these dispositions:

> Ritualization produces this ritualized body through the interaction of the body with a structured and structuring environment. ... Through a series of physical movements ritual practices spatially and temporally construct an environment organized according to schemes of privileged oppositions. The construction of this environment and the activities within it simultaneously work to impress these schemes upon the bodies of participants.[89]

The contemporary negotiation of the 'privileged oppositions' at play in the Republic of Ireland and Northern Ireland cannot be studied by looking at either the texts for Sunday morning's liturgies nor written historical accounts of liturgical practices on the island (even if such existed); nor can they be studied by asking people, after a liturgical event, what they thought was going on within it or what beliefs they thought it supported or expressed. Other things can be studied using these methods, and are of undoubted and significant theological and cultural value. But, because the ritual creation of subjectivity works below the surface of human consciousness,[90] the particular privileged oppositions at play in a (sectarian) landscape and the ways in which human beings negotiate (and are created by) them can only be discerned by embedding in their midst, and reporting from the front (and back) line.

Between September 2001 and September 2008, therefore, I visited 26 congregations in the Republic of Ireland and Northern Ireland. I always went to the Sunday morning service (or the later Sunday morning service, if there were several), and never to the Saturday night or Sunday evening services where such existed, simply to

89. Catherine Bell, *Ritual Theory, Ritual Practice* (Oxford: Oxford University Press, 1992), p. 98.
90. A premise of much of ritual studies; see Bell, *Ritual Theory*, p. 84.

create a more comparable sample. Consonant with current guidelines on the study of human subjects, apart from the two Cathedrals in the study (Galway and St. Patrick's in Dublin) and those churches where express permission was granted, I protect the anonymity of these communities in my report of what I observed there. However, because it is relevant to the argument, I do note the denominational background of each church in question, the region in which it is located and, sometimes, the date or time of year at which I visited. The factors of denomination, region and date are so vital to understanding the ritualization performed in these churches that the argument is impossible to make without mentioning them. I intended to visit each congregation only once, but I went back to half of them at least one further time, in some cases because I needed to check facts (e.g., is that flag *still* there?) and in others simply out of curiosity about how they had changed.

You see, in the course of this study, Irish society has changed massively. A country whose greatest export had long been its people, Ireland became during this period a major recipient of immigrants. Over the ten years prior to the current economic crash, many towns had seen a growth of 10 percent or more in their population claiming Eastern European heritage. The island also experienced astounding economic growth in this decade, taking the Republic from the second-poorest country in Europe to the wealthiest country in the world (according to GDP indices). And Northern Ireland and the Republic also encountered the peace-process. Northern Ireland bore the brunt of this process, to be sure, but it must be noted that the basis of *The Good Friday Agreement* required a referendum in the Republic, because its terms required a fundamental and historic change in the Irish constitution. Mistakenly, many of us who voted for that change conceived it as trying to do something about someone else's sectarianism, rather than our own.

The following chapter examines why it has been so very difficult to gain 'reconciliation' in Ireland when, on the one hand, sectarianism is always someone else's problem and one cannot, therefore do anything about it; and, on the other, theological models circulating in Irish liturgies allow only private and not corporate angers (the very sort that sectarianism trades in) to be forgiven.

Chapter Two

WORSHIP AND RECONCILIATION

'We couldn't even get peace at the altar.'[1]

If 'peace' takes the place of 'war', what takes the place of sectarianism? Treaties bind parties to ceasefires and new civic arrangements, but the sorts of violence that comprise sectarianism (violent thoughts, attitudes and everyday practices) remain intact; indeed, as the previous chapter noted, they are metastasizing.[2] Just as other recognizably damaging situations need to have some conceptual alternative to which to appeal (for example, in tackling crime we are able to refer to the concept of justice), so does sectarianism. Of course, the conceptual appeals that societies use to manage, and turn away from violence are only ever locally relevant and contextually effective. Justice works as a concept that can counter crime in specific western democracies, but other concepts (or other definitions of justice) are needed to moderate crime in other societies.[3] A quick survey of world sectarianism correspondingly reveals a wide range of moderating counter-approaches, some of which have also been tried in Ireland.[4]

1. Séamus Heaney, 'The Cure at Troy', *Collected Poems* (London: Faber & Faber, 2002).
2. In addition to the studies cited in the previous chapter, see, Helen Brocklehurst, 'Kids R Us? Children as Political Bodies' in Mark Evans (ed.), *Ethical Theory in the Study of International Politics* (New York: Nova, 2004), pp. 89–102. She writes that, 'Six years on [from the Belfast Agreement] sectarianism is still prevalent and hopes for peace low. Children remain caught up in paramilitary violence and their opportunities in society are still hopelessly inadequate', (p. 99). (And she quotes the *Northern Ireland Life and Times Survey* as evidence).
3. See, R. Scott Appleby, *The Ambivalence of the Sacred: Religion, Violence, and Reconciliation* (Oxford: Rowman and Littlefield, 2000).
4. Including: the concept of non-violent toleration; multiple models of partition (some including deportation); the notion of 'separate but equal'; strategies of enforced intermixing (such as busing to integrate schools); and models of consociationality (one of which was used in framing the Good Friday Agreement of 1998).

Thinking about the Irish–British situation from a Christian theological perspective, there is really only one moderating concept available, and that is reconciliation. Theologically, where there is hatred and violence, there is separation from God, and the only solution is neither a political strategy for toleration nor another for removing the problem, but reconciliation. Theologically, reconciliation refers to restoration of the right-ordering of relationship between God and human beings (briefly: the world was separated from God, its maker, by sin; God reconciled the world to Godself through the atoning life, death and resurrection of Jesus Christ) and to the right-ordering of relationship between human beings for theological reasons (only when in loving relationship with our neighbours are we able to live in full loving relationship with God).[5] Although theologies of reconciliation have varied enormously over time, geography and culture (and I will argue that reconciliation needs to be contextually conceived and developed) there is a basic common concept and it says: because God has forgiven you, you must forgive one another.

Christian theology thus has *forgiveness* at the heart of its various ethics of reconciliation, and this aspect especially has seeped deeply into colloquial and political conceptions of the meaning of reconciliation,[6] furthered at least in part by worldwide media attention to the South African Truth and Reconciliation Commission (TRC), with its controversial granting of 'amnesties' in response to confession. As several commentators have recently pointed out, the notion of forgiveness at play in the TRC (and dominating much of recent political, social and psychological research into reconciliation) is founded on exclusively Christian theological terms. In response to this, Solomon Schimmel has demonstrated how Jewish, Christian and Moral–Philosophical notions of forgiveness vary, sometimes quite radically, in both their philosophical premises and their assumptions about appropriate reconciling

---

5. The key text for which across denominations has been Mt. 5.23-4.

6. See, for example, Robert Enright and Joanna North (eds), *Exploring Forgiveness* (Madison, WI: University of Wisconsin Press, 1998); Donald W. Shriver, *An Ethic for Enemies – Forgiveness in Politics* (New York: Oxford University Press, 1995); Everett L. Worthington (ed.), *Dimensions of Forgiveness: Psychological Research and Theological Perspectives* (Philadelphia, PA: Templeton Foundation Press, 1998); plus the ongoing debate in *The American Philosophical Quarterly* throughout the 1980s and 1990s.

behaviours.[7] He thus argues that any political appeal to a supposedly neutral definition of 'forgiveness' is one that runs the risk of obfuscating important cultural understandings of the requirements for and effects of forgiveness.[8]

One might reasonably assume that in an Irish context this should not be problematic because nearly everyone is Christian and even despite recent declines in numbers, a relatively large number still attend worship on Sundays, implying common cultural understandings of forgiveness. How, then, do we explain the fact that it is indeed problematic?[9] Moreover, given that there is remarkable agreement not only on the fact that reconciliation is what lies beyond sectarianism;[10] given that there are contemporary theological articulations of reconciliation that have gained the assent of a wide array of thinkers in both religious and secular contexts; and given that so many grass-roots organizations have been working for reconciliation for decades, why is reconciliation so 'elusive'? I would like to suggest that the same thing Schimmel identifies as making Christian-based notions of reconciliation problematic in religiously-plural or secular situations turns out to be the very thing that makes it problematic in unusually-Christian Ireland: the ambivalent (or simply absent) place of contrition and restitution in its pursuit of forgiveness.

7. Solomon Schimmel, *Wounds Not Healed by Time: The Power of Repentance and Forgiveness* (New York: Oxford University Press, 2002).

8. His argument is that forgiveness is the way of ending the cycle of revenge, but it nearly always takes hearing repentance to be able to do it; Christian theology therefore needs to amplify its facilitation of repentance (and restitution) and resist the tendency to allow its radical forms of forgiveness (such as he sees displayed in the TRC amnesties) to become normative; Jewish theology needs to amplify its attentiveness to forgiveness (and he highlights theologians within the tradition who long ago also made such an argument, including early Mishnah teachings and the kabbalist Rabbi Moses Cordevero of Safed).

9. As Norman Porter has amply demonstrated. See, *The Elusive Quest: Reconciliation in Northern Ireland* (Belfast: Blackstaff Press, 2003).

10. For a survey of queries into whether reconciliation is, in fact, the answer to sectarianism, see Porter, *The Elusive Quest*. Also see, the *Good Friday Agreement*, which named 'reconciliation' as its ultimate goal in several places. The signatories pledged themselves to, 'the achievement of reconciliation, tolerance, and mutual trust, and to the protection and vindication of the human rights of all'... and to 'strive in every practical way towards reconciliation and approchement within the framework of democratic and agreed arrangements.' ('Declaration of Support' Nos. 2 and 5.)

In recent years, Irish and Northern Irish peace-workers have turned to a new set of theological treatments of reconciliation.[11] These specifically address the question of how contrition/restitution plays out in concrete experiences of forgiveness, and chief among them is Miroslav Volf's theological response to the war in his native Croatia. Although definitions of forgiveness are manifold in Christian traditions, as are the pastoral theologies that accompany them, prior to Volf *et al*[12] the more radical ones tended to have received the widest press in Ireland. Thus, at a popular level, it was common for the 'Christian' approach to a slight to be described as the demand that people totally let some injury go and love the offender as if they were a friend, whether the offender is a murderer or an abusive spouse or a dictator or whoever. By contrast, Volf describes Christian reconciliation using the metaphor of an embrace, unpacking four main movements: 'opening the arms, waiting, closing the arms, and opening them again'[13] and he excavates the interpersonal dimensions of each movement: how both giver and receiver feel, what is at stake for each, and what risk is required of both in each movement. As a metaphor, 'embrace' suggests a different mode of reconciliation than other metaphors in colloquial circulation (such as 'opening the door', 'setting the table' or 'adopting the higher ground'), and it makes the work of reconciliation directly inter-personal, challenging the individual to take the responsibility of embracing the enemy themselves rather than wishing others would fix the conflict on their behalf.

Volf's theology also repositions forgiveness in the sequence of necessary movements. Exegeting the story of the prodigal son (Lk. 15.11–32), he notes that, 'confession *followed* acceptance'. In Volf's reading, the father's arms went out to the son before he made any mention of his wrongdoing. However, because the relationship had been broken, 'for the embrace to be complete — for the celebration to begin — a confession of wrongdoing had to be made.'[14] The

11. Many of the key contributors to which are included in the great volume by David Tombs and Joseph Liechty (eds), *Explorations in Reconciliation: New Directions in Theology* (Aldershot: Ashgate, 2006).

12. Such as the contributors to Tombs and Liechty, *Explorations in Reconciliation*.

13. Miroslav Volf, *Exclusion and Embrace: A Theological Exploration of Identity, Otherness and Reconciliation* (Nashville, TN: Abingdon Press, 1996), p. 141.

14. Volf, *Exclusion and Embrace*, p. 160.

essential nature of this connection between celebration and confession, between reconciliation and restitution, has been explored in many recent commentaries, usually in discussion of the TRC. Widely applauded for its effectiveness in permitting South Africa to move beyond apartheid, the TRC was nevertheless also criticized in various quarters for its conception of and emphasis upon forgiveness. If somebody gave a full confession (told the truth) they would be forgiven (not prosecuted) for their actions. The amnesties' lack of a demand for either the expression of contrition or the punishment of crimes is what many identify as the peculiarly 'Christian' character of this model.[15] In Volf's developed model, however, we have a 'both-and': a model that allows the TRC method (of forgiving 'up front') but does not forego the place of contrition and/or restitution in the total economy of reconciliation. Contrition for wrongdoing has to be made for the process of reconciliation to be complete, but the victim is not condemned to having to wait for something that may never come before getting on with the ultimately self-healing step of 'opening their arms'.

In the autumn of 2005, in the absence of any state-sponsored truth and reconciliation commission in Northern Ireland, the BBC took it upon itself to invite individuals from both sides of the Troubles, victims and perpetrators, to meet at a table hosted by Archbishop Desmond Tutu, who had overseen the TRC in South Africa.[16] Most of the perpetrators in the documentary, despite having been given prison sentences of hundreds of years, were now free citizens due to the release clauses of the 1998 Good Friday Agreement (*GFA*), and they sat across the table from people who had, due to the actions of those same people, lost spouses, parents, children, siblings or limbs and other body parts, not to mention those losses that were more difficult to represent on film: sanity, livelihoods, community, security, the ability to sleep, to trust or to enjoy life. There were remarkable differences between each encounter and in each individual's behaviour, but one striking pattern was that none of the perpetrators cried, as the victims often

15. See, for example, Robert I. Rotberg and Dennis Thompson, *Truth v. Justice: The Morality of Truth Commissions* (Princeton, NJ: Princeton University Press, 2000).

16. The films of the conversations were broadcast by the BBC in Britain and Northern Ireland under the title 'Facing the Truth' on Saturday 4, Sunday 5 and Monday 6 March 2006.

did, and whereas the victims talked in directly personal terms, the perpetrators talked about their deeds in terms of their identity as agents of war. Many of the perpetrators insisted, 'we were badly affected by it too', strongly implying that they were also, in a strong sense, victims. At the end of each encounter, if both parties were still in the room, Tutu would guide the conversation toward the possibility of what he called 'closure'. He would suggest to the victim (obviously referring to preparatory conversations off-camera) the option of shaking the hand of the perpetrator, and the language of forgiveness and reconciliation was covert where it was not overt. It was a visible test of Volf 's image of 'embrace'.[17]

Personally, this moment always seemed to me both to arrive too quickly, and to be unwarranted in those cases where the perpetrator showed little or no remorse. Indeed, there seemed to be pressure (from Tutu) on the victim to forgive far more than there was pressure on the perpetrator to show contrition. But, my personal reactions were confounded time and again by the fact that so many victims did indeed approach the perpetrator, and so many shook hands. Based on their remarks across the table, what seemed to allow those victims who could do so to 'embrace' was in all cases their sense that they were both part of the same (externally imposed) problem, and in many cases an accompanying compassion for the perpetrator predicated on the understanding that he had suffered too, had had his life ruined too, in this specific, systemic, historic situation which had also harmed them. Forgiveness thus seemed to arise from awareness of a sort of imagined solidarity in the face of a mutual horror.

These victims seem to have discovered a way of responding to the question which is at the heart of this chapter: what do you do where there is no confession, and never will be a confession, or, as in some of these televised encounters, a confession without contrition, meaning admission of deeds but no associated remorse? The question is acute in Ireland/Northern Ireland because contrition/restitution is *never* going to come, for two reasons. First, regarding the Troubles, many of the perpetrators understand themselves to have been combatants in a war, rendering the rules of both engagement and restitution different than in other sorts of

17. Volf notes that in northern European cultures, a handshake is the appropriate analogy with what in America or southern Europe is performed with an embrace.

conflict.[18] Combatants might be able to regret that their actions inevitably caused grief for non-combatants (as the paramilitary apologies expressed[19]), but the terms of war mean that they are not able to apologize in the way one would in intra-civilian conflict. Second, even if (and it is a big if[20]) an apology could be garnered for every violent act from 1968–1998, it would not be contrition/ reparation enough to permit reconciliation because, as the last chapter showed, the sectarianism that requires reconciliation in Ireland and Northern Ireland is about so much more than the recent Troubles.

People on both sides of the sectarian divide in Ireland can open their arms in gestures of anticipatory acceptance, but who is ever going to furnish the anticipated confession, and to what? In a situation in which evil has festered for generations, the gnarl of blame becomes an impossible knot to untie. In Liam Kennedy's parodying acronym, the Irish are a bunch of 'MOPERS' (Most Oppressed People Ever)[21] and which Truth and Reconciliation

18. Here I differ from Nigel Biggar's recent commentary on Northern Irish reconciliation in two fundamental respects: first he repeatedly presents 'the Troubles' as being initiated by the IRA, not even mentioning, never mind addressing, the Republican perspective that the IRA were responding to and not initiating aggression/oppression; second, he conflates sectarianism with the Troubles and with paramilitarism, rather than seeing sectarianism as a society-wide affect that pre- and post-dates the Troubles. Nigel Biggar, 'Forgiving Enemies in Ireland' in *Journal of Religious Ethics* 36:4 (2008), pp. 559–80.

19. The loyalist paramilitary groups, when announcing their ceasefires in 1996, did apologize; in 2002, the IRA did similarly, apologizing for the hurt caused to all 'noncombatants' harmed during the war. While well-received by government representatives, because of their indication of seriousness about the cessation of violence, these apologies were not generally received as aiding forgiveness at a popular or church level. See, for example, Mark R. Amstutz, *The Healing of Nations: The Promise and Limits of Political Forgiveness* (Lanham, MD: Rowman and Littlefield, 2005).

20. A confession, never mind an apology, for the vast majority of the murders during the Troubles, remains missing. Over half the 3,600 deaths remain unsolved as murders and many of those deemed solved are known to be mistaken, as seen, for example in the encounter between Michael Stone and Sylvia Hackett (broadcast 7 March 2006), when Stone maintained he had only been present at Mr. Hackett's murder, and had not pulled the trigger — but had confessed to the murder because he knew he was going down (for 600 years) anyway, and by confessing he allowed the real killer to remain an agent of the struggle.

21. Liam Kennedy coined the acronym MOPE in *Colonialism, Religion and Nationalism in Ireland* (Belfast: Institute of Irish Studies, 1996), pp. 217–18.

Commission can unpack what some reckon to be 900 years of oppression resulting in Irish people's (righteous, if doomed) moping? In Ireland, we live with what Hannah Arendt described as 'the predicament of irreversibility',[22] in which (Troubles aside) wrongdoing is long-done and the memory of it is bedded-in, part of the fabric of social normativity, rendered unforgivable by its seeming un-pin-down-ability.[23]

Such is the legacy of 900 years of contested ownership of both the culture and the geography of the island that it is not going to be solved by a commission. Attention to individual cases is important and should be pursued as far as it is helpful to the victims, but for much of our hatred, there can be no tribunal. Republicans might identify Britain as the original invader and the long-time oppressor, and were the British to make a similar sort of apology to the Irish that the Australians recently made to the indigenous people of that land, it might help with the healing of history. However, the co-implication of peoples on the island goes back so long, and its history has so many—and conflicting—versions that such a move would prove incendiary to other significant constituencies of the island, not least those for whom the imperial threat has long come from Rome rather than London. We are going to have to get over it in some other way than a TRC, tribunal or an Australian-style indigenous apology, and this is where theological forms of reconciliation, with their call for confession/contrition in the economy of forgiveness, meet a challenge.

In the early days of post-colonial interpretation, it was common to find a narrative of a victim and their aggressor, a people and its colonizer, moving to redescribe themselves in the light of the oppressor's departure.[24] Such narratives were bitterly disputed in Ireland for a number of reasons, not least the fact that there are

22. Hannah Arendt, *The Human Condition* (Chicago, IL: University of Chicago Press, 1998), p. 212.
23. On the depth of this complexity and how it conditions notions of reconciliation or forgiveness in the Irish situation as well as others, see for example, Marie Smyth, *Truth, Recovery and Justice after Conflict* (New York: Routledge, 2007).
24. See, for example, Robert J.C. Young, *A Very Short Introduction to Postcolonialism* (Oxford: Oxford University Press, 2003. For a comparative study of very early post-colonial thinking in Ireland and India, see also: Julia M. Wright, *Ireland, India and Nationalism in the Nineteenth Century* (Cambridge: Cambridge University Press, 2009).

deeply contested notions of who is the oppressor and who is the victim; indeed, nearly everyone feels themself to be a victim.[25] As post-colonial discourses flourished in other parts of the formerly-British world, and the racism it identified became increasingly identified as a matter of visual culture, as a matter of colour, it was with some relief that Ireland could gain an exemption due to the fact that most skins were not dark, the famous line from *The Commitments* notwithstanding.[26] After 1998, we were free to pursue our economic aspirations like white people, and we ran with it, becoming colonizers ourselves as we rode on the back of the Celtic Tiger (a colonial animal if ever there was one) through globalizing capitalist markets.

But with the arrival of refugees (many of whom were darker-skinned people), an overdue awareness of the traveling communities in our midst, and the fact that cultural expressions of shame, aggression and rage simply kept repeating (clerical sex abuse, widespread illiteracy, binge-drinking, street violence and intimidation, not to mention large-scale poverty which had caused, first, mass migration and, then, destitution and despair under the belly of the tiger), the endemic nature of our relationship to empire became unavoidable. It seems important, therefore, to analyse Irish affairs as a post-colonial situation even though, as Leith Davis says, 'To apply the term *postcolonial* to an Irish context is to invite controversy'.[27] Yet to do so might also hold the key to understanding why Ireland has not and how it yet might encounter a strong enough version of reconciliation to move beyond sectarianism.

After forgiving, insists Volf, comes forgetting, and he argues hard against those who might find a path to reconciliation but not to actually letting the entire offending experience go. It is a complicated and in no way glib notion of 'forgetting'. His work

25. See, for example, Marie Smyth: 'It is not shameful to retaliate when one's family or community is attacked. Thus, a strong collective identity whereby individuals identify with wrongs done to their identity group, coupled with ongoing violence, creates the conditions for a pervasive culture of victimhood where, "everyone is a victim".' (*Truth, Recovery and Justice*, p. 80).

26. 'The Irish are the Blacks of Europe.'

27. Leith Davis, *Music, Postcolonialism, and Gender: The Construction of Irish National Identity, 1724–1874* (Notre Dame, IN: Notre Dame Press, 2006), p. 7. See also, Eoin Flannery, *Ireland and Postcolonial Studies: Theory, Discourse, Utopia* (New York: Palgrave Macmillan, 2009).

has been taken up by peace-seekers throughout the world, who report that the enactment of forms of forgetting after forgiving proved crucial to their being able to make sense of, and ultimately heal from, their conflicts.[28] The problem in Ireland when seen through post-colonial lenses is that we are practiced at forgetting without forgiving. All manner of historical episodes have been too-quickly hidden from sight, usually quoting the 'need to move on' as justification for their non-examination. With the help of pop-psychology, we thus reason that, for example: hardly anyone talked about the famine for a century because of mass-scale post-traumatic muteness; the Magdalen laundries were a display of an outmoded piety obviously not shared by the majority; migrants were highly-motivated self-seekers; and the sex abuse scandals were a result of the church's repression of homosexuality in the clergy. Each problem is localized, de-culturized (made non-endemic through isolation from the wider culture), and, most importantly, de-politicized as traces of imperial organizational structures and power-relations in government, education, gender and class-stratification are obfuscated.

Similarly, we nowadays encounter the seemingly *de-facto* impression that the Troubles were the product of a few 'savages' in Northern Ireland.[29] To interrogate the Troubles in a more extended sense, to excavate instead the landscape of sectarianism or racial/ethnic dis-ease across the island, is to be accused of 'harking on about the past', or 'standing in the way of progress' (the cardinal sins of modernity?), when what is supposedly needed is simply, as the *GFA* put it, 'a fresh start'.[30] The critic Colin Graham has noted that prior to the *GFA* there had been a widespread hope that, 'the cultural complexities of Northern Ireland would figure in, and maybe

28. See, for example, Everrett L. Worthington, 'Unforgiveness, Forgive-ness and Reconciliation and Their Implications for Societal Interventions' in Raymond G. Helmick and Rodney L. Petersen (eds), *Forgiveness and Recon-ciliation: Religion, Public Policy and Conflict Transformation* (Conshohocken, PA: Templeton Foundation Press, 2002), pp. 171–92.

29. 'Will these savages become model citizens in the "New Ireland?"' asks one of the contributors to the BBC's 'Talking Point'. http://news.bbc.co.uk/2/hi/talking_point/153675.stm. And David McKittrick's article at the time of the first Loyalist ceasefires was entitled, 'Savage killers who marked hatred in blood...' *The Independent (UK)* Friday, 14 October 1994.

30. *The Agreement: Agreement Reached in the Multi-party Negotiations* (Good Friday Agreement), 'Declaration of Support', paragraph 2.

even dictate, the shape of the future. But, by the time of the Agreement, a different political imperative had taken hold. "Culture" had been reduced to the issues of minority languages and the need to curtail the display of sectarian symbols' and he comments that 'this switch in strategy gambled on consigning the past to the rubbish-bin of history.'[31] The rubbish-bin of Irish history is brimming with similarly unconsidered pasts, the flip-side of which is a history of multiple 'fresh starts'. In our peoples' staggering drive to live a better way in a difficult world, we have developed the habit of being forced to forget without ever having been required to forgive. Consequently, we mistake a 'fresh start' for reconciliation.

Liturgical practices have an inevitably implicated relationship to this cultural situation. On the one hand, every single service that I attended during fieldwork from 2001–2008, across all traditions and geography, devoted a fairly large proportion of the worship time to reconciliation. It took different forms in different congregations, but all had in common a basic threefold pattern of repenting of one's sin, asking for God's mercy, and receiving/ remembering God's forgiveness. Such practices suggest that forgiveness is an essential part of the Christian life, and that Christians cannot proceed in their faith without the forgiveness of their sin and their reconciliation to God and to one another. On the other hand, so little is said of the specifics of daily life and the sectarianism it harbours, that the ritualization of reconciliation on Sunday mornings can convey the impression that it, too, is pushing more toward a fresh start than toward a serious interrogation of problems/sin.

The sin that is 'confessed' in most Irish churches, regardless of denomination, is either an abstract 'sin' (sin as the basic human condition of having fallen away from God) or else a very personal sin (the little ways we each individually fail in our relationships). The first sort arises in prayers like this: 'Father, having left Your love through sin, by Christ You reconciled us to Yourself'; the second like this: 'let us call to mind our sins, the ways we have fallen short this past week, the hurtful things we said and the things we did or failed to do to our families, our neighbours and in work'. Because

31. Colin Graham, '"Every Passer-by a Culprit?" Archive Fever, Photography and the Peace in Belfast', *Third Text* 19:5 (September 2005), pp. 567–80; 567.

these seem to be the only two 'norms' for thinking about sin in worship, it is rare that a connection is made between the realities of sectarian social attitudes or practices and a thing called 'sin'. When, then, people turn their attention to the peace process, it is without ever having interrogated sectarianism as sinful, or even as related to religion or the life of faith; it is, therefore, not conceived as something to be confessed or forgiven. 'Peace' is thus adopted, and embraced, but it is not *wrought*: the things (sectarian attitudes and practices) that made up the 'un-peace' remain (as Graham suggests through his analysis of contemporary Belfast photography) as 'archive' and not as *engaged* material — or spiritual — culture.

'Prima facie,' Norman Porter writes, 'reconciliation's absence is a disconcerting and puzzling reality given the sheer number of attempts that have been made to heal rifts between unionists and nationalists, or between Protestants and Catholics'[32] and he recites every sort of initiative tried, from the informal and neighbourly to the international and diplomatic. If one takes account of liturgical practices on the island, it becomes a lot less perplexing. People talking about reconciliation all seem to think they are talking about the same thing. There were not Protestant and Catholic definitions of reconciliation in the *GFA*, simply the use of the mutually understood term, reconciliation.[33] However, worship practices suggest that beyond the base-line of abstraction/triviality described above, Protestants and Catholics in Ireland in fact have remarkably different understandings of the theological economy of sin and salvation, and therefore a greatly diverse (and sometimes contradictory) set of understandings about what being reconciled to God or one another actually means. Accordingly, I suspect, what one group sees as reconciliation is not recognizable as such to the other, at least not easily; and, moreover, the very notion of 'relationship' is different.

For example, it is common in Presbyterian churches for the congregation to say together a prayer of confession, the words of

32. Porter, *Elusive Quest*, pp. 35–36.
33. 'The tragedies of the past have left a deep and profoundly regrettable legacy of suffering. We must never forget those who have died or been injured, and their families. But we can best honour them through a fresh start, in which we firmly dedicate ourselves to the achievement of reconciliation, tolerance, and mutual trust, and to the protection and vindication of the human rights of all.' *The Northern Ireland Peace Agreement* (10 April 1998) 1.2 (Declaration of Support).

which are framed as 'we' (what we confess to God to having done), and this is followed by the minister offering an assurance of pardon in which she/he reminds the congregation that in Jesus Christ, they are forgiven. In Catholic churches, the congregation all say a prayer of contrition, the words of which are framed as 'I' (what I apologize to others and to God for having done), and this is followed by an absolution from the priest in which he prays to God that through his declaration of absolution, these sins will be forgiven. Confession and declared-forgiveness is a very different matrix from contrition and absolution; and who God is perceived to be, such that God furnishes either, is correspondingly different, as is the degree to which the individual is responsible for their state in God's eyes. Moreover, the actual performance of these rites points to further differences in understanding of what reconciliation is about.

Catholics raced through the reconciliation liturgy fast, by rote, and in almost inaudible voices. *Kyries* were never sung (as they often are in Roman Catholic Churches in other countries), nor *Glorias* at the conclusion of the penitential rite, suggesting this part of the rite to be thought of as holding a low value, and to be completed as quickly as possible. According to the priests with whom I spoke, the work of repentance, reparation and reconciliation is supposed to be done elsewhere—in the confessional, on Saturdays. But there are three problems with this claim: first of all, most people no longer go to confession, so the work of reconciliation is not in fact being done there. Second, the confessional, when used in isolation and not in partnership with the Sunday liturgy, privatizes sin, ensuring that its social aspects remain obfuscated.[34] By retaining a focus only on the confessional, only personal sin 'counts' and problematic social attitudes (like sectarianism) remain 'just the way it is': 'I'll be as good/nice as I can within it, but I'd never dream of challenging it. Meanwhile I reap its benefits (righteous indignation, group belonging, identity affirmation, a sense of place, etc.)'. Third, it portrays forgiveness as the work of the priest alone, channeling God, and not also as the work of the people, one to another, by the grace of God. In summary, there is a high degree of denial common to all three problems.

---

34. In Roman Catholic teaching the confessional is not designed to be the sole locus of confession and absolution in the life of faith: the penitential rite in the Mass is deemed important as well.

Protestants spend longer on reconciliation in worship, say more about it, and allow intense or bleak feelings to arise around it. The time given to it, the volume of voices engaged in it, and the diversity and intensity of emotion it arouses are all such that the reconciliation aspect of worship seems of higher value in the common life of the community than it was among Catholics. The language is very different too: it is of triumph: 'the triumph of the cross'; the ways we 'rest triumphant' once forgiven; one concluding prayer in Belfast asked that we might be 'valiant'; and the congregational 'Amens' were the most rousing of the whole service. Across Northern Ireland, the language was of righteousness and of battle, and the voices were full and strong. While the battle in question is between good and evil, between God and Satan, between Christ's cross and our sin, it cannot be ignored that such language is taking place in a context of battle in which the same righteous attitudes ('eventual triumph', 'no surrender'), married to a profound belief that God is on our side, is echoed daily in political and media rhetoric.

Such radical differentiation in the ways Irish and Northern Irish Protestants and Catholics conceive of reconciliation (one the performance of a web of denial of sorrow, the other the pursuit of righteous triumph) maps quite closely onto the archetypal colonial self-understandings of each side in the Irish–British relationship. Hugh Denard has described such colonial discourse in the Irish case as a 'grievance-perpetuating myth',[35] with each group forever self-cast as victim and the other, victor. One can see in the worship practices described above that while human beings are ostensibly reconciled to God, any requirement for human beings to be reconciled to human beings is circumvented. The worship-going Irish or Northern Irish person, whether Catholic or Protestant, can thus continue to participate in cultural mythologies based on the perpetuation of a grievance while safe in the knowledge that they have done their personal work of repentance and forgiveness in church. Whether through absolution from the priest or alignment with the cross they have made sure they are okay with God, and are not required to do anything more *vis-a-vis* human beings. Thus, as Denard comments:

35. Hugh Denard, 'Séamus Heaney, Colonialism, and the Cure: Sophoclean Revisions' in *PAJ: A Journal of Performance and Art*, 22:66 (September 2000), pp. 1–18; 2.

Colonial discourse itself, as an interpretative paradigm or episteme, has served to lock Catholics and Protestants (and critics and analysts of the crisis) into accepting the seemingly inescapable, historically-determined roles of colonized and colonist respectively. These roles, manifested in a culture of victims and victors, have exercised a malign influence upon all aspects of life in Northern Ireland against which the politics of reconciliation continually has had to pit itself.[36]

Reconciliation is so 'elusive' in our context because the old Protestant–Catholic/British–Irish[37] grievance is seen as the air we breathe, not a sin we commit. It is, therefore, rarely if ever challenged as being antithetical to our right-relationship with God. Indeed, far from being challenged in liturgy, that grievance (and the sectarianism it perpetuates) can be bolstered by other symbolic aspects of the worship experienced in church. If reconciliation requires a turning of attention to these seemingly normative grievance-perpetuating mythologies, of which Christ and his cross are made emblems rather than redeemers, then the archives of colonialism will need to be exhumed from their forgotten state in Irish churches, because in this context it is colonialism and its complicated legacy that has rendered our mythologies of victimhood normative. Concomitantly, it has also created a liturgical theology of reconciliation that privileges too much the status of the individual victim and too little the social and corporate aspects of our human frailty. Thus it is to post-colonial theory that we now turn, to query whether and how there may be something in our collective past that needs to be forgiven even long after it has apparently been forgotten.

If, as David Lloyd has suggested,[38] post-colonialism is effective as a set of projects rather than a theory, the question becomes: how might Christian reconciliation practices, particularly those that occur in church during Sunday morning worship, be understood as constructive projects in the new Ireland? Offering a clue for constructive thinking such that would stem the elusiveness of the

36. Dennard, 'Séamus Heaney, Colonialism and the Cure', p. 2.
37. On the complexity of language in the attempt to even name the distinctions/obfuscations of the various constituencies in this context see, Joseph Ruane and Jennifer Todd, *Dynamics of Conflict in Northern Ireland: Power, Conflict and Emancipation* (Cambridge: Cambridge University Press, 1996).
38. David Lloyd, 'Regarding Ireland in a Post-colonial Frame' in *Cultural Studies* 15:1 (2001), pp. 12–32; 13–14.

quest for reconciliation in Ireland, Denard turns to Seamus Heaney's translation into English of the Sophoclean epic poem, *The Cure at Troy*, and remarks that:

> neither of the mythically "pure" identities of colonist and colonized remain intact indefinitely; the process of colonialism in fact produces a hybrid, "post-colonial" consciousness in both the historical colonist and colonized. *The Cure at Troy* allows us to observe what happens when this shared hybridity is recognized and is made the basis of new relationships based on respect for both the wounds and the worth of the historical "Other".[39]

He finds in Heaney's allegorical reading of Philocletes a richly-layered reconceptualization of grievance in which both communities are justified in claiming victimized status; and he suggests that Heaney's accentuation of the highly ambivalent nature of such claims allows the entry of a new flexibility in the conception of the relation of past to present in Northern Ireland. Denard founds such a perspective on the notion of hybridity, a term associated most closely with the Parsi–British intellectual Homi Bhabha,[40] and it will be necessary to look in some depth at Bhabha's employment of, and complication of, the idea of hybridity before making some suggestions about its usefulness to Irish worship.

Bhabha's foundational concern is with *difference:* how it is conceived, managed, and articulated. Unlike Said, his forerunner as the major thinker of post-colonialism, his interest resides with the deconstruction of colonial mythologies through their reappraisal and not in the eventual claiming of (ultimately intact colonial) power by the underdog. As a consequence, his gaze is focused more specifically on the forms of life (such as those found in a culture's arts and letters) through which damaging mythologies about differences were constituted in social life. 'What is theoretically innovative, and politically crucial', he wrote in *The Location of Culture*, 'is the need to think beyond narratives of originary and initial subjectivities and to focus on those moments or processes that are produced in the articulation of cultural differences.'[41] To

---

39. Denard, 'Séamus Heaney, Colonialism and the Cure', p. 2.
40. Although he is not the originator of the concept. See, for example, the introduction to the term in Patrick Colm Hogan, *Empire and Poetic Voice: Cognitive and Cultural Studies of Literary Tradition and Colonialism* (SUNY Press, 2004), pp. 1–3.
41. Homi K. Bhabha, *The Location of Culture* (New York: Routledge, 1994), p. 2.

enable him to do so, he became what David Huddart calls a psychoanalyst of modernity,[42] interrogating the vocabulary of a culture to re-construct the processes by which it had been formed. Such processes are, in his view, always shot through with the promotion of colonial ideologies *via* myths that persuaded whole peoples of the supposed inevitability of modernity's lifeworld. Arguing for a hermeneutic that would open up paths to viable alternatives, he insisted that, 'We must never forget that the establishment of colonised space profoundly informs and historically contests the emergence of those so-called post-Enlightenment values associated with the notion of modern stability.'[43]

Addressing the problem of what to do about *difference* and the attempted organization of it inevitably instituted by modernity's various manifestations, his vision is of 'a cultural hybridity that entertains difference without an assumed or imposed hierarchy.'[44] By thus de-coupling difference from hierarchy (a move one might argue he borrows from feminist theory), he can undo certain key factors of the colonial worldview. For example, chief among colonial thinking's toolkit is the stereotype, and Bhabha was among the first to point out that far from being an indicator of a supposed norm, a stereotype in fact always points to the thing it is not:

> Fixity, as the sign of cultural/historical/racial difference in the discourse of colonialism, is a paradoxical mode of representation: it connotes rigidity and an unchanging order as well as disorder, degeneracy and daemonic repetition. Likewise the stereotype, which is its major discursive strategy, is a form of knowledge and identification that vacillates between what is always 'in place', already known, and something that must be anxiously repeated … as if the essential duplicity of the Asiatic or the bestial sexual license of the African [*or the Barbaric unruliness of the Irish Catholic; or the sober pomposity of the Ulster Protestant*] that needs no proof, can never, really, in discourse be proved.[45]

Stereotypes, in Bhabha's unmasking, are thus understood to be based in *ambivalence*. Ambivalence serves as a crucial term in Bhabha's particular conceptualizations of hybridity, and the aspect (of ambivalence) that I will employ as a hermeneutic for interpreting

---

42. See David Huddart, *Homi K. Bhabha* (London: Taylor & Francis, 2005).
43. Bhabha, *CSP*, p. 64.
44. Bhabha, *The Location of Culture*, p. 5.
45. Bhabha, *The Location of Culture*, pp. 94–95. Italics mine.

worship in Ireland is that which unrelentingly unmasks the *constructed* nature of supposedly self-evident (or, in the case of worship, 'divinely authored') modes of social interaction.

By becoming alert to the need to search for the peculiar ambivalence to which any stereotype inadvertently points, one can begin to fathom things differently. Not only is colonial discourse itself made apparent as an agent in discourse,[46] but the supposedly normative identities of ritual agents are exposed as being far more diverse, and having a far greater degree of agency, than the pre-post-colonial interpretation would have had it. Where Bhabha's notion of hybridity becomes truly involving, then, and where his theory proves most pertinent to current liturgical practices in Ireland,[47] is in his contemplation of how such ambivalence functions in *identity formation*. 'Hybridity' he writes, 'is the revaluation of the assumption of colonial identity through the repetition of discriminatory identity effects.'[48] This works on (at least) two levels in Irish liturgy. The first is the sense (also common in much liturgical theology)[49] in which liturgy is thought to *form* identity, and the ways this supposedly benign process is corrupted in Ireland because liturgy can, in this acutely Catholic/Protestant-colonial context, form people as sectarian agents. The second creates a new way of conceiving of history, and this is helpful in cutting through the seemingly unique, discrete and variant practices of reconciliation and, through *remembering* (i.e., not forgetting) something both unique (our version of history) and common (the situation in which we have all been implicated, and which we continue to live into/ manufacture), being able to take a forgiving step.

Such a re-view of history offers two significant epistemic openings for reconciliation practices: first, what might be described as

46. 'neither the narrative of the colonist, nor that of the colonised, is exclusively dominant, thus reflecting the primacy in Northern Irish culture of the Catholic–Protestant divide', Bhabha, *The Location of Culture*, p. 6.

47. It is also what differentiates my use of hybridity from Volf's, because it rejects the notion that the victim is involved in the sin.

48. Bhabha, *The Location of Culture*, pp. 94–95.

49. There has been an emphasis in much recent liturgical theology that the liturgy's main purpose is formative, and that human beings' prime concern should be to be conformed to the liturgy and not to conform the liturgy to their own whims, tastes or agendas. See, for example, E. Byron Anderson, *Worship and Christian Identity: Practicing Ourselves* (Collegeville, MN: The Liturgical Press, 2003).

'standing alongside', and second, what might be described as an emphasis on 'process as product'. Both could be accomplished entirely within the terms of existing norms for worship in the four main churches in Ireland; indeed they are feasible by simply doing what is already mandated for Sunday worship. They may require, however, a conscientization about the point where the fullness of theologies or rubrics for worship meet the local context. If Roman Catholic churches did not omit the *Kyrie* (and sang it), if calls to confession in Protestant churches erred as much on the side of humility as righteousness, and if all churches ceased to neglect to interrogate sectarianism as sin, a great start would have been made. Then, the churches could begin to name what is actually going on, replacing safe and sentimental calls to confession/examinations of conscience with real questions about the dynamics of hatred, holding those whom one would rather simply ignore *in mind*.

To illustrate both, take for example my attitude to the former leader of the Democratic Unionist Party: I can no more generate the will to embrace Ian Paisley than I can to cut off my left arm, but I do not think that has to mean that I am not serious about a strong version of reconciliation, a version that includes forgiveness. I may not be able to hug Paisley, but (and here is the *alongside* view) in Christian worship, I can stand in a room and say prayers *with* him, say a confession *with* him, hear an assurance of pardon *with* him, *offer* him a sign of peace (a hand shake and a, 'peace be with you'), and break bread *with* him. And all of that liturgical conspiring might lead me, in time, to being able to embrace him. But—and this is where the notion of hybridity can qualify the symbol of embrace for the Irish context—I do not think embrace is the goal, the thing that would make the other things either possible or valid. I think the liturgical gestures on their own are strong enough to count as reconciliation, especially when performed in such a variety of ways, and every week, and by many people. They are to sectarianism what peace is to war because (and here is the point about process not product), they enact the seven times seventy-seven method of forgiveness: not a single moment of arrival at a new state but a perennially-repeated set of actions that articulate the joint-ness of previously estranged agents. It becomes characterized as a lifetime of acting it out, making it by making it, but probably never seeing it 'made' in any empirical sense.

Hybridity, it was noted above, decouples difference from hierarchy. By doing so, it shifts the emphasis from individual grievances to whole-group effect. This suits Ireland partly because, in contrast to other western cultures, it is relatively group-oriented: very social in both behaviours and notions of identity.[50] It also suits Ireland because it unmasks the supposedly normative mythologies of victimhood in our context, something that is a real stumbling block to our various (and make no mistake, they will remain varied) theologies of reconciliation (and relationship). If the group which has been so long sorely threatened or oppressed can be re-seen, re-identified as mutually-constituting of the supposed other, then the individuals within that group can honour differences but not endlessly have to heal them, attempting always to reconcile the irreconcilable. Instead, by recognizing that these are mythologies, the product of colonial discourse, which have seeped into most aspects of cultural meaning-making, they can be dismantled not just because they are destructive, but because they are false.

An acknowledgement of hybridity (and particularly the way it decouples *difference* from *hierarchy*) thus leads to a change in (perception of and accounts of) subjectivity. It prioritizes intersubjectivity. Before there is an individual subject, there is the intersubjectivity of the wider unit of the self in relation to other, or group. Therefore, we might venture the following in a liturgical theology for Ireland/Northern Ireland: before individual forgiveness can be asserted/performed, there must be group forgiveness. Volf, using an individual-based model writes,

> As Christians [we] must develop a will to embrace and be reconciled with our enemy. This will to embrace is absolutely unconditional. There is no imaginable deed that should take a person outside our will to embrace him, because there is no imaginable deed that can take a person out of God's will to embrace humanity — which is what I think is inscribed in big letters in the narrative of the cross of Christ.[51]

It is not that this is wrong. It may be right. It all depends on context. And in Ireland it is not enough. In Ireland, because of the lack of

---

50. See, for example, Michael Cronin (ed.), *Irish Tourism: Image, Culture and Identity* (Bristol: Channel View Publications, 2003). Many of the essays consider reports of Irish 'sociability'.

51. Miroslav Volf, 'To Embrace the Enemy', *Christianity Today*, 17 September 2001, http://christianitytoday.com/ct/2001/138/53.o.html

the possibility of confession, contrition or reparation, because of the group-nature of the cultural dynamics, and because of the role of sectarianism in identity-formation itself, something else is needed before we can arrive at the point of being able to will individual embraces. What the BBC programmes show us is that the only times a person could shake the hand of the perpetrator was when they had developed a sense of 'hybridity'. When they had contextualized their own grievance in the fact that something heinous was engulfing not just them but also those who perpetrated the crimes. When they could see that all parties were, indeed, badly affected. That does not take away one bit the fact that one person was terribly harmed and the other did the harming.[52] Nor does it result in a feeling of 'unity' with the other person or group. Nor does it diminish in the slightest the very profound differences in identity between the various groups, or the legitimate grievances held by groups on account of their histories. It simply contextualizes the path forward in a different way than either revenge on the one hand or an individually-manifesting expression of contrition or forgiveness ('embrace') on the other.

This is what liturgy in Ireland has to do. Stop using the cross of Christ to create an individually-constituting narrative of victimhood (which in Catholic mythology parades as martyrdom and in Protestant mythology as a triumphalist/supremacist view of Christian identity), and start creating a narrative of the cross of Christ appropriate to each community that knows *all* peoples to be nailed to the same cross. Such alterations in liturgical performance need to come not only in the texts our confessions, so that we actually name the sectarianism and specific events that are going on around us (i.e., stop the silence about local matters — something I expose in the following chapter), but in so very many other aspects of the liturgy too. For example, far greater attention needs to be granted to how the cross is positioned, how people are oriented in

---

52. I am not arguing, as Volf does, for 'the non-innocence of the victim'. On the contrary, it is the victim's innocence that qualifies them as victim, and the perpetrator's guilt that makes them the perpetrator; I am, however, arguing for something in addition to and not instead of that economy, something that permits a move. An analogy might be provided by the game of netball, when a player cannot make a throw, but something beyond their own ability to manage the situation happens, like a free throw, a gap in the opponent's defences, or a fall, and that enables the throw to be made.

relation to it, and how it is talked about not only in sermons and prayers but also in slight and passing references, spoken and sung.

Furthermore, for the cross to make sense in reconciliation liturgies in church, it has to be used appropriately outside church: if the cross of Christ is paraded through a neighbour's community in a display of intimidation, goading or provocation, masked under the seemingly reasonable rationale of 'expressing cultural identity', then it will not work as a mechanism of reconciliation no matter how nice are the new prayers that are written about its supposedly reconciling power. Our cultural identity as Christians requires us to find love on the cross, not pride. We will not find it if we do not look for it. We will not look for it if we do not have faith it is there. And this most hybridized of attitudes, finding love on the cross, I suggest, is what will get us as close to reconciliation as we can manage in Ireland this side of the parousia.

But, speaking of parousias … In *The Cure at Troy*, in Heaney's translation, the ultimately effective medium of reconciliation is a transcendent intervention, a 'visionary possibility'.[53] The poem adjures us to 'Believe in miracles/And cures and healing wells', and it might seem incredulous to employ it in an ecumenical text, given most Irish Protestants' attitudes to cures, never mind holy wells. And yet it might in fact point to the very thing, the only thing, which can forge forgiveness. It may well be neither confession nor contrition nor reparation but only some 'miracle' that can wrest forgiveness from our specific predicament of irreversibility. Fr. Alec Reid, responsible for brokering many of the negotiations that led to the peace process, when asked as part of a consortium organized by leading politicians and scholars what he thought was the main thing that brought about peace in Northern Ireland replied straight away: 'the prayers of the ordinary people, over years. I have no doubt about that. Prayer.'[54]

This is more than giving over the 'final reconciliation'[55] to God, thus permitting us to open our arms in the offer of an embrace. This is a belief in God's power to forge change in the situation right

53. Denard, 'Séamus Heaney, Colonialism and the Cure', p. 15.
54. Conversation at Yale University, 6 November 2008.
55. Unlike in Volf's metaphor of embrace, in this post-colonial envision-ing, final reconciliation is not deferred: it is imagined, and thus in a strong sense made real, immanent.

now. It might be better understood through comparison with Derrida's description:

> Must one not maintain that an act of forgiveness, if there is such a thing, must forgive the unforgivable, and without condition? ... Even if this radical purity can seem excessive, hyperbolic? Because if I say (as I think) that forgiveness is mad, and that it must remain a madness of the impossible, this is certainly not to exclude or disqualify it. It is even, perhaps, the only thing that arrives, that surprises, like a revolution, the ordinary course of history, politics, and law.[56]

It 'arrives' — i.e., it has agency independent of our ability to conjure it — as a 'surprise' or, as Arendt had it, as a 'miracle'.[57] However, Arendt insists that to be open to it requires setting aside the desire for vengeance. This is exactly the point we are at in Ireland. The violence has stopped. We have a 'cold' peace.[58] To allow a miracle actually to happen, we must now work on our *thinking*.[59] Just as you can commit adultery in your mind, so with acts of war; just as fidelity consists not merely in where you put your body but in how you think your way through your world, so reconciliation consists not merely in refraining from physically harming your neighbour but in how and what you think about them. It is this, rather than the search for confession or the demand for contrition, that the work of forgiveness requires in our context. Dr. Harold Good remarked, in conversation with Alec Reid above, that, 'The end to the armed conflict is marvelous, just marvelous; but what we have now is a battle for hearts and minds, and that's what needs to change now, the hearts and minds of the ordinary people.' This involves for us, as it did for Arendt in the aftermath of the holocaust,

56. Jacques Derrida, *On Cosmopolitanism and Forgiveness* (New York: Taylor & Francis, 2001), p. 39.

57. 'the miracle of rebirth that saves the world'.

58. Jonathan Tonge, *The New Northern Irish Politics?* (Houndmills: Palgrave Macmillan, 2005).

59. John Swinton's recent work on the place of thoughtfulness in the enacting of forgiveness of interest here. See, *Raging with Compassion: Pastoral Responses to the Problem of Evil* (Grand Rapids, MI: Eerdmans, 2007). Although he, like Volf, argues for a method by which Christians can 'live faithfully with unanswered questions as they await God's redemption of the whole creation', rather than the hybridity-based response to colonial discourse which holds out hope for a here and present miracle and, by imagining it, transforms reality.

making and keeping new promises, and this happens, crucially, at the level of everyday attitudes and practices, in other words, through *thinking* but also through acting—and perhaps especially through *ritualizing*.[60]

The result, Arendt predicts, will be not merely 'getting over' but 'undoing'. Speaking out of the South African context, Nancy Scheper–Hughes articulates the distinction like this:

> Although individuals can "get over" a personal and collective history of violence, "undoing" demands a more Herculean task of mending, healing, repairing, remaking, even rebirthing the world. If the term carries a touch of the sorcerer's magic, we can excuse it. World repair cannot be accomplished through the applications of reason and the rule of law alone.[61]

What are the liturgical instruments of this sort of World repair? What are we confessing/expressing contrition for? That we told three fibs this week and drank too much on Friday night, or that we are part of a desperate situation that leads us to normatively and indignantly view our neighbours with thinly-masked contempt. What are we being assured/absolved of? That God has always already forgiven us so we are free to get on with habitual righteous sectarian hatred or that God's forgiveness is useless if we are not open to its radical—for all people—presence in the world?

By first of all admitting that there can and will be no apology for sectarian division in Ireland and Northern Ireland, this chapter has presented a particular choice: we have the choice either to hang on to a definition of reconciliation in which contrition and restitution are essential to its economy and thus ensure that reconciliation remains ever-elusive on our island, or, to discover an indigenous attitude to reconciliation that can think and act its way to a forgiven and forgiving culture, despite the inevitable absence of reparation. In the post-colonial notion of hybridity one finds the offer of a world-view that permits an end to the 'grievance-perpetuating

60. Ritualizing has an inbuilt intersubjectivity (between us as individuals, between our individual selves and God, between God and our group, between all the elements of creation and between the entire created order and its maker), such that identities are always explicitly being formed jointly there.

61. Nancy Scheper–Hughes, 'Violence and the Politics of Remorse', in Joao Biehl, Byron Good, Arthur Klienman (eds), *Subjectivity: Ethnographic Investigations* (London: University of California Press, 2007), pp. 180–229; 192.

mythology' that comes with the victor–victim way of framing history. Both communities are seen to have suffered losses, but, more importantly, as having affected one another at deep, cultural levels. Neither can then be thought of as an ethnically or culturally 'pure' representative of a particular history or set of beliefs.

What we have in Ireland at the moment is an archiving of notions of difference (culturally distinct markers, and their growing significance) matched with inter-cultural indifference: 'you do your thing, we'll do ours'. It is doomed as a strategy for peace-making. But it is also inaccurate as a presentation of relationship and identity in our particular context, as Chapter Six (on music) will make especially apparent. It may be helpful to consider an analogy with a very different context: considering the theological ethics of African American movements, Marcia Riggs alerts us to the distinctions of various forms of group-organization: 'Exclusionary separation is divisive, functional separation recognises differences as meaningful for interrelationship between groups; homogenisation creates an artificial unity.'[62] Exclusionary separation, whether physical or attitudinal is what we have with sectarianism, and homogenization is what we have with the 'archiving' of the past in the drive to a (market-driven) 'fresh start'; while a recognition of difference *in the service of greater interrelationship* remains largely unexplored.

Without remembering our differences, and without detaching them from the hierarchies that have so marked their definition, we will be sectarian for as long as we can see. Perhaps the notion of hybridity can therefore help us reconcile even as it helps us acknowledge there was never a conciliation to re-turn to, because it opens space for the discovery of something entirely new through the examination of something doggedly old. And God is *always making all things new.* Perhaps that is what we should be announcing in our absolutions/assurances every Sunday morning. Such a statement could help us acknowledge our differences while letting go of our (internalized, colonial) mythologies about them, thus allowing them to be merely a source of difference, and not a source of sectarian hatred or violence. Such would be its own forgiveness.

Reconciliation practices do not have to be made homogenous in order to accomplish this. Catholics and Protestants can and will

---

62. Marcia Riggs, *Awake, Arise, Act: A Womanist Call for Black Liberation* (Cleveland, OH: The Pilgrim Press, 1994), p. 96.

continue to have differences as well as commonalities in christologies, soteriologies, etc.; and these will continue to be visible in Sunday morning worship. What matters is not that they are made identical (as if that were even possible) but that they take account of hybridity, in their different ways, as a way of honouring difference. For example, much can be accomplished in this regard by a more careful use of language, and Chapter Four will examine this in depth, advocating, among other measures, avoidance of the terms 'the other community' and 'opposite religions'.

But much can also be accomplished through commission as well as omission. Calls to confession can be written with specific mention of sectarianism as a sin. Initiation of the examination of conscience can ask not just 'how have we offended those we love?' but 'how have we failed to love our enemies?' They can press us to ask (and it will be more to the point for a notion of reconciliation true to our own context): how have we kept people in the category of neither beloved nor enemy, simply those we do not deal with, do not engage, the great mass of historicized, objectified and de-individuated people whom we reserve the right to feel benighted by at any turn, but whom we refuse to put a face upon and so classify as neither enemy nor friend. The great problem in Ireland nowadays is not so much difference as *indifference*, and postcolonialist practices of reconciliation, ones that actually remark difference in the service of deepening relationship to God and to one another can help us begin to address it.

Chapter Three

SPACE, GESTURES, BODIES AND VISUALS

When theologians study worship, they usually think first about what words are said or sung. However, much of our experience in worship derives from its non-verbal aspects, such as: how the space smells; who else we see in the space and where they are positioned (some may be elevated, some may be not quite 'inside' — standing at the boundary with the street, etc.); what we see in the space (flowers, furniture, the floor, things hanging on the walls or from the rafters, etc.); how the seating is arranged; how it feels to sit or stand in there, especially in relation to other people; whether our feet make a noise or not; whether we can hear ourselves or other people singing; how amplification affects us, and so on. Also under this vitally important category of the non-verbal come the gestural habits that shape the worship of the congregation: how people dress, move, and indicate, and how they interact bodily with one another and with the things used during the time of worship. All these things, and so many more, condition not just the basic 'knowledge' we have of worship but also our knowledge of God.[1]

---

1. A point pressed by many who have contributed to the revival of 'liturgical theology' in the past twenty-five years. Notably, Alexander Schmemann who worked 'to make the liturgical experience of the church again one of the life-giving sources of the knowledge of God.' *Introduction to Liturgical Theology* (Princeton, NJ: St. Vladimir's Seminary Press, 1986), p. 19. Also, see for example, E. Byron Anderson and Bruce T. Morrill, *Liturgy and the Moral Self: Humanity at Full Stretch before God. Essays in Honor of Don Saliers* (Collegeville, MN: Liturgical Press, 1998). In their Introduction they write: 'In the liturgy, tradition gathers through the present toward the future, just as God brings all creation toward Godself. This gathering and bringing in liturgy and life is what theology "knows" of God. This knowledge, while it is certainly cognitive, is never merely rational or even linguistic. The range of what we know about liturgy's embrace and God's giftedness requires our ability to name God in all that we do.' (p. x).

Greeting Gestures

Greeting gestures vary enormously across and within denominations in Ireland, as they do in the rest of the world. However, the following observations can be made about those churches studied in my research: in Roman Catholic churches, the only greeting is usually given by the priest to the assembled people at the start of the formal part of the liturgy, while in Anglican, Methodist and Reformed congregations, there are usually several greetings: the initial ones by people standing at the back of church greeting each person as they enter; worshippers greeting one another in the process of taking their seats; and then the minister greeting the assembly as the service begins.

There was greater variety of practice among Protestant and Anglican churches than there was among Roman Catholic churches, but not so much that one cannot also easily discern a common form: one, two or three people (nearly always women) stood inside the doors of the church, said hello, and handed something to those coming in (in Anglican churches, a prayer book; in other churches, an order of service, a hymn book, a newsletter, and/or a brochure about the church). How they did this varied. In some places, such as the Church of Ireland parish in Co. Mayo, they stood to one side of the entry-point, said something matter-of-fact, like 'Hello; here's the hymnal', and indicated with their body language that you should just walk in past them and find a seat. In other places, such as a Presbyterian Church in Dublin, they were very warm, reaching out to shake your hand and saying something like, 'Good morning, you're welcome here, thanks for joining us today. You'll need this bulletin. You can sit anywhere you like' and gesturing you to go on in. However, in yet other places in both Northern Ireland and the Republic, the greeters physically blocked the entry by putting their bodies between the newcomer and the worship space, they said 'Good Morning' and then asked who you were, where you came from and, occasionally, why you were there.

Concentrating on this latter pattern of practice, the means by which personal information is elicited can be subtle or seemingly incidental: in one church in Armagh I was asked to sign a Visitors' Book before going in (I said, 'I would rather not.' She said, 'We require it.'), while in another in Dublin I was asked for all this information because the greeter insisted that I needed to wear a name-badge 'like the rest of the congregation' (about half of whom were wearing a name tag). But it is not always subtle or incidental and in two churches (both in Northern Ireland) I was asked these questions directly, without conversational niceties and without the medium of a Visitors' Book or name-badge. In one of these churches, I was not allowed to proceed into the worship space, despite my insistence that I had the minister's permission to observe the service as part of a study.[2] In the other, I was allowed inside but it was strongly suggested I sit at the back (where the greeters proceeded to keep an eye on me throughout the service). My experience in these four congregations was of being vetted rather than greeted.

Going into Roman Catholic churches there was very rarely someone standing at the entry-point whose role was to greet people coming into Mass. In all but one of the Roman Catholic churches I attended, I could park the car and walk up to the church, through the narthex and into the pew without speaking to any other person. There was usually a table of some sort inside the doors containing a stack of orders of service (sometimes called missalettes, or service leaflets), without which a newcomer cannot join in the unison prayers, and these were usually pretty obvious once I was in the narthex; however, in three churches I never found this table, and just muddled along without the order of service. In some places I had to squeeze myself through a fairly large group of men standing on the threshold of the church, none of whom said hello, but many of whom gawped at me, and in just one location an older man standing outside the doors said 'Hello' to me and to everyone else, handing out orders of service to us as we passed by him. In one of the Roman Catholic churches there was no greeting whatsoever — not from another congregant, nor from a person with service orders, nor from the priest at the start of the rite; but in all the others, the priest began with a greeting immediately after walking into the space. He would greet the congregation with the words, 'The Lord be with you' and, in half the churches studied, he supplemented this by saying 'Good Morning' and making a few introductory remarks. My experience in the Roman Catholic churches (apart from the one where I was greeted by the layman who handed me a bulletin) was of being anonymous, un-oriented (meaning, unsure where to sit or what to say or how to navigate the situation) and of

2. And so, when I say I studied 26 churches, without this one, where I never got beyond the door, it would be 25, but I include it because it is a valid — and telling — experience of worship.

being treated with indifference by the other human beings in the room.

There is fairly widespread consensus in liturgical polity, across denominations, that the first words from the minister during Sunday morning worship should be some sort of greeting, although there is debate over the relative merits of the biblical, 'Grace and peace from our Lord Jesus Christ!', the traditional, 'The Lord be with you!' and the colloquial, 'Good morning! Let us enter a time of praise and worship'.[3] However, practical theologians and local worship committees alike have had considerable discussion in recent years about the greeting practices that happen at or near the doors, and there is a significant lack of consensus about whether and how the lay members of a congregation should welcome one another.[4] What constitutes ushering to some feels like herding to others; what feels welcoming to some feels invasive to others. Every congregation has to come to its own conclusions on how best to meet its needs, based on its specific context and resources (e.g., Do you have a lot of newcomers? Do you have laypeople who would be good at this role? What does this role look like given the specific needs of your congregation?)

Yet these discussions are not conditioned solely by local pastoral needs and resources. The issue of whether and how to greet is an extension and expression of the ecclesiology of a church, and the contrast in practices encountered in my fieldwork reflects the differences in ecclesiologies between churches. For example, it was entirely appropriate that in an Evangelical parish in Dublin I was greeted and welcomed individually and my name mattered and my reaction to the service mattered, because the people who were greeting me were part of a church which believes that each person comes to God individually, and their ministry is to help other individuals have a one-to-one encounter with the living God. When they gather, it is as a community, but it is not the assembly who is addressing God; it is, rather, every individual in that assembly moved by the Spirit, one by one. In the Roman Catholic church in

---

3. See, John Witvliet, 'The Opening of Worship: Trinity' in Leanne Van Dyk (ed.), *A More Profound Alleluia: Theology and Worship in Harmony* (Grand Rapids, MI: Eerdmans, 2005), pp. 1–30.

4. See, for example, Karie Ferrell, *Guide for Ushers and Greeters* (Chicago, IL: Liturgical Training Publications, 2008), and Gerald Spice, *Ushers and Greeters: A Worship Handbook* (Minneapolis, MN: Augsburg-Fortress Press, 2002).

Athlone, by contrast, the majority of people walking through the door understand that by doing so they are entering into the formation of a people and that the actions they are about to engage in cannot be done privately and can only be done in and by a group: their personal relationship with God matters but the primary purpose of this gathering is to form the assembly which is *ekklesia* in the world. Equally appropriately, then, the entry point required no individual attention to be given: by walking through the doors, crossing themselves with water in the narthex, and walking into the main space, the individuals entering this church become part of the mass. These are just two (of many possible) ways of being church and so it is inevitable that different things will happen at the physical point of assembling the worshipping people on a particular Sunday morning.

But in addition to the ecclesiological forces at play, one must also take into consideration the fact that norms of human behaviour also vary greatly across cultures. Being asked one's name, or greeted with a handshake, are not discrete activities that can happen just the same in one culture as in another, nor are they even things that can be easily translated across cultures. Behaviour that is 'warm' in one place is 'hostile' in another. How locals greet one another going into church in Johannesburg or Moscow or Tokyo depends hugely upon etiquettes of greeting that pertain in the wider cultures of those locations, as well as upon the different ecclesiologies of the churches in those contexts. Indeed, how locals greet one another does not easily translate even between England and Ireland, those cultures having such substantially different notions of private and public, of the boundary between individual and group and, therefore, of behaviour *vis-a-vis* hospitality — all of which are at play at a church door. For example, many Irish people say 'you are welcome here' as their first words to someone visiting their house while English people rarely do; or, as another example, English people stand farther apart from one another in public (in queues, for instance) than Irish people or people from continental Europe do. What feels a 'proper distance' to an English person is considerably farther away than for an Irish person.[5] All of this sort of normative behaviour and expectation in the local culture

5. See, for example, Dean Foster, *The Global Etiquette Guide to Europe* (New York: Wiley, 2000), p. 39: 'distance between [Irish] speakers is usually less that between other northern Europeans.'

immediately affects how people greet one another, and how they expect a newcomer to behave, when they come into a church.[6]

It is for this reason that I wish to interrogate both the 'vetting' and the 'indifferent' practices that I experienced going into those churches described above. Because they are happening in the Republic of Ireland and Northern Ireland, where such practices have particular resonances in the wider cultures, they become occasions with potential sectarian resonance. If such practices happened at the church doors in another country, they would have different resonances; but they are happening in a culture wherein 'vetting' and 'indifference' play very specific, complex and strong roles in the maintenance of sectarianism. Of course, it is not simply the case that what happens in the wider culture affects what happens in churches. On the contrary, interactions between human beings inside and outside church have developed in tandem and have mutually informed one another. Indeed, the case could be made that what happens in church in Ireland has had a primary shaping role in human behaviour in the wider culture, given the historically high rates of participation in church by the society at large, and given the authoritative place church has had in civic life and national identity.

That said, Irish and Northern Irish people constantly vet one another for their Protestant/Catholic, English/Irish identity profiles. Vetting by name is a prominent aspect of Northern life, as mentioned in Chapter One, and most people have a story of being vetted, and not just at a check-point on the border, but in classrooms, pubs, workplaces, sports grounds — indeed in every aspect of public life. Liechty and Clegg put it like this:

> In terms of inter-personal attitudes, there is the almost unconscious series of questions or checks people go through when they meet a stranger in order to ascertain to which "side" they belong and therefore how they should treat them: name, accent, school, place they live, how they pronounce the letter "h" etc. Then there are the areas people instinctively avoid, the street they do not walk

6. Something that one Church of Ireland parish in South Dublin sought to address directly. A leaflet on 'Welcoming Immigrants' on the table in the narthex (authored by its Rector) educates about cultural differences; for example it advises the parishioners not to take offence if Africans do not respond to invitations to come over to dinner on a given evening (a standard Irish practice), explaining that the blessing for the African is not in the acceptance of an invitation but in the unexpected arrival of guests.

down, or the pubs they do not drink in. For most, these are nearly unconscious reflexes.[7]

Like most people who have lived in Ireland, therefore, I have many such examples, but to give just one: teaching undergraduate Theology in Galway, a mature student asked me in front of the whole class, 'Where were you born?' I answered, 'near Liverpool, England'. Despite my name, looks, parentage, residence, accent — all of which he knew — and the fact that I was teaching him, he then turned to the rest of the class and said, 'See, I told you she was a Brit.' The information allowed him, he thought, to reject my authority. Of course, not all vetting mechanisms are so overt or easily identifiable. It took an artist friend of Anglo-Irish descent, born and raised and resident all her adult life in the west of Ireland, 20 years to admit that the reason her work hung in major collections in the UK, while she could not even get a show at her local gallery in Ireland, was because her 'posh' accent and 'Protestant' name meant that people thought she was British — and therefore to be kept at a distance, not entitled to markers of belonging that would ordinarily, were she Catholic (and therefore supposedly authentically Irish), be an occasion for local pride.

The above illustrations imply that identity can be simplistically known and judgments made on the basis of that knowledge and this is, of course, not true.[8] Yet we in Ireland persist with such an illusion. The notion that I, or anyone, can be 'Irish and British, both', with dual citizenship while resident in Ireland, is not acceptable to most Irish people. We in Ireland persist with vetting, opening conversations by discovering what allows us to accept or reject the other, because it allows our sectarian identity (and the comfort that derives from the peculiar hatreds and prejudices that are part of it) to remain. Such vetting allows us to exclude or accept people and this allows us to feel safe. But, more than that, even in situations where no danger is present, as in the situations described above,

7. Liechty and Clegg, *Moving Beyond Sectarianism*, p. 107.
8. As has been amply demonstrated at a grassroots level by the high number of crimes against people of 'mistaken identity' and, at an academic level, by the sorts of post-colonial examinations of hybridity discussed in Chapter Two. The quasi-theological and historically anti-Irish remark dubiously attributed to the Duke of Wellington is relevant here: 'If a gentleman happens to be born in a stable, it does not follow that he should be called a horse.' John Simpson and Jennifer Speake, *The Concise Oxford Dictionary of Proverbs* (Oxford: Oxford University Press, 1992), p. 162.

we persist in it because it reattaches us to strong and reassuring forces of identity-definition.

And so, when I felt vetted at the point of being 'greeted' in church during fieldwork, it registered as 'normal': I knew I would either make it through and feel the pleasure that comes from a moment's acceptance (although it is a guilty pleasure, because you know something is wrong with it: others may well not gain acceptance in the vetting process and you are colluding with that process), or I would be left as the butt of suspicion and feeling the sting of exclusion. If we vet people, even subtly, when they come to church, we make sure that the insider feels safe and the outsider feels rebuffed, if not actually rejected. If this is the first experience a person has as they enter a church in Ireland then, I contend, the entire experience of 'going to church' is framed in sectarian terms. Church becomes no different to a Republican pub, for example, that employs a bouncer whose job it is, without actually breaking any discrimination laws, to assess whether or not you will be allowed free passage into the social space.

By seeing my ID Card, a bouncer at such a pub would let me straight in (on my name alone, Siobhán Garrigan being widely perceived as not only Irish, but nationalist—the choice of an indigenous name, spelt in Irish, being a supposed sign that I come from a family interested in reclaiming Irish identity in a post-colonial world). If I did not have ID, he might ask me any old question, just to hear my accent, and in that case there would be a good chance he would not let me in because mine is a hybrid English-Irish accent (which shows I lived in the UK for a long time, making me supposedly less-Irish) and it is also quite 'posh' by regional standards (putting me on the wrong side of the strongly class-based identifier that is 'Republicanism'). If he was left wondering, he might ask where I was from, or who I knew inside, or whether I was staying in the area. All of which are seemingly nice questions to ask a tourist, but all of which are in fact trying to ascertain whether I am Catholic and on what terms, if any, I should be allowed in. On a camping trip to Achill in 2002, my travelling companion, a local Irish man, said simply as we approached the door of what I thought was just any other pub, but was in fact a Republican one, 'If you want a drink tonight, you'll let me do all the talking'.

I was reminded of that piece of advice while undertaking the research for this book, and I wished at several points that I had a 'local' who could gain me access to situations without my having to experience the discomfort of the vetting process and all its potential rejection at various thresholds. However, it is this discomfort that affords the key insight of this study: that church participates in sectarianism even—and perhaps especially—at those seemingly benign moments, like saying hello at the church doors, when we think it does not, or should not. I was not studying that minority of radically independent congregations who openly prohibit people from any 'religion' but their own. On the contrary, the official polity of all the churches in my fieldwork affirms the place of any other Christian as a visitor and witness in their worship, even as one cannot participate in all aspects of it (such as receiving communion). Moreover, all the churches that I visited recognize baptism in one another's churches as valid. And so to be vetted at the church doors, in a cultural context in which vetting is one of the main ways in which sectarian relations are reinforced, alerted me to the implication of church life in both the vetting and the sectarianism at the heart of the vetting.

My point is not simply that by vetting a newcomer/visitor, these congregations engage in sectarian behaviour as normative behaviour. My point is not just about how churches greet newcomers and visitors. Because, just as when I passed right by the bouncer in the pub in Achill on the strength of my companion's 'authenticity' and felt that *frissance* of 'insider-ness' (even though it was a lie, I was not an insider in that context), so for the majority of people each week who sweep past the church greeters without having to answer any questions, even as they know others are being required to answer them: they are participating in the matrix of sectarianism, the first stage of which is sifting. There is a confirmation happening, a 'we're all okay so long as we stick together', a 'we belong here' that is not 'affirmative' belonging (we all choose this, so this binds us together) but that rather comes at the expense of someone else's non-belonging. If this were not so, then no one would be met with suspicion, watched, made uncomfortable under the pretence of being made comfortable, or turned away on the grounds of suspected non-belonging.

Turning from the 'vetting' strategies I experienced in four Protestant/Anglican churches I shall now examine the 'indifferent' treatment I experienced in the vast majority of Roman Catholic churches I attended. Such treatment would be barely worthy of note in countries or cultures where the experience of walking into a civic space and not being greeted in any fashion is normal. But in an Irish and Northern Irish context it gives pause for reflection because in almost every other interaction in public life — shopping, going to the pub, in the bank or credit union, or even just walking down the street (if it's not a busy city street) — people nearly always greet one another: if not actually talking to you (which is common) then at least giving you a nod of recognition. There are obviously marked differences between villages, towns and the major cities, with greeting practices in the latter liable to be more muted; and yet, as travel guides to The Republic and Northern Ireland consistently remark, whether in rural or urban environments, Irish people interacting with all other people on the street generally come across as 'warm and friendly'[9] to people of most other cultures: they habitually 'crack on'. Some guides even warn travelers not to mistake an Irish person talking to them as 'over-familiarity', explaining that they not only routinely greet one another, but also often stop for actual conversation.[10]

Moreover, for someone in an Irish context to walk into an interactive space (such as a pub, a shop or a classroom) and not receive any form of acknowledgement of their presence may be tantamount to a snub. Indifference being so far from normal in the wider culture, except as a snub, it was therefore remarkable to experience it repeatedly when going into most Roman Catholic churches. Watching a group of Irish Catholics greet one another in a pub and then watching them do so in church makes the paucity of warmth or connection or even just acknowledgement in the church practices demanding of further enquiry.

Perhaps people going into Roman Catholic churches are so catechized in the idea that they are going to church to interact with God directly, or to interact simply with the priest, that other people are deemed irrelevant and ordinary human modes of interaction are suspended. Or perhaps people were in fact greeting one another, the ones known to them, in some very subtle way that I was not

9. For example, Professor Henry Weisser, who wrote the *Hippocrene Companion Guide to Ireland* (New York: Hippocrene, 1990), notes 'the warmth, hospitality, humor and friendliness of ordinary people' on the book's back cover.

10. For example, 'People stop each other on the busiest of streets and engage in rich dialogue.' Weisser, *Hippocrene Companion*, p. 82.

aware of. Both are quite possible. However, my point remains (and is supported by travel guides): in other aspects of Irish public life, the person who is not-known is nonetheless acknowledged, and acknowledged even to the extent of the whole country being characterizable as being a place which is 'very friendly' to visitors.[11] As a visitor to church, then, my experience of not being acknowledged in all but one church is significant.

What is immediately communicated by this indifference is the notion of Mass as a location in which you are either an insider or an outsider: there is no category of 'guest'. By being required to come into the interactive space without the comfort of usual courtesies, you are left alone, and you have to fend for yourself. You are also required to navigate not just the situation but also the strangeness of its interpersonal dimensions relative to ordinary life, wondering what is wrong that normative behaviour (courtesies, etiquette, eye contact, nods, handshakes, greetings, and basic interpersonal acknowledgement) should have been suspended. And you might also feel a snub, although I did not do so personally.

Specifically, what is communicated is that you are not meant to be part of what is going on unless you are a competent insider. You are free to enter (there is no vetting process whatsoever), free to take a seat anywhere, and free to stay for the whole thing. Yet this seeming 'openness' masks the fact that if you do not already know exactly what to do, you will not be able to participate at all. Unless you are already a ritually observant Roman Catholic, then without knowing that you need to collect an order of service and knowing where they are kept, you will not have a clue what to say—and even if you are a daily communicant Roman Catholic you will not know what to sing. What is being perpetuated by this practice of 'indifference' is the reinforcement of the idea of church as a closed club: some are in (and they know what to do) others are out (and they are kept in a place of not knowing what to do).

Seen in this light, greeting practices of 'indifference' are not all that different to those of 'vetting' in that they both furnish a similar

11. Not only does Frommers note: 'That the Irish are friendly is not the best-kept secret of the century', but it goes on to recount numerous ways in which Irish people 'reach out to the stranger', gushing that it is 'Their particular brand of friendliness—that's what often comes as a surprise.' Susan Poole, *Frommers Comprehensive Travel Guide: Dublin and Ireland* (New York: Simon and Schuster, 1991), p. 5.

result: a visitor or newcomer being informed that they do not really belong in this environment. Having lived in other parts of the world, I know this is not what greeting practices accomplish in these same denominations' congregations in other countries or cultures, and so I speculate that in The Republic and Northern Ireland our sectarian worldviews are conditioning, and being conditioned by, this entry-point to our churches. But even if one had not lived abroad (and so many Irish people have lived abroad, it is even more striking that we persist in these behaviours only at home), it would be difficult to find any justification for the 'club' mentality in the ecclesiologies of any of the four main Irish churches. On the contrary, there is an emphasis in each of these denominations' theologies on the fact that the church is not a club, and that hospitality to the stranger is the church's constant calling.

We do not have to look far for alternative practices, ones which are consonant with the teachings of the churches: the Roman Catholic church where the older man outside said hello and handed me an order of service—one word and a simple gesture—made a radical difference to my ability to engage in the liturgy in that place; and in those Roman Catholic churches where I could come in, get a nod of a hello if I made eye contact with other people, and find an order of service easily, I at least felt permitted to be there. Likewise the Anglican and Protestant churches in which no vetting happened: I felt allowed-to-be there, not strange, and even welcomed (even too effusively sometimes for my personal tastes; but that is just a matter of taste, it is not related to a spectrum of reactions caused by experience of sectarian filtering). Such greeting practices, no matter what form they take, not only live out the gospel calling of the church but also actively undo both our instinctive, routine habit of mutual-assessment on sectarian grounds *and* our fear of being met with and excluded by it.

Seating Arrangements

All around the world, seating in Christian churches can be found arranged in two banks of chairs or pews, with a centre aisle, facing toward a 'stage' area. However, although this seating arrangement may look the same to an observer, it registers differently with people in different places depending on local norms of spatiality; what it 'means' is therefore different all over the world. In a similar way to that in which a bodily gesture, such as an embrace, may happen in all human societies and yet convey significantly varied meanings and be ruled by greatly varied conditions, so seating might 'look' the same, but in fact be operating in ways discrete to its particular location. In liturgical history, this is perhaps most acutely evidenced in those churches where deliberate changes have been made as a result of thinking critically about the resonances of dual bank seating. For example: puritan settlers in New England got rid of the central aisle, had a large bank of people all in a central block with two side aisles and smaller rows of seats on the two side blocks,[12] while Catholic catechists in mid-twentieth century Latin America had no pews and arranged ordinary seats in circles.[13] Each of these changes was understood theologically: to better orient the congregation to the Word being proclaimed and/or the sacrament being celebrated.

In Northern Ireland and the Republic of Ireland seating almost always conforms to the dual bank/centre aisle model, although it might be supplemented by a relatively small amount of seating in a side chapel or to either side of the dais. There do exist a few churches with circular or other arrangements for seating (such as the Roman Catholic Church in Boyle, Co. Roscommon) but they are a tiny minority. In all but two of the churches I visited, seating was in the form of pews, and in *all* the churches, whether the seating was provided by individual chairs or wooden pews of varying lengths, they were in the dual bank/centre aisle formation. Even in the Dublin church which described its Sunday morning service as 'Praise and Worship' and its ecclesial structure as 'pods',[14] and which had as the whole central section of its service a time of small group sharing and prayer among the congregation, the chairs were all in rows, with a central aisle, facing the 'front' (the place with two

12. For a history of the movement from the box pews of the puritans (owned by individual families) to the long central pews, and even long, seated, curved pews with all seats facing the pulpit, see, for example, Jeanne Halgren Kilde, *When Church Became Theater: The Transformation of Evangelical Architecture* (New York: Oxford University Press, 2005).

13. See, for example, Sara Margaret Evans, *Journeys that Opened Up the World: Women, Student Christian Movements and Social Justice 1955–1975* (Rutgers, NJ: Rutgers University Press, 2003), pp. 37–28.

14. A married couple (male-female only) hosts a house church each week for a group of 8–12 church members and this is 'where the work of church is done', according to the 'Welcome Leaflet' one is handed as one enters the church.

microphone stands where the keyboard and guitar players, who also led the prayers and scripture reflections, came and went). During a time of extended sharing and prayer, people turned around or lent forward uncomfortably in their seats, conducting conversations across the rows of chairs, but never moving them. Indeed when a child, running around at this time of conversation, collided with a chair and shifted it, the parent readjusted the chair to sit straight in its row before he picked up the child. The chairs in this church – lightweight, foldable, plastic chairs – were thus patrolled in such a way that they were *de facto* pews.

While seating formations were remarkably consistent, the ways in which people took their seats varied considerably along denominational lines. In all the Protestant and Anglican churches in the study, people arrived in advance of the advertised start of the service (so, for a 10.30am service, there was a steady stream of people arriving between 10.15 and 10.30am and almost none thereafter). When worshippers arrived, they walked in quite slowly, said hello to the greeters and often to one another, then spaced themselves out through the entire church, left and right, front and back. In the Roman Catholic churches, by contrast, most people arrived exactly at or a minute or so prior to the appointed time, which made for a great number of people pouring through the doors all at once. Also, many people (sometimes up to a third of the final congregation) arrived after the Mass had started. People came in quickly, rarely talking to one another, and sat mostly in the back half of the church.

I witnessed something in many Roman Catholic churches in the Republic of Ireland that was common practice in Northern Ireland and in mainland Britain: rather than walk up the centre aisle or down the side aisles to reach empty pews, people remained always in the back half of the church and simply went to the end of a pew already full of people. Then, when the people were standing, the newcomers squeezed themselves into the end of the pew, standing half in the pew, half in the aisle; thus, when the time came to sit, everyone adjusted slightly, so that room was made for the new person to sit down. However, more often than not there had been hardly any room to begin with, and so people became squashed extremely tightly up against one another: children were put on laps and couples moved so as to sit sideways-close to one another. Occasionally someone let out an exasperated sigh but in general there was hardly any complaining about being shunted along and pressed tightly against the next person.

Whether people enter the space slowly, occupy its length and breadth and sit with ample room to stretch (Protestants), or whether people enter it hastily, stay near the back and squash in next to someone else (Roman Catholics), once they are seated, their way of behaving becomes surprisingly uniform within and across denominations: they end up sitting side-by-side, interacting with someone in an elevated place in front of them, and they have almost no contact with one another. Even taking into account the ways in which most Protestants and Anglicans greeted one another during peace-passing, and the ways in which most Roman Catholics moved to make room for one another in highly populated pews, once the service began there was relatively little interaction of any sort between worshippers for the whole of the remainder of the services: they sat in parallel lines, aware of their neighbour only laterally, out of the corner of their eye, facing the backs of the heads of the people in front of them and, beyond these, if sightlines allowed, the worship leaders.

It can no doubt be argued that worship happens like this in many other places in the world, and there is nothing therefore exceptional about the Irish case. However, analysing these seating practices on the basis of the wider matrix of meaning-making in Irish cultures, I contend that from the moment worshippers go into most churches in Ireland, they acquiesce to being subtly placed in a binary set of relationships: either one side, or another, and this placement contributes to the formation of lenses that see the world in similar fashion. Indeed, as I hope will gradually become apparent through the following chapters, this binary worldview affects every aspect of Irish religious self-understanding. There are rarely three ways. There is rarely a circle. There is rarely movement across the aisle/ divide. There is one side or the other.

It is not merely the two-ness of the binary that I wish to highlight, it is also the oppositional framework it implies: one *or* the other. I thus perceived in my site visits a bodily habit that mimicked the ways in which Irish and Northern Irish cultures play out in manifold venues. The fact that people come in and choose one side or the other, then sit there largely passively, interacting with the elevated, distant, authority figure but not with one another seemed closely related as a performance with a standard, dialectical worldview in

Irish society. Moreover, this standard mode of behaviour is, I suggest, normatively sectarian, because in our context, the either/or has been conditioned by our religious, ethnic and national identity categories of Catholic or Protestant. One side of a Roman Catholic church is just as Roman Catholic as the other; but I am not arguing that the choice in church is itself between sectarian options. Rather, I am pointing to two factors that form the bedrock for other thinking (including potentially sectarian thinking): first, the fact that there are only ever two options and, second, our passivity (including our habitual looking for leadership from others who operate at a distance) once we take either option.

Textile Placement

At the start of my research, an American colleague asked if I was going to write about flags, given the recurring controversy over flags in worship spaces in the USA.[15] I replied that because there were no flags in Irish churches, it would not be an issue. Imagine my surprise, therefore, to walk into the first church in my fieldwork, the national Cathedral in Dublin, and see the heraldic arrangement of the Royal Arms of England, Scotland and Ireland, known as the Royal Standard hanging there at the front of the main nave. In fact, it hung on both sides of the choir, front and centre to the congregation and, on closer inspection, there were many of them, in ranks, bedecking the choir stalls on both sides. During the offertory collection, I went to the kindly ushers at the back who had greeted me when I arrived and whispered: 'I see the old British flag up there [pointing]; is there a Tricolour (the national flag of Ireland) in here also?' 'Oh yes' he replied, 'now where was it?' And I followed him as he discreetly walked up the side aisles, looking, until he pointed up at a great host of flags in the North transept. 'Nope', he said, as I looked at more Union flags than I could possibly count hanging throughout the space (many of them the remnants of regiments). We walked all the way back up the Cathedral, the offertory procession well under way by now, and as we reached

15. One recent example of these debates, which flare up every few years: in May 2007, a United Methodist clergyman and member of the Board of Church and Society in Washington DC called for the removal of US flags from Church sanctuaries. See, for example, http://www.dakotavoice.com/2007/05/united-methodist-church-official-calls-for-removal-of-us-flag-from-churches/

the back side door, he turned around, perplexed and then spotted the Tricolour halfway along the south west wall: 'There!' he exclaimed, 'I knew we kept one somewhere!'

In half the Protestant and Anglican churches I visited, there was a Union flag, often in the nave or apse/chancel, and in only one of these (a Church of Ireland community) in the Republic, was there a Tricolour as well. In the Roman Catholic cathedral in Galway, there were two small Tricolours—one under the mosaic of former USA President John F. Kennedy and the other under the mosaic of Pope John XXIII, both mosaics being situated in a small side-chapel-space just off the nave. There was also a USA flag ('Stars and Stripes') beside the candle-trays where people knelt to pray. Several other Roman Catholic churches in Ireland and Northern Ireland had the Irish national flag (and never the Union flag) visible in the space— although usually, as in Galway, it was off to the side, on side altars, and not in the main nave or apse.

Some of the things I examine in this book are subtle and even abstract, but the presence and placement of flags in Irish and Northern Irish sanctuaries is not. If you have the primary symbol of nationhood in your sanctuary, you are making a strong claim about the place of the state in the life of faith, and the place of faith in the life of the state. If you have some other country's flag in your space, ditto. In Ireland, as elsewhere, such occurrences are performances of identity, both in its formation and its celebration, rather than, necessarily, manifestoes for specific forms of church-state relationship. They tell people about the ethno-national identity and allegiances of the community that worships there and, as such, they allow a quick political read of the sorts of things one can expect of that community. Yvonne Naylor, of the Irish School of Ecumenics (ISE)[16] told me that it is not just the presence of flags, but also their absence from churches in Northern Ireland that is taken as an indicator of ethos to newcomers: because people are so used to looking for the flag and being able to tell where the community stands (how overtly sectarian it is) by its prominence, when there

16. Interview at the Irish School of Ecumenics, Belfast, 19 March 2006. Naylor directed the *Transforming Sectarianism — Sustained Education Encouraging Diversity (SEED) — Project*, 2000–2006, which equipped teachers and church leaders, particularly Christian education ministers, to guide children in their thinking about a whole host of cultural artifacts, including flags in church.

is no flag they can conclude that it is a 'lukewarm' church and can decide to stay or leave as their politics—or faith, because at this point they are closely merged—allows.

But more than that, flags have a particular history, an extraordinarily strong set of meanings, and a great deal of valence or importance in Irish life. To a tourist they might look to be simply the appropriate national symbol of their respective nation-states (or to historical or aspirational nation-state configurations, as in the personal emblem of the Crown—the English Crown, that is—in the National Cathedral in Dublin), but to those who live on the island they are far more layered and conflict-ridden in their meaning. For example, to this day the Tricolour in Ireland carries party rather than national associations, seen as standing for 'the republic which Sinn Fein had fought for and the Free State government had betrayed'.[17] Thus there are multiple venues in which alternative national symbols are displayed where the national flag would ordinarily be, a harp on a clear background being the most common.

Furthermore, the British Union flag in Northern Ireland is freighted with a history unknown to the other 'provinces', as has become clear in the controversies over whether and how to display it in all manner of venues in Northern Ireland after the 1998 Good Friday Agreement (GFA). Unionists argue it should be flown alone because Northern Ireland is part of the UK. Nationalists argue that it should be flown alongside the Tricolour, or that a new, common symbol should be found (such as the image of the flax flower for the Assembly), or, failing agreement on those, that no flags be flown at all.[18] The issue remains far from resolved at the time of writing: for nationalists, the Union flag is a symbol of Unionism, and it is not appropriate to fly the flag of only one of the two traditions in Northern Ireland. Flags in Ireland, as Ewan Morris has recently suggested, 'make possible the imagining of nations, the marking of inclusion in and exclusion from the nation, and the development

17. Ewan Morris, *Our Own Devices: National Symbols and Political Conflict in Twentieth-Century Ireland* (Dublin: Irish Academic Press, 2005), p. 44.
18. See Dominic Bryan and Clifford Stevenson, 'Flagging Peace: Struggles over Symbolic Landscape in the new Northern Ireland' in Marc Howard Ross (ed.), *Culture and Belonging in Divided Societies: Contestation and Symbolic Landscapes* (Philadelphia, PA: University of Pennsylvania Press, 2009), pp. 68–84; 77.

within nations of solidarity without consensus.'[19] When flags are in prominent places in our churches, this 'solidarity without consensus' is subsumed under a seemingly divine authority: all the flag stands for (all 'the imagining of nations') is presented as part of the architecture of faith, one of the special symbols that enable our worship.

A great deal could be gained by removing flags from sanctuaries in Ireland, because as long as they are present they are making a nationalist statement to a sectarian situation, and giving it a divinely-ordained implication that it ought not to have. Not that there is anything necessarily wrong with acknowledging one's national affiliation in church. Congregations in the Church of Sweden, for example, often display the Swedish flag in their sanctuaries, and no one is hurt by it. The problem with Ireland is that it (the island, Ireland) comprises two countries, geo-politically speaking, and one of those countries (Northern Ireland) is ultimately owned by another (the UK). Moreover, this is a relatively new arrangement, and one that many residents remain unhappy about. So whereas in Sweden the church can pray for its national leaders as its public figures, because the borders/boundaries of church and state coincide, in Ireland by contrast, the four main denominations being all-Ireland in ecclesial polity traverse two countries (Irish Republic and Northern Ireland) and include two national jurisdictions (Irish Republic and United Kingdom); and, more to the point, all three entities have been embroiled in hostile relations for many years. To raise only one country's flag in church in such a context sets up a very, very different picture to raising the Swedish flag in a church in Sweden.

The Cross

In all the churches in this study, there was a (sculpture of a) cross in a very prominent position in the space. In all the Roman Catholic churches there was an image of a person, usually but not always identifiably male, hanging on the cross. In about half of the Anglican churches this was also the case. In the remainder of the Anglican and all the Protestant churches, the cross was just a cross. In the Roman Catholic and one of the Anglican churches, people would

19. Bryan and Stevenson, 'Flagging Peace', p. 7. See also the un-numbered section of photographs in the centre of the book.

genuflect or bow to the cross at several points during their time in church, while in the other Anglican and Protestant churches people made no explicit gesture toward the cross. Except, of course, in all cases, from wherever the worshippers stood or sat, the cross was visible straight in front of them, so it could be said they stood or sat in front of the cross. It might equally be said that they positioned themselves in front of the altar or the worship leaders, because these were always right in front of, or right beneath, the cross. However, you can take the altar away (and some churches did) or the worship leaders can move 'off stage' (as they always did at some point, in all cases), and what always remains is the cross in front of the people.[20] Thus it seems reasonable to remark that in all the churches studied, the people in the congregation adopted as one of their fundamental bodily gestures (standing or sitting) a relation to (facing) the cross.

Roman Catholic and higher-church Anglican congregants made 'the sign of the cross' (using their right hand to trace a cross on the upper part of their body, starting by touching their head, moving their hand down their torso and touching their sacrum, moving their hand to left and then right and touching each shoulder). A majority of people did this at the start of the service and, in most cases, at several additional points in the service as well, although the precise timing of these varied considerably: for example, some Anglicans did so at the words in the creed 'resurrection of the body', some Catholics did so while the priest gave the absolution, and many Roman Catholics and a few Anglicans did so after receiving communion; there was no uniformity of practice within or between churches.

Protestants did not make the sign of the cross on their bodies, but all, without exception had an image (a drawing) of the cross on the front of the service leaflet or Book that they were holding as a guide to worship. Even the non-text using churches (which used a screen for words to songs and prayers), handed people a 'Welcome Leaflet' on the front of which was a cross. So, while Catholics and some Anglicans make the sign of the cross with their hands, Protestants hold the cross in their hands for almost all of the service (these leaflets/Books were put down only at occasional points in most services).

20. And, in most Roman Catholic churches, the tabernacle.

In all cases, then, people's bodily interactions with the space involved (or one might even claim was mediated by) their physical relationship to the cross. This is not surprising, given the importance of the cross in Christian theology. The cross is the symbol of the death and resurrection of Jesus and upon it hinges, therefore, the central Christian theology of salvation (particularly the doctrines of atonement and redemption) and Christology in both their Catholic and Protestant articulations. The theological interpretations of the cross and associations with the cross are rich and varied across cultures and I did not discern any peculiarly Irish 'meaning' in the cross or the people's interactions with it.

However, while the cross was interacted-with a very great deal in worship, it was not actually ever talked about in worship (although 'the cross' was a strong theme in the hymn texts used in the Anglican and Protestant churches, something which is addressed in Chapter Six's discussion of music). The words with which a community surrounds a symbol frame its interpretation, and there is a danger in allowing a strong and multi-dimensional symbol to loom un-reflected upon. It will be important in moving beyond sectarianism to pay attention to the associations that the cross is allowed to silently carry. I say this because in Ireland and Northern Ireland, it may be that the cross is failing to serve primarily as a reassurance that God is with us in our suffering (as it often is, for example, in Spanish-speaking cultures where the Christ figure is depicted with graphic wounds, and people touch, stroke and weep over the figure on the cross); and it may be failing to serve primarily to increase our compassion for the *whole* world (as it has been crafted to convey in, for example, Scandinavian churches with the intertwining of the cross with images of creation placed in a prominent place in the worship space); and it may be failing to serve primarily as the site/memorial of a personal implication in sinfulness and option of forgiveness (as it has been used to depict — in tandem with preaching that message — in Calvinist churches in Scotland for centuries).

Could it be that, in the Republic and Northern Ireland, the cross might be serving primarily as a reminder of and reinforcement of a whole community's victimhood? If Jesus's victimhood is given centre-stage by the placement of the cross in the space or in the hands, and also by the lack of direct language to contextualize it, then, combined with social understandings of want, lack (hard-done-by-ness) and the desire for justice or security, this dominant image potentially justifies and/or reinforces a community's victimhood.

Geographers in recent years have paid increasing attention to the concept of space and the ways in which spaces work. Peter Shirlow and Brendan Murtagh, writing about Belfast as a place, notice the ways in which notions of victimhood and expressions of violence co-produce one another spatially. They suggest that:

> The ability to consolidate identity, however loosely, remains dependent upon the capacity to govern the memory traces of conflict through a series of notions of belonging. It is a process of strategic management that is still based upon convincing sections of each respective community that resistance to the "other" community is a historical struggle and that the residents of harmed places are the makers of a profound history. Without doubt the mono-cultural imaginings of victimhood undermine the possibility of progressive political movement. ... Despite the extensive attempts to control localized narratives of victimhood it is evident that the capacity to do so has been blunted by alternative, if concealed, notions of collective loss.[21]

I suspect that the cross functions in many Irish churches as one of these 'concealed notions of collective loss' and it would thus serve to reinforce, causally, people's sense of victimhood as well as their feelings of righteous indignation in the face of it. More than that, it gives such feelings divine credibility. The corollary of 'This is our God, the victim, scorned by those who hated him, now central to our worship and central to our faith' produces the distorted but powerful theology: 'our victimhood is the central characteristic of our relationship with God; it is for this reason God loves us; God is on our side.'

Furthermore, the cross is rarely a shared reality. It is debatable whether Catholics and Protestants understand themselves to believe in the same God, and this produces a peculiar double-think in popular apprehension of the cross: as a historical figure, there was only one Jesus, and therefore only one cross-event; but as God, Christ—whether remembered through the cross or through an image of a body on the cross—is conceived in partisan terms, as is

---

21. Peter Shirlow and Brendan Murtagh, *Belfast: Segregation, Violence and the City* (London: Pluto Press, 2006), pp. 75–76.

God the Father also. While the ecumenical movement claims the cross as a common symbol, meaning a symbol all Christians share, in Irish worship there is a pervasive sense that *our* cross is different, and means something wholly different, to *their* cross. This is no wonder, given the combination of these two facts: on the one hand, the aspect of the cross that is deep in the popular imagination is most often its metaphor of victimhood (through hymn texts and image-handling in Protestant churches, or devotional practices such as kissing it or kneeling before it in Roman Catholic churches); and on the other, Catholics and Protestants both feel they are the real victims, the greater victims, and each at the other's hands. So, each side asks, if Christ as victim saves us victims, then how can the oppressor claim that Christ saves them too?

As Liechty and Clegg have demonstrated, such split-thinking can be broken down through conversation. But only a very small minority of people brings this thinking to the level of consciousness, perhaps because there are currently so very few venues for the sort of conversation Liechty and Clegg envisaged, especially between local congregations.[22] For most, the cross functions at only a symbolic, bodily level and co-conspires with other things to form habits, attitudes, beliefs and practices in their daily lives. All the more important, then, in leading worship, to preach the cross in ways that de-emphasize it as the apotheosis of victimhood, and to instead present it along doctrinal lines which are more orthodox whether one is Protestant or Catholic (none of whose theologies of the cross resolve or conclude at victimhood alone).

Moreover, it is vital to proclaim its commonality as a symbol shared by all Christians. This does not have to involve lengthy sermons; on the contrary, it can be accomplished in small remarks and passing references, such as, 'like Jesus [point to cross] who died that *all* people might have life' or, 'as we bring our cares and concerns of this day and lay them at the foot of the cross, we are reminded that this cross bears the pain of *all* peoples.' Basically, surrounding the cross with the language of '*all*' (and not '*our*') takes one significant step toward preventing its adoption as an emblem of righteous victimhood.

22. Maria Power, '"Of Some Symbolic Importance, But Not Much Else": The Inter-Church Meeting and Ecumenical Dialogue in Northern Ireland, 1980–1999', *Journal of Ecumenical Studies* 43:1 (Winter 2008), pp. 111–23.

Furthermore, not only through words, but also through practices of handling or gesturing toward the cross, communities can broaden their understanding of Christ's cross and the place of their histories in its story. The existing worship practices for Good Friday in all denominations use the cross as their central symbol (i.e., veneration at the afternoon service in Roman Catholic churches, or walking with a large cross through the town or from town to town that is most often organized by Protestant and Anglican churches). As such, they offer potentially powerful inter-denominational possibilities. Good Friday is the only day of the year that Eucharist is not celebrated in the Roman Catholic Church, and it thus removes that habitual sticking-point (the prohibition on inter-communion). Furthermore, having a multi-denominational cross-carrying (as a few communities already do) on the morning of Good Friday allows those with afternoon services to still attend them. All these suggested practices, verbal as well as non-verbal, will take imagination and critical reflection (for example, if Roman Catholics invite Protestants to a service venerating the cross, do they keep the figure on it?), but they will also help to undo the habit of making the cross a sectarian spatial identity-marker, based on distorted theologies of victimhood.

Peace-passing

Most congregations in Ireland, in common with Protestant and Catholic congregations throughout the world, have in their worship guidelines provision for a time when the minister can invite all the people in the assembly to share a sign of peace with one another. In Ireland this usually transpires as a handshake, or the odd kiss for a family member, accompanied by the words 'peace be with you', or 'God's peace' or just 'peace'. It is scripted to occur at different points in each respective tradition's services, so in Roman Catholic churches it comes after the Eucharistic prayer, right before the '*Lamb of God*' and the distribution of gifts, while in Anglican Sunday morning services it usually comes earlier, following the confession and before the Eucharistic Prayer (if the Eucharist is being celebrated). In Protestant churches it can come in both these places, but also at a range of other places, depending on whether or not there is communion, such as immediately prior to the offering or at the very end of the service.

The ways in which peace was passed in my field studies were not uniform, but, again, patterned throughout the island according to denomination (i.e., there were only denominational and not regional differences in practice). In most of the Roman Catholic churches where peace was passed, the priest would say the biblical words of Jesus, 'My peace I give you, my peace I leave with you', invite the sharing of a sign of peace, and then the people would turn only to the people on either side of them, and offer a quick handshake or kiss on the cheek. They rarely turned behind them or reached across one another, and they never reached across the aisles. In the Protestant and Anglican churches, by contrast, people moved around a great deal, greeted many people, used hugs as well as handshakes, and made obvious effort to reach out to those who were alone, at the back, or less mobile.

However, in a significant number of the congregations I studied (two Protestant and seven Catholic), this exchange of the peace was not invited. The minister, arriving at the time at which the invitation to pass the peace might normally happen, would just run onto the next thing. In those Catholic churches where it was omitted, the priest said the preamble: 'The peace of the Lord be with you always,' to which the assembly responded, 'And also with you', but then he neglected to lead what conventionally comes next: 'Let us offer one another a sign of peace'. And in the two Protestant churches, no mention of the peace was made at all. I could not tell if this was an accidental omission on the days I was visiting or a regular habit, and so at coffee hour in both Protestant locations, I asked the congregants. In one church, I speculated that maybe the peace was like communion, only happening once a month or once a quarter, but those with whom I was chatting responded that they did not know how often it happened or whether it was related to communion: their sense was that it was 'random'. In the second church, one man said he could not remember the last time the minister invited it, it was so long ago, and he did not mind personally because he thought it was a stupid practice, and another man said they did it every week and the minister must have just forgotten today: this was in the same church. None of the seven Catholic churches where no peace was passed had a coffee hour or any other venue for meeting worshippers after the end of the service, and so I could not ask what people thought of its absence.

If there were not a provision for passing the peace in the worship books, if it were not practiced routinely in the other congregations of these denominations around the world, or if it were omitted for a reason that the congregation understood, then I would not take this absence of a practice so seriously. But it seems significant that, in a country that struggles to imagine, never mind achieve 'peace', there are such a relatively high proportion of churches that omit the convention of passing the peace in their services.

Peace-passing as a liturgical act is thought to have derived from the earlier practice of kissing as a marker of group belonging. Following Christ's command to 'leave mother and brother and follow me', the earliest Christians adopted the sign of filial bond (a kiss on the lips usually being reserved for one's immediate family members only) to indicate that the people with whom they gathered in Christian community were now their family.[23] While Christians once kissed at a whole host of points during worship in the first and second centuries, by the fourth century, the kiss had become associated primarily with forgiveness and reconciliation (something it had not been used for in earlier years).[24] Having fallen out of favour for a number of years in the Roman Catholic church, congregational peace-passing gestures were reinvigorated through the reforms of Vatican II and became standard practice in churches throughout the world by the end of the 1970s.

Of course, the man who described it as 'stupid' is far from alone: as anyone who listens to comments about worship at a congregational level knows, complaints about having to pass the peace abound. Many people feel that it is an awkward moment, they do not know what to do, they do not know why they are doing it, they feel it makes worship too 'ordinary' and so on. But, at the same time, there are many people who value it as one of the high-points of Sunday worship. And there are also many people who while not exactly loving it, know that it is important and that it accomplishes something worthwhile over time.

23. See Edward L. Phillips, *The Ritual Kiss in Early Christian Worship* (Cambridge: Grove Books, 1996).

24. See Michael P. Penn, *Kissing Christians: Ritual and Community in the Late Ancient Church* (Philadelphia, PA: University of Pennsylvania Press, 2005). Tertullian was the first to call it 'the kiss of peace' or 'the peace', and Augustine coins the phrase 'the sign of peace'. See Penn, *Kissing Christians*, pp. 44–45.

Ireland is no different to other contexts in any of these regards or reactions. It is different in this though: in a third of the churches I studied, no peace was passed at all; and, moreover, in those Catholic churches where the peace was passed it was done in as minimal and half-hearted a fashion as imaginable. Northern Ireland has, in the period of this study, gone through a (very public, internationally-sponsored) 'peace-process', and so it is also striking that in all of the churches where peace was passed, no verbalized connection was ever made between the peace passed in church and the peace process happening outside of it. Why, in a country in which a peace-process was underway (and no one could have been ignorant of it—it was constantly in the media, discussed in schools, and had required whole-country referenda in both the Republic and Northern Ireland), was the connection between liturgical peace-passing and civic peace-making not made in any of the churches, and why was the peace not even passed in a third of the sample?

Ireland and Northern Ireland are countries that have struggled hard with creating peace. The 'peace-process' involved an extraordinarily contested set of descriptors of 'peace', and alienated many communities from their previous functional notions of peace in the service of consociational civic arrangements. As noted in the preface to this book, the peace-process may have left us with fairer civic structures and greatly diminished scales of organized violence, but it is a very 'cold' sort of peace. Such a situation cannot be an accidental relative of the absence of peace-passing in so many Irish churches and the very perfunctory performance of it in so many Roman Catholic ones.

It may not have been the case that those who argued for the passing of the peace among the congregation to be reincorporated into the liturgical life of the churches did so with actual situations of civic conflict, or unresolved historic grievance, in mind. But it is nevertheless the case that we have, as part of our worship services in Catholic and Protestant churches alike, a time prescribed for the peace to be passed; furthermore, when one is worshipping in a situation of conflict, endemic or otherwise, that conditions how the peace-passing gesture in the ritual is performed: it affects its meaning.

If the peace we were 'signing' in church were simply a matter of our individual peace with God, then we would not need to pass the peace with our neighbour in the pew. And if our peace-passing were meant to reconcile us simply one to another strictly within the limits of a closed-community (reinforcing the bonds among the club), then the biblical words that precede and frame the conventional invitation to pass the peace would be rendered meaningless. However, because it is the peace Jesus left, it is God's own gift of peace that we are called to signal to one another. It is a universal peace in which we are invited to participate by God's grace, not just some gesture for our little denomination to feel self-satisfied about. It is potentially the most reconciling gesture in the whole of Christian worship and, as we discovered in Chapter Two, this could account for the problem: we want peace, but not reconciliation; hence our minimization of this particular liturgical act. It seems that the peace is being omitted or under-played for very plain reasons.

The standard theologies underpinning and arising from the practice of peace-passing vary according to denomination, and this is reflected in where it comes in the service. For some it is an essential step in the process of confessing and being forgiven our sins and so it is a vital part of the reconciliation portion of the liturgy. For others, sharing a sign of peace with one's fellow worshippers is an extension of confessing our sins to God and being forgiven by God (i.e., it is not a direct part of that transaction, but a consequence that is deemed sufficiently important not to leave to the imagination but to make concrete). For others it is related to the Eucharist, harking back to Jesus' command that you must make your peace with your neighbour before coming to the altar. And for yet others it is not to do with our need to be reconciled at all, neither with God nor with our neighbour, but is rather an acknowledgement of the peace God has already given, in Jesus Christ, of which we are ever called to grow in awareness.

Until we face our desperate need for workable theologies of reconciliation for our unique situation, theologies capable of articulating the very great diversity of past hurts, present meeting-places and future hopes, passing the peace will remain an avoided act in many Irish and Northern Irish churches. But passing the peace, if re-introduced in a nuanced way, a way that acknowledges the problem, might also serve as a physical strategy for discovering what shape those theologies of reconciliation might take. Passing the peace every time we gather for worship, instead of being yet one more charade of coercion or conformity, might be an effective way of rehearsing, living into, feeling the discomforts of, negotiating and tailoring a definition of what peace means in this context because, quite clearly—like the reconciliation it points to and potentially—it means, and will always mean, different things to different people. And this is the nub of the matter. Being able to fashion a lived sense in which all meanings are held under the umbrella of God's peace might be very useful, accomplishing a peace-process with something additional to political definitions of peace. It might 'warm up' the peace underpinning civic engagement.

Moreover, for those churches that already invite some form of peace passing, it might be worth, homiletically, in the prayers, or, in those traditions that are not strictly scripted right around the time of the peace-passing, to have the minister say something short but direct that connects this peace in church with the peace beyond its walls. Not the soft version, but the hard version, the version that involves actually naming people's stories and realities—a very problematic aspect of Irish worship to which we are about to turn in the next chapter. It would be understandable if people felt disturbed by the hypocrisy of the juxtaposition of a display of theological peace on Sunday and a parade of sectarian prejudice on Monday, and that may be part of the reason why the peace is so often omitted or under-performed: because doing so streamlines things, keeps their integrity. What is needed at this juncture in history, I suggest, is a streamlining in the other direction: passing the peace needs to be reconceived as an occasion for intentionally reaching-out, literally, to our neighbours at a time when reaching-out is what is most needed. This is unlikely to be achieved unless the reconciliation that the liturgical peace gesture has always pointed to is actually capable of the task, and is actually talked about. It is to talk, and to what is in fact talked about in church, that we now turn.

Chapter Four

WORDS

'In our prayers, above all, there must be reality.'[1]

The ways in which words are chosen and spoken in worship services in Ireland and Northern Ireland varied enormously within as well as between the denominations I studied. While some Church of Ireland congregations followed the Book of Common Prayer (BCP) to the letter, resulting in only four points in the service which were not pre-scripted (a small part in the prayers, the sermon, the peace and the welcome), others drew on the BCP only occasionally, their leaders speaking spontaneously and/or communicating through the use of words displayed using *PowerPoint* on screen. Likewise in the Presbyterian and Methodist Churches, while not exhibiting such radical differences in style as the Anglicans, there were some that stuck closely to the orders of service printed on the service leaflets or in the Hymnals and others who used these more lightly, with the leaders speaking (without reading) many of the words as they went along. The sorts of things they adlibbed included interjecting theological reflection here and there (e.g., why we take up this offering), introducing the day's scriptures before they were read, offering some words to help orient the children as they returned from Sunday School (and covering the noise of them settling into their seats besides their families), and, in two cases in Northern Ireland, preaching extemporaneously (and brilliantly!).

Despite this great variety, there was nevertheless an enormous amount of common vocabulary as well as grammar between all the congregations, as one would expect from religious rites that historically have evolved in direct relation (including reforming and critical relation) to one another. However, analysing the data once the bulk of site visits were completed, I was surprised to find

1. J.A.F. Gregg quoted in The Church of Ireland's *General Synod Journal*, lxxxiii (1949), p. iv.

particular patterns of naming and, especially, not-naming recurring across the full spectrum of churches I visited. Churches which were radically different in almost every ethnic, national, denominational, political and aesthetic aspect of their character and foundational identity turned out to be using very similar if not identical words and phrases in moments of spontaneous speech, praying for the same issues, and, to my amazement, not praying for the same issues. The same name or subject that was included or omitted from the prayers of a conservative Presbyterian congregation in Northern Ireland was also included or left out of the prayers of a progressive Catholic congregation in the Republic.

O Ireland, Where are You?

"Father, we ask you to look after the people of Zimbabwe, the poor Blacks who were held down for so very long, but now also the Whites who are being turfed off their farms. May peace come to that turbulent land and may the current violence stop."

Roman Catholic, Midlands, IR

"And we pray especially today for the people of Indonesia and everyone down there near the Indian Ocean. They're still struggling to recover from the tsunami and all they lost in it."

Methodist, NI

"Lord, in your mercy, hear our prayers for those who gather this week at the G-8 summit in Germany. Instill these our leaders with humility as well as courage, and guide them to construct policies that will protect this earth, our island home, from further abuse or catastrophe."

Church of Ireland, NI

Throughout the Republic and Northern Ireland every Sunday morning, prayers are said for the lands and peoples of the whole world. The three examples above date themselves easily by the specificity of the concerns they express: anyone could go to a search engine, tap in the people and places named in the prayers and identify the year, if not the exact week, I recorded these words spoken in a church in Ireland. And yet, in all my research, from 2001–2008, I never heard the word 'Ireland' (nor 'Northern Ireland', obviously) used in the non-authorized-text speech of any of the churches I visited. In Ireland, I was very surprised to discover, Ireland is rarely mentioned in church. Sermons would talk about 'at home', 'around here' and 'our leaders' but never named the locality, or the country, or the government. Prayers would be made for 'justice' and 'peace', but never for any specific issue, person or place. On just three occasions (in three different churches across the spectrum in the sample) prayers included mention of 'the peace process' in 'the North' but nothing more specific about it than that; indeed on one of those occasions (in a Roman Catholic church in Cork in 2001) the prayer made sure to relativize even this expression: 'for the peace process in the North, and all peace processes around the world'.

When it came to naming Irish needs, concerns and fears, the language became vague or generalized, or both. This is in stark comparison to non-scripted prayer in Christian worship services in other countries, where the needs of the native region or nation are mentioned directly and frequently. And it is also in stark contrast to the ways in which Northern Irish and Irish people pray for the very specific needs of people and events in other very specific places, as seen in the three examples above. To me, this is fascinating. Irish newspapers are full of Irish news as well as world news; why are the Irish aspects of our world not mentioned in church?

In part, this non-naming of Ireland and Northern Ireland may be a way of saying: 'we are connected to a much bigger world', or 'we want to identify with a much bigger world as a way of not just being ourselves'. Such statements stem from lessons learned from history that Ireland could not afford to be isolated (as seen in the peace process), is not isolated (because of the diaspora and all the money as well as international connection it has sent home), and will not be isolated (hence the Republic's strong association with the EU and the Loyalist North's strong association with Great Britain). Irish concerns, when mentioned, are emphasized as being in common with many others around the world, not purely or exclusively Irish matters. It is almost unanimously agreed that without its connections to the much bigger world, the peace that exists in Ireland would not have been gained. Significant international pressure promoted the actions of the respective governments and substantial international investment created the economic conditions in which political conversation might stand a chance of practical application.[2] Not only through the diaspora of emigrants and their generations, but also through a sudden surge

2. See, for example, Steve Coleman, *The End of Irish History? Critical Reflections on the Celtic Tiger* (Manchester: Manchester University Press, 2003).

of worldwide interest in and empathy for Irish culture, Ireland and Northern Ireland by the mid-1990s were in the world's eye as never before. And so perhaps Irish church leaders picked this up, and began only ever talking about Ireland in the context of its wider world-location.

However, more may be at stake here. In addition to the undoubted importance of its international-connections in its recent history and self-perception, there is a self-abnegation about Ireland and Irishness that is also worthy of remark. Writing about the film *The Commitments* and the way the characters immerse themselves in popular (North American) culture, Luke Gibbons remarks that, 'The absence of the Catholic Church, the lack of "picturesque" local colour and, for Alan Parker, the indifference to the Northern conflict, all add to the universalism of the film, to the likelihood that it could have been set anywhere (the highest form of praise, it would seem, for an Irish film in recent years.)'[3] Analogically, the highest aspiration of 'good worship' in Ireland and Northern Ireland seems to be a universalizing of both self-reference and sense of belonging.

This may be due to traces of older liturgical aesthetics, inherited colloquial norms about 'how to pray', discernable in two noticeable characteristics that work in tandem: the first is the idea that you do not pray for yourself and your needs directly; and the second is that you never name any one particular person, group or place, for fear of leaving out others equally worthy of the prayer. However, it may also and worryingly be a sort of self-erasure, the product of the desperation at play for so very long; desperation that knew that a specifically Irish, or Northern-Irish, notion of belonging could only be self-defeating in the long-run and so cut-out all specific self-reference in the hopes of salvation in universalism.

This points to the possibility that there may also be some fundamental insecurities about geography as well as culture being displayed in Irish ways of praying. Perhaps we do not know who to pray for as 'ourselves'. The four denominations I studied being all-island in their governance, one might expect that their solution, when praying for their native location would be to say 'Ireland, North and South' or 'Northern Ireland and the Republic of Ireland'.

3. Luke Gibbons, 'The Global Cure? History, Therapy and the Celtic Tiger' in Peadar Kirby, Luke Gibbons and Michael Cronin (eds), *Reinventing Ireland: Culture, Society and the Global Economy* (London: Pluto Press, 2002), pp. 89–108; 92–93.

But this does not work because although the churches are structurally all-Ireland in their management, few ordinary Christians in Ireland perceive themselves to be part of an all-Ireland daily geo-political reality. With the exception of Roman Catholics in the North, the four main churches' parishioners/members generally do not see themselves as inhabiting shared territory: the Southern Catholic's country is Ireland, the Northern Presbyterian's country may be Northern Ireland or Ulster (although the latter is not a country, and includes some counties in the Republic: Cavan and Donegal) or it may be Britain (which is not, technically, a country, either), but it is not usually 'Ireland'. Crossing the border into Northern Ireland, the road signs are blue, distance is measured in miles, and you must pay for your petrol in Pounds Sterling; crossing to the South, the road signs are green, distance is measured in kilometers, and you must pay for your petrol in Euros. The ultimate authority for many matters in Northern Ireland is British, even after devolution, and the authority in the South is Irish, and the effects of their differences in authority extend far beyond road signage and currency.

By not naming Ireland or Northern Ireland in worship, Irish Christians may be performing the reality that they are caught in, which is an un-nameable (or at least un-named) situation. The church in which they are worshipping is all-Ireland in its self-identity. The country in which they are living is most definitely not. Church and state not only have different borders but deeply contested borders, these very borders having been the subject of much of the last century's pain. On the one hand, this allows Irish people to explore their eschatological location in ways that few in the western world, with their easy assimilation of church and state, are ever able to. Without the ability to name their geo-political location in ways that line-up with their ecclesiology, they have become adept not only at evasion, but at naming the alternative reality thus formed. Irish prayers for 'this place', 'here on earth', 'this island home' (meaning the whole earth, and echoing a phrase in the *Book of Common Prayer*), locate Irish congregations in a place that is at once both non-parochial and universal. Perhaps in liturgy, then, Irish and Northern Irish worshippers are not so much citizens of any worldly geo-political entity as they are dwellers on God's earth, their only country being God's own, with its limitless boundaries and presence not only through space but also through time.

On the other hand, however, repressing the conflict inherent in not knowing quite where their limits lie seems only to add to the conflict that so conditions the place where they live. Sectarianism thrives most, as Liechty and Clegg demonstrated,[4] where it is least acknowledged, and this problem of not knowing how to name our place, and so not naming it, cannot be separated from the sectarianism in society at large. As with 'Ireland' because we do not know how to name it, because our efforts to name it result in such gauche statements, such seeming over-statements, making more than is there and not just getting on with the job of living in peace, we prefer not to name it. And then, appalled when a child comes home from school talking about the 'Proddy-dogs' or the 'Fenians', we are suddenly thrown into a world of knowing we must speak but having no notion what to say. Liturgical borders simultaneously break open cosmic borders: the eschatological borders of heaven and hell, the existential borders of divine-human relations, and the theological borders of language (through praise); but this breaking-open is concrete, not abstract; it is not a 'no man's land'. Liturgical borders inevitably happen within worldly borders, and while they are not bound by the imagination of the nation-state, they nevertheless have developed in tandem with it and, insofar as they require speech, must take their geo-political and national-cultural location into accurate account.

Praying for Irish and Northern Irish concerns seems, therefore, to be urgently needed. Moreover, we need to name them with the same ease with which we name those of Zimbabwe, the countries bordering the Indian Ocean, the member nations of the G-8 and their discussions, or all the other concerns for which we routinely pray. By naming ourselves, we take responsibility for ourselves in the sight of God, eschewing the popular temptation to obliterate the difficulty and divisiveness of our crises of identity through a media presence (for profit, sold back to us as commodity) on a world stage. Moreover, and importantly, by setting out our actual store in the eyes of God, we lay ourselves open to receiving God's help, both in the act of naming and the re-naming to which all Christian prayer ultimately points through its desire for transformation.

4. See, for example, Joseph Liechty and Cecilia Clegg, *Moving Beyond Sectarianism: Religion, Conflict and Reconciliation in Northern Ireland* (Dublin: Columba Press, 2001), pp. 9–10.

Anniversaries

The same reluctance to mention things Irish can be seen in the fact that in none of the churches I attended were any anniversaries mentioned. As a culture, anniversaries are of great significance to Irish and Northern Irish people. On the one-month marker of a loved one's death in the Roman Catholic community, the family, friends and parish gather for the month's mind mass, and mass is said for them again at the one-year anniversary (often followed by a meal for family, friends and neighbours), and then usually again, for many subsequent anniversaries. This means that on any day in a Roman Catholic parish, there is a good chance that mass will be being said for somebody's anniversary. Anniversaries are thus intricately woven into the fabric of daily life for Roman Catholics. Protestants also honor an intricate web of rituals that run the gamut of domestic-civic-ecclesial anniversaries. For example, Orange Order marches (and other public actions such as bonfire making) happen on many significant historic anniversaries (the most notable of which is the commemoration of the Battle of the Boyne on 12 July), or other ceremonies of civic commemoration, such as that on the anniversary of the armistice on 11 November each year.

However, when it comes to anniversaries related to recent Irish experiences, they are rarely mentioned in worship; the sole exception to any historical anniversary being 12 July, and the context in which this was mentioned during my fieldwork was in prayers on 1 July 2001 in a large Presbyterian Church in Belfast for a peaceful parade the next weekend, and for an avoidance of a repeat of the problems at Drumcree. Most strikingly, on 20 August 2006, I went to two churches on the same morning in Donegal (one Catholic, the other Methodist) both of which prayed hard for the coming anniversary of Katrina (which happened in the USA in September of the previous year) but neglected to mention at all the anniversary of the bombing of Omagh, which had passed that very week and had happened just up the road in 1998. It is simply not the case that our memories only run one year, so this lack of mention of important regional or national anniversaries in church must be about something else. The reference to anniversaries of American rather than Irish events may stem from the same desire to be part of American history that can be witnessed in many other aspects of media and cultural life. But I suspect the pattern of not naming anniversaries to do with the life of the nation has more to do with just not wanting to deal with ourselves; or, rather, not knowing how to, and so not doing it.

It seems to me that honouring significant anniversaries in recent (as well as ancient) Irish history needs to become a vital part of the liturgical year in Ireland. Not to do so is to fail to root our worship in our own culture, because anniversaries constitute such an important aspect of our particular society and its social and temporal norms. Moreover, if it became a common practice for *cross-community* anniversaries to be honoured in all the churches in Ireland and Northern Ireland, significant gains in moving beyond sectarianism could be made. Worship that marks anniversaries such as Omagh (15 August) are a potentially powerful ecumenical bridge because of their very cross-community nature, due to the fact that members of all communities lost people at the same time and still mourn it at the same time. Worship that marks anniversaries such as New Year's Day are also a potentially powerful ecumenical bridge because they unite the community-at-large in a day of celebration, and new-beginnings. By knowing that people from all sides care about, remember, celebrate and pray for the same specific things, at the same specific times, great strides can be taken in realizing that we hold far more *in common* than we do in opposition. Taking a cue from common experiences in those aspects of life that are shared on both sides of the sectarian divide, churches can use anniversaries as a moment for noting their common experience, shared concerns and mutual prayer, across denominations.

Don't Mention the War, Or Any Other Problems

During the years of my research, and those immediately preceding it, Northern Ireland and the Republic of Ireland encountered a range of changes that history will remember as an extraordinary period in the island's life. The sexual abuse scandals rocked the Roman Catholic Church in Ireland to its foundations, changing the nature of clerical-societal relations but also contributing to the radical decline in the numbers of native-Irish people attending church on Sundays. Mass emigration ended. Both jurisdictions received large numbers of immigrants and from a great many origins around the world, sowing the seeds of greater cultural diversity. Refugees found new homes in the Republic, but also found racism, and new legislation was needed to address their status. The economy of the

Republic suddenly grew at a rate of almost 7 percent for six consecutive years from 1996 onwards, making one of the poorest countries in the western world suddenly one of the wealthiest (due to the so-called Celtic Tiger). Northern Ireland became substantially wealthier, too. There was a peace-process, and an Agreement, followed by devolved power-sharing government, a new police force, an end to armed campaigns, and the development of regional initiatives throughout Northern Ireland. This constitutes massive social change.

Yet in the course of my fieldwork, I heard only one sermon that mentioned (lightly, saying it should talk about it but could not due to lack of time) the sex abuse scandals that had decimated the Roman Catholic Church in that period (in an Roman Catholic Church in Dublin in March 2005). I heard only two prayers for a specific moment in the peace process (both were in fact prayers for David Trimble, who was not mentioned by name, but just as the leader of his party, and both were in Church of Ireland parishes, one in Dublin, the other in the Midlands in June 2004) and I heard the phrase 'the Troubles' in prayer only twice (in 2001 and 2002), although I saw it in the newspaper nearly every day from 2001 to 2005. I never heard prayers for on-the-ground experiences related to the Troubles (whether they were named as such or not), things like usury, drug-related-crime, threatening behaviour, people who had to flee fast, the security forces, knee-cappings or any form of sectarian violence, contentious Orange marches, intimidation at school gates or rising local crime rates—all of which were going on during the time of the study (as we knew from the papers), but none of which were mentioned in church. In the South, only in the last year of the study did prayers start to appear for the new immigrants (and then only in Dublin, although across denominations), and everything else was met with quiet.

Prayers were either incredibly broad ('for an end to injustice', 'for peace on earth', 'for guidance for our leaders at this time', 'for healing from all the suffering of this life') or incredibly local ('for a good result in the match this afternoon', 'for the teachers in the school', 'for *Name*, who died this week', 'for the sick of this congregation, especially *Names*') and very often about the weather ('for good weather for the marching next weekend', 'for a bit of decent weather for the tourists', 'for rain, in due season'). Since the end of the fieldwork stage of this research, I have heard more mention made of specific concerns: for the victims of sexual abuse and the well-being of refugees. It seems that ten years or so after the epicenter of both crises, it is now occasionally safe to pray for them. But what would have been so dangerous about praying for them at the time? At the time, the churches, or at least the ones I visited, were slow to react, slow to know how to name what was going on in prayer.

Liturgical change is often incremental, consensual (the product of scholarship and consultation) and slow. And the churches in Ireland are, furthermore, notoriously slow to implement changes. For example, regarding the *Irish Church Hymnal*, used in almost all Church of Ireland parishes, only in the year 2000 was the note 'for use in Northern Ireland' added to the British national anthem, 'God Save Our Gracious Queen'; and also only in that year were a few hymns in the Irish language included (that is: 129 years after disestablishment, 78 years after Independence, and 51 years after the 26 counties' departure from the Commonwealth).

But was it just habitual tardiness that led to it taking ten years to pray for specific people involved in specific Irish crises? Unlike the problem of silence in the aftermath of the famine, which will be discussed in the next chapter, the period cannot be characterized as an inchoate situation where speech is impossible due to the effects of profound trauma. Newspapers were full of naming strategies for our situation every day of the week, so it was not as if a common vocabulary for describing the people and their needs did not exist. Perhaps it was due to a feeling of inappropriateness that such matters were not to be examined too closely in church. Perhaps it was the inevitable product of a world spinning faster than the conserving institutions within it could keep up with. Perhaps it was racism on the one hand and denial on the other. Or perhaps it was the paralyzing effects of deep shame. It is impossible to say for sure. But the pattern is worthy of remark even without being able to identify a certain cause, especially because it is not just that specific concerns were not being mentioned in intercessory prayer; thanks was not even being given for the fact that the children were no longer leaving (the tide of emigration having turned), roads were being built, headage was high,[5] and the country was becoming

5. Headage was a subsidy received by farmers in support of rearing live-stock. Nearly all the funds for this scheme came from the European Union, as did nearly all the funds for the major infrastructure developments in these years, most notably the road system.

remarkably prosperous. So, neither the 'bad' nor the 'good' were directly named in any church I attended.

One possible reason for this phenomenon is that ministers, priests and others leading the un-scripted aspects of worship do not want to cause offence. To mention something specific in a situation of profound, multi-faceted and historically-long conflict, about which passions run high under closely-guarded surfaces, and about which so little is actually openly said, is to run the risk of furthering sectarian feeling in some quarters. As the old saying goes, 'Whatever you say, say nothing.' Better not to mention the referendum directly than to risk sounding like you're suggesting the conflict is all over now; better not to mention the sex abuse scandals than to risk the idea that you, too, are jumping from the ship while it's going down; better not to mention the ombudsman's efforts to create fair and transparent structures of accountability than to risk being seen as selling out your own community and its historic ways of doing business; and better not to mention the refugees than to be perceived as giving them preferential treatment over all those native-born people who still struggle to find and keep work and housing while the Celtic Tiger roars most loudly for the wealthy.

The flip-side, however, with its vast generalizations and universalizations on the one hand, and its comfort with the minutiae of mundane and innocuous local concerns on the other, is that it allows major issues of the day to go unspoken and the problems associated with them to fester. Ironically, what starts out as an instinct not to cause offence, not to rattle sectarian bones, ends up reinforcing latent attitudes of ignorance and hatred by not laying them out in the sight of God and of one another. Priests and ministers do not have to come down on any one side of a discussion, and in other countries they can get round this by mentioning the issue and acknowledging that there are differences of opinion about it, and stating that we can therefore pray for this crisis in the midst of difference of opinion about it, because we all agree it's a crisis, even as we cast blame in different locations. This is almost impossible in Ireland and Northern Ireland due to the particular matrixes of foundational, homogenizing mythologies discussed in Chapter Two, mythologies that require us to be utterly 'opposite', our opinions on everything from sex to governance supposedly lining up always on opposing sides of the fence.

Not mentioning the war, or anything else, in our prayers in Ireland does not make it go away; indeed, it takes away a vitally important public location for its possible solution and healing. Former Archbishop of Armagh and Primate of all Ireland J.A.F. Gregg ensured that public worship in the Church of Ireland changed to reflect the constitution of the new state (after cessation from the Commonwealth in 1949). Most controversially, he recommended the replacement of prayers for the monarch (which were said as part of the form for every Sunday's worship) with prayers for the leaders of the Irish nation. The old prayers for the crown should now only be kept in Northern Ireland, the Archbishop argued, because, 'in our prayers, above all, there must be reality'.[6] This is a very interesting statement: it both implies that there are discourses where there might not be so much need for reality, and that prayers are a privileged sort of discourse. Why, in our prayers, above all, must there be reality? Because in our society, prayers are conditioning politics, as well as politics conditioning prayers.

Accuracy in prayer is essential, first, because it is ultimately an act of trust in God, and trust in God is what needs to be rebuilt at this time in our history (immediately post-violence but with stringent divisions remaining), just as it did when Gregg spoke in the aftermath of World War Two. For Roman Catholics, trust in the church needs to be rebuilt too; however, for Catholics and Protestants alike it seems that cultivating healthier types of dependency upon the church would help. A large number of people living in close proximity to one another and each being fed the line that their church is the one true means of salvation is, inevitably, a recipe for disaster. Mature and loving relationship between churches changes the character of belonging within them. Churchgoers belong no longer to one rigidly demarcated bastion of truth but, rather, to the place that ministers most directly to their needs but which is always already in relation to the place down the road which does not. Only by saying where we are, and who we are, will we be able to get to the point where we can be in relation with 'the other'. Brushing it all under the carpet of unspecificity, even if only for fear of causing offence, undermines the opportunity to claim who we are *in relation to* others.

We therefore need to get real in church, in our prayers and in our preaching because by keeping church free of our actual problems, we abnegate responsibility for our situation. Church has been seen as 'a relief from all that', as a place where the harsh realities of the

6. J.A.F. Gregg quoted in *General Synod Journal*, lxxxiii (1949), p. iv.

world 'outside' can be escaped for a while, or simply set in stark cognitive relief. By not naming 'reality' in our prayers, sermons and liturgical announcements, we deny God his/her proper role in our lived situation. (The same could be said about other peculiarly Irish issues, too; for example, 6,000 Irish abortions a year taking place in the UK because it is illegal in the Republic and Northern Ireland and no debate about taking responsibility for this.)[7] Churches would not need to say much in order to offset the dangers of not-talking about such big issues, nor would they need to 'take sides' in order to simply pray about it. Worship leaders could, for example, say simply, 'may your Spirit inspire the bishops gathering at Lambeth this week' and leave a long pause. During the pause, a great range of opinions in the minds of the worshipers can find their diverse place in the assembly while being 'united' in a whole congregation's prayer in the same time and place for a very specific matter.

Like John Cleese's character in Fawlty Towers who, when a group of Germans arrive for dinner, repeatedly commands his staff: 'Don't mention the war!' only to end up referring to it in the most offensive terms possible through his own subliminal utterances, our worship is all the more likely to make faux-pas, all the more likely to reinforce rather than heal divisions between Catholic and Protestant, by trying not to mention the war, or any other of our problems. I turn now to two specific examples of such potentially divisive naming.

'The Other Religion'

"Lord, in this week when we break up for the summer holidays, look after all our schoolchildren and keep them safe over the summer. And the children from the other schools, keep them safe too."

Prayers of the People, RC, Cavan, IR

"help us to stay open to your grace in our lives, even when we are faced with disappointment, illness or other hurdles. Help us to be loving parents, good neighbours, and help us to be decent to those who are opposite to us."

Time of Prayer, Presbyterian, Ballymena, NI

7. The average for the past 15 years has been steady at about 6,000. According to the Irish Family Planning Association, 6,217 Irish women travelled to the UK for an abortion in 2004, 103 fewer than the previous year. Additional numbers of women travel to Holland (where an early abortion costs up to 300 Euros less than in the UK).

"It is you who hold us up. It is you who keep up going. It is you who shows the way. You are all we need. Whatever religion we were from before, take us now into your truth."
Call to Worship, Evangelical CofI, Dublin, IR

"This week finds us in the international week of prayer for Christian Unity and so on Wednesday night we'll be gathering in the church hall for a bible study with the folks from St. Mary's, followed by tea and biscuits, of course. Please make an effort to come out for this very important night and show our warm welcome to our brothers and sisters from the other religion."
Announcement, RC, Armagh, NI

It was my impression, hearing the four statements above, that each was meant with the kindest and most sincere and most charitable of intentions. The evangelical mission was trying to say: we may be an Anglican foundation, but even if you were raised Catholic, you have an absolutely equal right to be here this morning because there is only true authority, Jesus Christ. The other three remarks were, as I encountered them, not only significant statements of considerateness for their fellows in faith, but they also seemed to stem from a deep commitment to reconciliation in those congregations. They were among the most moving prayers and announcements I encountered in all of my research. They were saying a new thing, they were reaching for new words, they were creating new models of relationship and imagining a new world, being made new by God, in which previous divisions were healed. Each was said with a tone of earnestness, warmth, and profound hope, as if some new world was seriously within reach.

And yet, the way in which Catholics referred to Protestants and vice versa was as 'the other religion' and this is a profoundly inaccurate term of reference; a term whose inaccuracy stems from and reinforces the sectarian landscape all around it. It is not just in worship that one commonly hears Catholics refer to Protestants as 'the other religion' (and vice versa); this naming is also frequently encountered in the media and in politician's remarks on both sides of the border.[8] A few days after I turned 30, I was admitted to the orthopedics unit of Galway General Hospital with a sports injury.

8. For a selection of examples of statements about 'the opposite religion' from civic leaders in the Republic as well as Northern Ireland, see B.K. Lambkin, *Opposite Religions Still? Interpreting Northern Ireland after the Conflict* (Aldershot: Averbury, 1996), pp. 39–47.

The nurse completing the admission raced through a series of questions and ticked a box on her form for each of my replies. For the last question, she asked, 'religion?' I replied, 'Christian.' She said, 'We don't get many of them in here; there's no box,' and hurried off. A few hours after surgery, a priest came into the room, then turned and left, then popped his head back in: 'So sorry', he said, 'We've no one in this part of the world of your faith.' I asked what the choices might have been. 'Protestant or Catholic. But nowadays also Jewish, Buddhist and a couple other little ones.' In the rest of the English-speaking world, 'religions' refers to entities such as Buddhism, Islam, Judaism, Hinduism and Christianity, and 'denominations' refers to the different organizations of Christians such as Roman Catholics, Presbyterians, Anglicans and Methodists. In Ireland, however, these denominational differences are named as 'religions'.[9]

Naively, perhaps, I was surprised to encounter this nomenclature used widely in churches. I had expected that because priests and ministers have a better understanding of the difference between a religion and a denomination from their theological education and ordination processes, they would name their fellow Christians more accurately in worship. It is, however, such an ingrained way of naming — and, thus, way of thinking — in the culture, that although ministers and priests know, rationally, the difference between the meaning of 'religion' and 'denomination' or 'general type',[10] referring to Protestantism and Catholicism as 'religions' is just how they, and their congregations, speak. In speech in Ireland, as the nurse's form made clear, Protestant and Catholic are different 'religions'. Moreover, not only are fellow Christians referred to as

9. A habit that is thought to go back to the Reformation debates over 'true' and 'false' religions. For a history of why Irish people understand themselves as participant in different religions, see Lambkin, *Opposite Religions Still?* pp. 26–35.

10. And the difference between Catholic and Protestant is one of general type. In Ireland 'Catholic' is to refer to Roman Catholics and 'Protestant' is used to refer to everybody else (including, in occasional contexts, and to the amazement of observers, Jews and Muslims). Although common in popular speech, these names for the general types of religion in fact mask serious anomalies: 'Protestant' is being used as an umbrella term to cover substantially different denominations, from the Church of Ireland, Presbyterian and Methodist to Unitarian, Quaker and Evangelical; and many Anglicans consider themselves 'Catholic'.

belonging to a different religion, they are sometimes referred to as 'the *opposite* religion', as can be seen in the prayers and announcement above. Indeed, even where 'opposite' was not explicitly said, it is an *oppositional* sort of otherness that defines 'the other religion' in Ireland. It is not an *additional* sort of otherness, or a *strange* sort of otherness, or a *different-but-related* sort of otherness, or an *unknown-entity* sort of otherness; it is very peculiarly an *opposite* sort of otherness: in common parlance, there are two main religions in Ireland and the one is still conceived as being in direct, and oppositional, relation to the other.

Whilst the context in which these words (other/opposite religion) were used in the examples above was, I felt, one of hospitality and a desire for genuine relationship, the words and phrases themselves nevertheless carried a certain antagonism in their very meaning. B.K. Lambkin confirms that such 'split-thinking' is commonplace in Irish speech, and concludes that it is the result of Irish and Northern Irish people making the transition from the Reformation paradigm to the Ecumenical paradigm of Christian self-understanding far more slowly than the rest of western Europe: 'During this critical intermediate phase [before ecumenical awareness]... The majority are uncertain, confused, or uncommitted, in the manner of floating voters. They switch or, more accurately, they modulate between the opposite-religions, opposite-communities paradigm and the one-community, one-religion paradigm, according to changing social circumstances.'[11] There are, however, as Lambkin himself remarks, few indications that Northern Irish people are actually making such a transition. They seem content to remain in a state of permanent 'paradigm ambiguity' — and why should they transition? 'Why forsake the status quo, which is in effect a finely attuned mixture of sharing and separation, for the uncertainties of any radical change?'[12]

No doubt there are a raft of issues in political life that warrant the 'modulation' between notions of separation and sharing amid opposite entities; but when it comes to Christianity in the twentieth century, such language must be examined for its patent inaccuracies. Protestants and Catholics may disagree on a range of matters, but they hold a very great deal in common in terms of beliefs, values and practices and the principal churches across the world, even

11. Lambkin, *Opposite Religions Still?*, p. 39.
12. Lambkin, *Opposite Religions Still?*, p. 62.

those with profound historical schism from one another, acknowledge that they are part of the *same* religion, sharing, on balance, more than they disagree upon. Liechty and Clegg remark that the phrase 'opposite religions', far from being a quirk of colloquial Irish naming habits is, in fact, 'a striking and chilling sign of a culture's customary mindset becoming infested by sectarianism, which typically seeks to magnify difference as far as possible.'[13] With the best will in the world, you cannot, therefore, refer to your fellow Christian as 'opposite' or as being from an 'other religion' and not in fact disown them in the process. Creating distance rather than promoting mutual understanding, such naming is in fact self-sabotaging: it keeps the neighbour with whom one seeks to connect in a place that is in fact 'other', or even 'opposite': ultimately different and perennially separated.

But even more than that, because of the meaning of *opposite*, such naming makes the other people and/or keeps them as the *enemy*. For most of the Christian world, the opposite of God is Satan, the opposite of believers are atheists, the opposite of the faithful are detractors, the opposite of salvation is damnation, the opposite of love is hate, and so on. Moreover, down the years Christians have turned these vocabularies with absolute vitriol on all manner of people, so that the Jews became Satan, the Protestants atheists, the Catholics antichrists, and the one who is not part of us is damned: abstract oppositionality is re-inscribed on the worldly enemy, falsely making that enemy a fierce opponent of God—and not just a neighbour from whom one differs. If in Ireland, the *opposite* of Protestant is Catholic, and vice versa, then the other is being set-up as an enemy. Never mind the extreme inaccuracy of such a move theologically (both sets of believers being, in fact, Christian), it ensures that any notion of relationship between these entities is construed on purely antagonist lines. Thinking about how this operates at the level of identity-formation, Claire Mitchell concludes that when it comes to theological reflection in Ireland, 'conflict and power struggles encourage not the unity of all Christians, but oppositional notions of community.'[14]

13. Liechty and Clegg, *Moving Beyond Sectarianism*, p. 37.
14. Claire Mitchell, *Religion, Identity and Politics in Northern Ireland: Boundaries of Belonging and Belief* (Abingdon: Ashgate, 2006), p. 73.

There is a great deal of oppositional language about communal identity in the broader culture.[15] But as Lambkin asks, 'After the fighting, is the fundamental opposition of Catholicism and Protestantism resolved, or does it persist?' It would seem, from the ways in which Catholics and Protestants referred to one another in worship in my research, even as they were trying to be nice about them, that it does indeed persist. The extent to which we in Ireland do genuinely think of one another as 'opposite' is not to be underestimated: it may seem like an accidental figure of speech, but it bespeaks a very deep and prevalent worldview.

The depth at which other Christians are conceived of as 'opposite' in Ireland helps to explain the peculiar problem faced by the people of Northern Ireland at this time (and perhaps harks back to the binary ways we sit in church, mentioned in the previous chapter). The political peace that is being forged at a civic level (by the various implementations of the 1998 *Good Friday Agreement*) is based on the model of 'consociationality' (supported by a web of shared arrangements between separated communities), a model designed to permit the co-habitation of radically different parties. However, religious peace makes no sense whatsoever on these terms: Christianity is not about being called to live in carefully policed co-operation across fundamental separation from one another; it is, on the contrary, a call to live *in fellowship* with one another.

This is why the notion of 'opposites' is so pernicious in the Irish context: because religion is a significant factor in sectarianism, unless this notion is challenged and dismantled it is going to ensure not only that the peace that is accomplished remains chillingly 'cold', but also that the type of Christianity witnessed and confessed in Ireland has a significant heresy at its heart. In order to avoid lives of heresy, Christians in Ireland need to correct their misunderstanding of the nature of their difference from one another as being that of 'opposition'. Christians are different from one another across traditions, very different in some cases, but at no point is any denomination 'opposite' to another.

15. See multiple examples in Lambkin's book, *Opposite Religions Still?*, especially the remarks of children aged 11 to 15 (p. 2). Also, as they demonstrate in their book on anti-Catholicism among Loyalists in Northern Ireland, media reports are saturated with the language of Catholic-Satanism: John D. Brewer and Gareth I. Higgins, *Anti-Catholicism in Northern Ireland, 1660–1998* (London: MacMillan, 1998).

The heresy of Christians living as 'opposite religions' in Ireland will need to change if anything other than separate arrangements are to be imagined let alone accomplished. Furthermore, reconciliation is, I would argue, truly impossible on such terms. As we saw in Chapter Two, there have been some world conflicts that have proven beyond reparation, and if Protestants and Catholics were truly 'opposites' in their faith, with one on the side of God and the other on the side of Satan, it would be an example of *irreconcilable differences*. However, because it is fundamentally inaccurate to think of Protestants and Catholics as opposites, the conflict insofar as it relates to such a worldview is not irreconcilable.

By ceasing to use this vocabulary in worship, by educating worshippers about the ways in which it is inaccurate, and by devising other vocabulary that accurately expresses the relationship between churches (different, but of the same religion), we can engage in the work of re-conciliation. Of course, sectarianism has little patience for the niceties of questions of accuracy: it feeds on so much more than the technical aspects of theology and ecclesiology. And so I am not naively suggesting that by changing this one thing others will all fall into reconciling place. But I am nevertheless suggesting that by changing this one thing, we would be addressing a fundamental problem (a misconception of opposition), and in a fundamental way (linguistically); it should therefore be a contribution to moving beyond sectarianism, an active process of reconciling, even as it is no magical solution.

The Language of Community

"Almighty God, help those in our community who are unemployed or without work, and let them still be good role models for our children as they grow up..."

Church of Ireland, Dublin, IR

Because of the above analysis of the language of 'other religion' in Irish and Northern Irish discourse, the small phrase 'our community' demands particular attention. This phrase was used in the non-scripted speech of worship in all but three of the churches I visited and it had a more complicated meaning—and a more implicated place regarding sectarianism—than was at first apparent. In a culture saturated with multiple references to 'community' in the media (from just one newspaper on just one day, I found 'the post-modern community', 'the American Idol community', 'the lesbian-gay community', 'the international community'), and on an island that is part of the European 'Community', and in a time of resurging interest in things spiritual which often find expression in the language of 'community life', *community* is evidently a rich and multi-faceted concept.

However, in a culture within which groups have historically been so strictly divided along Catholic-Protestant lines (by law and governance in the past, and by schooling, marriage, and housing patterns in some areas, up to the present day), the language of 'community' takes on a particular nuance, especially when prefaced with the one word, 'our'. When priests and ministers refer to 'our community' in the context of Sunday morning worship, it is therefore unlikely to be one community among many; rather, it is one out of two, the 'two communities' of religious self-understanding in Ireland being Protestant and Catholic. Add to this the layers of injustice, fear, and resentful feeling, not to mention violence, that have accrued to the notion of the 'two communities' and it becomes possible to understand why the language of 'cross-community' relations meets with so many difficulties when it is uttered.

In a similar way to the phrase 'the other religion' or 'opposite religions', the phrase 'our community' sits at a critical theological-sociological juncture. Socially speaking, it is not necessary for communities to be 'shared spaces'. Indeed, socially speaking in contemporary Northern Ireland, it seems to be to many people's best advantage for spaces to be separated, schools being a particular case in point, as we saw in Chapter One. While theologically, Protestants and Catholics are members of the same umbrella community (Christianity), they divide into differentiated communities of self-organization with substantial disagreement on everything from doctrine to polity to liturgical aesthetics.

Nevertheless, the language of 'our community' is more ambiguous than that of 'opposite religions' because of the multi-faceted meanings it carries from popular culture, such that, unlike the language of 'opposite religions' it is not a matter of accuracy or error. It denotes a far more complicated social world than a mere denominational rift: 'our community' might be taken to refer to a neighbourhood, or a region, or an affiliation group, as much as to a single or opposing 'religion'. Indeed, the language of 'two communities' is accurate: two communities are exactly what Protestants and Catholics in Ireland and Northern Ireland have historically constituted (and as we saw in Chapter One, it is the main marker of identity for the majority of people who live on the island).

And yet, while it is accurate, it is not necessarily benign: what is being referred to by this phrase is not merely a sociological boundary but also a sectarian one. It is one of those items in this study that defies empirical proof but which many readers will nevertheless recognize as being true: when a minister prays for 'our community' in a worship service in the Republic or Northern Ireland, their words are very often is marking a boundary which is at least in part created and maintained by religion, and which reinforces Protestant-Catholic division. One cannot 'prove' that the minister is referring to a belonging-network framed by a single denomination, but in a context in which civic boundaries are fundamentally conditioned along Protestant-Catholic lines, those listening hear a sectarian divide.

This divide may seem like the simple and inevitable distinction that results from the choice between two modes of community life, and as such it might seem harmless. For example, my father is a member of a Catholic men's society in Liverpool, England, which meets to network and support one another professionally: because Catholics could not get jobs or contracts, because positions of authority in civil society were nearly all held by Protestants and kept for Protestants only, Catholic men formed alliances to create bonds of mutual support and what we might today call 'networking' — helping one another find work, creating business, etc. However, in a post-violence world, this 'sticking together', 'looking after our own', 'cultivating the health of our community' or just plain 'surviving' attitude (along with its associated practices), many of which did great good in people's lives, runs the risk of perpetuating the notion that one lives in a basic oppositional dilemma and 'our community' has been established at least in part to protect us from 'your community' or 'that other community'.

It is what Liechty and Clegg describe as sectarianism's most insidious effect, the manufacture of inter-community hatred as a by-product of a community's best intentions: 'Our motivation is not to be sectarian, it is to build strong communities, but because our efforts fall within the boundaries set by sectarianism, our best pastoral efforts can end up strengthening the sectarian divide.'[16] And as they go on to say, the responsibility for dismantling such a worldview falls squarely at the churches' door: 'so long as the churches see challenging the sectarian divide as a marginal responsibility, or no responsibility at all, or a responsibility we will address when everything else has been settled, the sectarian system will go on employing well-intentioned, positive, community-building activities as sustenance for itself.'[17] My contention is that worship has an important role to play in this regard because words used in ritualizing contexts have such power in framing our world.

The alternative to 'opposite religions', I suggested, was to educate about 'religion', and then to use in liturgy words that accurately reflect the relations between denominations in Ireland, eradicating the phrases 'the other religion' and 'the opposite religion' from use in worship; it required actually dismantling a way of naming that was indentured with mistaken concepts. I suggest that the alternative to 'our community', by contrast, is to be specific, to name the exact community that is being imagined by reference to geographic or other social markers; for example: 'people in this neighbourhood/city/region/village who...' To name the specific group of people or landscape that one has in mind is to avoid the risk of sectarianism that creeps in with the ambiguity of simply 'our community'.

It does not require losing the words 'our' or 'community', but it does require qualifying them so as to dismantle any sectarian references they may have carried. Furthermore, it is not just the ambiguity of the phrase as a term of reference that is worth excavating; it is also its long and prominent association in the speech of political rhetoric. When a priest prays for 'those in our community who...', there are few people in the congregation who have not also heard politicians and other civic leaders using that same phrase on the radio or TV to refer to the Unionist-Protestant or Nationalist-Catholic matrix of political positions and concerns in civic life.

A further way of countering the sectarian associations of 'our community', therefore, is to emphasize the relationship *between* the two communities. So claim, and pray for, 'our community' but do

16. Liechty and Clegg, *Moving Beyond Sectarianism*, pp. 13–14 (quoted in Chapter One).
17. Liechty and Clegg, *Moving Beyond Sectarianism*, p. 14.

not leave it at that. As the priest in the example at the top of the section said 'we pray for the children from the other schools, too.' Schools in that particular town (like almost every town in Ireland) being strictly segregated along Protestant-Catholic lines, this Catholic priest was making sure that it was not just the Catholic children who were prayed for as they began their summer holidays. All the children in that town, Protestant and Catholic, were prayed for. He might have gone a step farther, however, and prayed for 'all the children in this town', making the town, and not the two communities (Protestants and Catholics), the paradigm for thinking about that 'community'. By doing so he would help to dismantle a worldview that sees people as Catholic or Protestant *first* and as neighbour, citizen or fellow-Christian second (or never).

By referring to the town as the thing that binds us, or to the neighbourhood as the arena that defines belonging, we do not deny our Catholic-Protestant affiliations one bit, but we do de-centre them; we make them no longer the primary way in which we organize our thinking about ourselves and our relation to other people in the world. Especially given the fact that our cities are becoming home to people of multiple religious affiliations, as well as those of none, it seems more important than ever to find a way of claiming 'community' that works for the contemporary world, especially given the classic and long-held Christian vision of not merely fellowship, but fellowship *amid difference*.

In church, the language of 'our community', including in prayers that follow the form 'for those in our community who...', reinforces a sense in which our church is: a) separate from and b) more worth praying for than that of others. Often the language used in prayer is taken directly from long-held defensive positions designed to protect a community's interests. As such it mimics the sectarianism embedded in those histories. It may not be *intended* this way; it may simply be falling into the 'don't mention the war' trap. In the Republic and Northern Ireland prayers for 'our community' may sound the same as in other English-speaking countries, but they do not necessarily mean the same. Even where they are spoken with something other than a sectarian worldview in mind, they are not *heard* that way (meaning being the product of the way speech is heard), the vocabulary of sectarianism being so pervasive in the common culture; and so priests and ministers must make adjustments accordingly when leading worship.

Chapter Five

MEALS

One of the most striking differences in the ways people worship in Ireland on a Sunday morning is that Protestants and Anglicans who celebrate the Eucharist[1] share the cup among the congregation, while Roman Catholic churches do not.[2] At the distribution of communion in Roman Catholic churches, most of the people in the congregation leave their pews and form a single-file queue in the aisle in front of the priest or Eucharistic Minister (EM). The priest or EM holds up the host (a small, thin, round wafer which has been consecrated) and says, 'The Body of Christ' to which the congregant replies 'Amen'. The priest or EM then either puts the host on the person's tongue or into their open, cupped, hands. The person turns, making the sign of the cross as they do so, walks back to their seat (or out of the church), and the next in line steps forward. Communion is distributed quite differently in Protestant and Anglican churches, with many variations in how people sit, stand, kneel, come to a central point or remain in their pews, as well as in what they say to one another during the process, and what happens afterwards. Nothing in the Protestant and Anglican churches' diverse ways of sharing communion warranted analysis in this particular context, but the fact that no congregant in any of the Roman Catholic churches

1. Some Church of Ireland congregations celebrate the Eucharist every Sunday morning, but others retain the practice of celebrating Morning Prayer most Sundays and Eucharist once a month. Most Methodist and Presbyterian churches in Ireland celebrate the Eucharist once a month, at most. Roman Catholic parishes, by contrast, have Mass for every single one of their Sunday services and very rarely offer a public non-eucharistic worship service nowadays (in contrast to pre-1980 or so when Benediction and/or Veneration were common).

2. I understand that there do exist Roman Catholic churches where the cup is distributed among the congregation, as well as others where the cup is available off to one side of the altar and those who wish can make their way up there to receive it; but such churches seem to be a distinct minority.

studied received the cup demands considerable attention. This chapter therefore examines this Roman Catholic habit in some depth.

There were hundreds of years when Roman Catholics around the world could not receive the cup as well as the host. The practice was re-introduced by the reforms of Vatican II, as a result of theological arguments made on the basis of emerging historical research into early church practices which suggested that the common meal among Christians usually involved the sharing of wine as well as bread. With the rise in understanding of the Eucharist as essentially a *meal*, the decline in the practice of sharing of the cup (and even, for much of the Middle Ages,[3] the host as well) was seen as regrettable, as a loss of connection to both the full theology of the ritual moment and the lineage of tradition itself.[4]

The practice of cup-sharing was reintroduced amid much initial opposition that it was a 'Protestant' thing to do, but throughout most of the English-speaking world it nevertheless became the norm. Eucharistic Ministers were trained, and congregations were educated about the theological and ecclesiological reasons for the practice as well as the practical mechanics of how to do it.[5] In Ireland, however, such widespread catechesis accompanied by changes in practice did not happen and, unlike other English-speaking countries including the UK, the USA, Australia or New Zealand,[6] it remained

3. This move to view the host rather than to eat it had happened by a relatively early stage: 'By the late fourth century not only had the original meal long since been reduced to symbolic proportions but at least for some of those who were there it had now become more often something to be watched and worshipped from afar than to be consumed.' Paul F. Bradshaw, *Eucharistic Origins* (Oxford: Oxford University Press), p. 156.

4. See, Herbert Vorgrimler, *Sacramental Theology* (Collegeville, MN: Liturgical Press, 1992).

5. The history of the reception of the cup in various parts of the world, is a fascinating one, but it is too big a story to tell here. Of particular interest is its relationship to public health. For example, 'The role, if any, of the common cup in the transmission of disease has been the subject of debate and scientific enquiry for many years. The "Spanish Influenza" pandemic in the wake of the First World War and the emergence of HIV/AIDS in the 1980s gave rise to periods of particular interest in the common cup.' The Church of England's *Memorandum on Administration of Holy Communion During a Flu Pandemic* (23 June 2009), p. 4.

6. Although, of course, practice in these countries is not uniform. While all had the support of their Councils of Bishops for the sharing of the communion wine by 1980 (unlike Ireland), and while it was the majority practice in

almost unheard of for parishioners to be offered the cup as well as the host on a Sunday morning. Indeed, in the Republic and Northern Ireland it is still common to hear Roman Catholic clergy saying to a couple during their marriage liturgy, 'Well now today is that very special day of your life, because it is one of only two days in your life when you receive communion under both species' (the other being First Holy Communion).

Roman Catholicism teaches that, due to the sacramental action of the priest in the presence of the people, and by God's grace, the bread and wine offered in the Eucharistic liturgy become the body and blood of Jesus Christ. The catechism puts it like this: 'It is Christ himself, the eternal high priest of the New Covenant who, acting through the ministry of the priests, offers the Eucharistic sacrifice. And it is the same Christ, really present under the species of bread and wine, who is the offering of the Eucharistic sacrifice.' It is important to remark that in the above statement, it is not understood that Christ's body is present in the bread while his blood is present in wine; rather, Christ's body (and all that makes up his body: his soul, divinity, flesh and blood) are fully and equally present in *both* the consecrated elements. The catechism explains that, therefore:

> Since Christ is sacramentally present under each of the species, communion under the species of bread alone makes it possible to receive all the fruit of Eucharistic grace. For pastoral reasons the manner of receiving communion [through the ages] has been legitimately established as the most common form in the Latin rite. But the sign of communion is more complete when given under both kinds, since in that form the sign of the Eucharistic meal appears more clearly. This is the usual form of receiving communion in the Eastern rites.[7]

The last sentence, added in the most recent edition of the Catechism, reflects the growing ecumenical sensibilities of the Roman Catholic Church in the twentieth century. By pointing out commonality with the Eastern rites, the church highlights its desire for its faithful to

those countries' parishes (unlike Ireland), there nevertheless remained priests and/or parishioners who were reticent about serving/receiving the cup.

7. *Catechism of the Catholic Church*, 1997: paragraph 1390. The quotation in the text is from the *General Instruction to the Roman Missal*, p. 240. '[Through the ages]' is my addition, to clarify the distinction I understand the document to be making on the basis of the official teachings of the Church on the Eucharist in the years preceding this revised Catechism.

see themselves as connected through their practices to a greater communion than perhaps previously conceived. It is in stark contrast to earlier Catholic teaching which had pronounced that receiving only the host was a unique marker of Catholic identity (with its strong though not always explicitly stated concomitant that the habit of regular receipt of the cup at communion was something belonging to the supposedly not-'true' churches).[8]

In fact, in English-speaking countries, communion under both kinds has not become the universal practice that Vatican II anticipated. It is, however, the majority practice in all English-speaking countries apart from the Irish Republic and Northern Ireland.[9] In my field research the opposite was true: nowhere was the cup distributed among the congregation. Recognizing that peculiar patterns regarding the Eucharist had developed in their churches (compared to other countries),[10] the Irish Bishops commissioned a report on improving Eucharistic participation from the National Centre for Liturgy in Maynooth in 2004. They responded positively to its recommendation that: 'Faith is strengthened by good celebration of the liturgy, and the effects of the contrary should also be heeded. Following appropriate catechesis there should be encouragement of the introduction of

8. A persistent misunderstanding that Garry Wills discerns as the legacy of the Council of Trent, or, rather, the widescale popular dissemination of its teachings over many centuries. 'The council could not bring itself to endorse the "Protestant" practice of laymen receiving the cup, nor the "Protestant" practice of allowing lay people to read the Bible for themselves. Garry Wills, *Why I am a Catholic* (Boston, MA: Houghton Mifflin Harcourt, 2003), p. 169. The latter belief, that reading the Bible is a Protestant practice and Catholics should therefore not do it, was one with which even my parents' generation was raised. However, it has almost completely disappeared in the past generation; which goes to show that the misunderstanding about cup-reception could disappear too, if the Irish church wanted it to.

9. There are no statistics on this parish by parish, but one gains a sense of the Bishops' preferred practice from what happens in the Cathedrals and *mesa* parishes, and these are almost unanimous in their offering of the cup as well as the host to the congregation.

10. A BBC Northern Ireland report on 2 November 2007, included jocular speculation that the threatened zero-tolerance drink-driving law might force the priests to share the cup with the congregation, given that they could not do their other duties, many of which included driving, if they had drank the entire contents of the cup at morning Mass. Diarmuid Fleming, 'Eucharist Could Mean "Water into Fine"' (http://news.bbc.co.uk/1/hi/northern_ireland)

Communion under both kinds on a more regular basis',[11] and some of the Irish Bishops began a process of implementing the report's recommendations that continues to this day.[12]

The continuing widespread absence of the distribution of the cup begs the question: what is at stake in Ireland on this issue? At a local level, when I asked priests at the churches I visited, they gave one of two answers: either that there were just so many people that it was not practicable or else that the bishops had not authorized it. But the bishops have allowed it, and very large congregations in the rest of the world have found ways of managing distribution, so neither response adequately accounts for the phenomenon. Given that clericalism was being identified as a major problem in Roman Catholic life in Ireland at the time of this research,[13] was the priest's retaining the cup for himself and not sharing it with the congregation[14] a means of navigating the choppy waters of clerical power in Ireland?

Querying the possibility that the non-sharing of the cup is a strategy in the negotiation of clerical power has a certain precedent in Christian liturgical theology. In the fifteenth century, Jan Hus and his companions argued that all the laity should receive the cup

11. Fr. Hugh P. Kennedy, 'The Year of the Eucharist'. This document and its recommendations, of which this is but one, were invited by the Irish Bishops in preparation for the meeting of *Episcopal Commission for Liturgy* on 25 November 2004. The meeting was in response to the Pope's mandate for study and action for the international 'Year of the Eucharist', October 2004–2005.

12. The Archdiocese of Dublin has, this year (2009), published a thorough set of resources to encourage distribution of communion under both kinds. See: http://www.litmus.dublindiocese.ie/secmenudisp.php?MID=216

13. See, for example, Donal Dorr, *Time for Change: A Fresh Look at Sexuality, Spirituality, Globalization and the Church* (Dublin: Columba Press, 2004), particularly Chapter 12; see also Peadar Kirby, 'The Death of Innocence: Whither Now? Trauma in State and Church' in *Studies: An Irish Quarterly Review* 84: 335 (Autumn, 1995), pp. 267–65. Further, regarding clericalism as a problem in liturgy specifically, see Aidan Kavanagh, 'Liturgy (Sacrosanctum concilium)' in Michael A. Hayes and Liam Gearon (eds), *Contemporary Catholic Theology: A Reader* (New York: Continuum, 1999), pp. 445–52; 451.

14. Of course, according to historical Catholic teaching, the priest is not merely drinking from the cup for himself alone—he is understood to be doing so as *mediator Christi* and, thus, his drinking is for the people. However, just observing the practice and its effects, especially when also considering the fact that this official teaching has been universally revised, it is difficult not to query the appropriateness of this teaching in the contemporary context.

as well as the host at the Eucharist, and also that they should receive the elements frequently and not just once a year, as had become the custom across most of Europe by that time.[15] Many of the subsequent Reformers followed Hus in identifying clerical power or, rather, the *abuse* of clerical power, as the reason for the absence of cup-sharing, as well as a whole suite of practices from the sale of indulgences to the prevention of the laity from reading the Bible. Luther, for example, speaking explicitly about the practice of withholding the cup, sees the abuse of clerical power as the central and key issue:

> The papists highly boast of their power and authority, which they would willingly confirm with this argument: the apostles altered baptism; therefore, say they, the bishops have power to alter the sacrament of the Lord's supper. I answer: admit that the apostles altered something; yet there is a great difference between an apostle and a bishop; an apostle was called immediately by God with gifts of the Holy Ghost; but a bishop is a person selected by man, to preach God's words, and ordain servants of the church in certain places. So, though the apostles had this power and authority, yet the bishops have not.[16]

However, in the years during which the fieldwork for this study was undertaken (2001–2008), Irish clergy were held in very low regard in the media in Ireland and in many quarters of both the courts and the general public, due to the scale and severity of the sex abuse crisis, and morale among the clergy was at an unprecedented low. In response, bishops and priests in Ireland were doing everything they possibly could to promote and publicize their right-use of power, their servanthood in the community, their trustworthiness, and their willingness to minister to contemporary needs. This was expressed in a large number and variety of ways at a local level, many of which had a direct impact on liturgical matters: for example, Prayers of the People were written by people other than just the priest; there was a significant increase in lay

15. See, Carolyn Walker Bynum, *Wonderful Blood: Theology and Practice in Late Medieval Northern Germany and Beyond* (Philadelphia, PA: University of Philadelphia Press, 2007). For example, 'In fifteenth century Bohemia, the demand for the eucharist in both species (*sub utroque specie*) gave its name to a group of the followers of Jan Hus, the Utraquists, also known as Calixtines (from cup or *calyx*)' (pp. 94–95).

16. Martin Luther, *Table Talk* (trans. William Hazlitt; 1857); (Philadelphia, PA: The Lutheran Publication Society: www.theapologiaproject.org), CCCLVIII.

ministries (including ministries for young people), such as reading the scriptures in Mass; financial matters were more widely reported in church newsletters; and pastoral councils were formed to create clerical-lay collaboration in ministry. It would seem that if the congregation not receiving the wine was perceived to have anything to do with the 'old ways' of the priests, or the misuse of clerical power, then it, too, would have been changed during these years.

If the distribution of the element of wine was understood by neither the laity nor by the clergy as primarily a strategy of navigating clerical power (the usual reason history has revealed to account for similar practices), then the question is: why was it so persistent, so widespread and so 'normal' as a religious practice in the Republic and Northern Ireland? The fact that it is a peculiarly Irish problem, and one that plays out along entirely denominational lines (all Protestant churches share the cup, no Catholic ones do), suggests the need to interrogate the practice in the light of the sorts of background attitudes to sectarianism and reconciliation outlined in the first two chapters.

In 1996, for the first time in modern history, the Republic of Ireland recorded a higher number of immigrants than emigrants. Many of them were former emigrants or the children of emigrants. There were 141,000 such returning emigrants in 2002-2003 alone, including 27,000 returning emigrants and just under 41,000 asylum seekers.[17] This number remained high in subsequent years due to the relatively large numbers of refugees that Ireland accepted during the Romanian and Nigerian refugee crises (especially before legislation was passed to curb the scale of intake), as well as through the high numbers of migrant workers from first Spain, then Estonia and then Poland who came as a result of the combination of an economic boom in Ireland (lots of construction) with the relaxation of laws governing working abroad in member countries of the European Union. Among both returning emigrants and new immigrants, a high proportion of whom went to Mass (relative to the population as a whole), the fact that the element of wine was not offered at communion was often different to what they had been familiar with in their country of origin. But after a short while, receiving only the bread became the norm, along with a whole raft

17. Martin Ruhs, 'Ireland: A Crash-Course on Immigration Policy', *Migration Policy Institute Papers* (Washington DC, 2004). See: www. migrationinformation.org/USfocus/display.cfm?ID=260

of idiosyncracies of Irish life to which the newcomer or returner had to adjust, not the least of which included (for those from the UK) having to pay to see a doctor and a median income tax rate of 45 percent.

Getting used to not being able to receive the wine is just like getting used to so many other distinctively Irish cultural effects precisely because not receiving the wine is understood *as* a habit in Irish life. It accidentally functions as a marker of uniquely 'Catholic' identity and, as we saw in Chapter One on the relation of religion and sectarianism, the elision of 'Catholic' with 'Irish' permeates a great deal of normative popular—and constitutional—thinking. There is a folk perception (held even by some bishops as well as other folk), dating back to the Counter Reformation, that 'The Protestants, they receive the wine. We do not.' And, in some quarters, even: 'If we received the wine, we'd be just like Protestants.' This is generally unspoken, and therefore largely unexamined, but it is there nonetheless. However, in an Irish context, for reasons we are about to examine, it is a far more complicated and rational attitude than such a patently misinformed statement might at first imply, and this helps us to understand why it has persisted in Ireland while it has disappeared in other countries.

When one considers the distribution of communion, the basic bodily actions in play are eating and drinking, and the basic genre of activity is a 'meal'. Even allowing for the distinctions in genre between a ritual meal (which is seen as an economic, symbolic instantiation of the basic concept of meals as communal feeding), part of the problem in interpreting the non-reception of the cup is that the Eucharist's 'meal'-like quality does not seem to be widely countenanced. Also, even allowing for the notion of symbolic eating and drinking, Irish worshippers historically have scant sense that the consumption of the elements relates to other bodily habits of eating and drinking; instead, the laity understands eating and drinking to be what you do at home (or in pubs or restaurants) and communion to be a different genre of behaviour. Communion is adored precisely because it is not quotidian, because it is of God's own world. Much of the *meal* emphasis in Eucharistic theology that has flowed from Vatican II[18] has so far been lost on Ireland because

18. The literature on this point is vast. For but one example, a compilation of excellent commentaries, see, R. Kevin Seasoltz (ed.), *Living Bread, Saving Cup: Readings on the Eucharist* (Collegeville, MN: Liturgical Press, 1982).

it is based on a connection between eating and drinking in life and eating and drinking in church; and the latter is, in Ireland, still popularly understood in almost entirely mystical, pre-Vatican II terms, non-meal terms.[19] While the rest of the western world has integrated meal theologies of the Eucharist with prior emphases on sacrifice and mystical communion, Irish Catholics may not even see the bread as 'food' and the 'wine' as drink,[20] never mind the gathering as a meal.

This is perhaps not very surprising, given that in Ireland (unlike the rest of the English-speaking world) eating and drinking are uniquely contested cultural subjects because of two problems that other modern countries have not had: a famine in the recent past and reports of an exceptionally high level of alcoholism in the general population. These problems have been compounded by two coterminous factors: the remarkable lack of critical analysis of either of them in the popular public realm, and the characterizing function of each in articulations of national identity. It seems that only in the past ten to 15 years has there been any concerted effort to study or to raise critical awareness of the historic and contemporary effects of either. Furthermore, as we will see, both problems — the famine and endemic alcoholism — have strongly nationalist components, related to both the legacy of British authority in Ireland and the sort of nation/s that the island has become in recent years. I would like to explore the possibility that both problems, and the lack of discussion about them at a critical level, have radically altered

Phillip Rouillard, in his essay 'From Human Meal to Christian Eucharist' (pp. 126–56) summarizes the shift thus: 'We cannot understand the full meaning of the eucharistic meal if we do not reflect first on the meaning of the meal as a human reality' (p. 126) and he traces it from Old to New Testament and through church history. For an equally comprehensive but more catechetical presentation of the meal debates, see also: Teresa Whalen, *The Authentic Doctrine of the Eucharist* (Kansas City, MO: Sheed and Ward, 1993.)

19. Post-Vatican II theology did not abandon the sacrificial and thanksgiving understandings of the rite; they merely sought to highlight that it is the meal quality of the rite that enables both (so, it is a sacrificial meal, like Melchizidek's; so it is a Eucharistic (thanks-giving) meal, like the Last Supper).

20. Canon law is clear that they must be real food and real drink, of the sort one encounters in ordinary life: it stipulates for Ireland: fresh 'wheaten bread' and wine that is 'natural, made from grapes of the vine, and not corrupt'. (Code of Canon Law, Book IV, Part I, Title III, Chapter I, Article I, Can. 924, Nos. 2 and 3.)

Catholic understanding of what is going on in the celebration of the Eucharist in Ireland and Northern Ireland.

Famine

After a series of small famines throughout the nineteenth century, the *gorta mór* (literally: big hunger, or Great Famine, as it has become known) began in 1845 and lasted for five years. At that time, Britain had complete administrative oversight of Ireland (no portion of it was independent, as the 26 counties became after 1922), the Church of Ireland (Anglican) was the established church of the whole island, and the population, which numbered nearly 9 million, was overwhelmingly Catholic.[21] It was also mostly poor, due to a number of factors, not least of which was the system of regional governance maintained by the British since the Cromwellian land clearances of the sixteenth century, the result of which was that the peasantry lived as subsistence farmers, working the landlord's land and paying rent to do so. In 1847 came the Gregory Clause in the Poor Law legislation, which required families to give up all rights to their land (tenancy of their land) in order to receive any state-sponsored relief, such as admission to the workhouse. 'Thus landlords who wanted to move from tillage to livestock or dairy farming would now have a valuable opportunity to do so,'[22] and thus the problem of evictions (and especially the problem of the *threat of* eviction) was added to the already acute problem of inadequate food supply. The population was decimated by somewhere between 20 percent and 25 percent from 1845–1851 due to starvation and its resulting emigrations and deaths, and by about half from 1851–1906[23] due to the aftermath of famine. As Amartya Sen has remarked, '[in] no other famine in the world [was] the proportion of people killed as large as in the Irish famines in the 1840s.'[24]

---

21. See, Mary E. Daly, *Social and Economic History of Ireland since 1800* (Dublin: Longman, Browne and Nolan, 1981).

22. Colm Toibín, *The Irish Famine* (London: Profile Books, 2001), p. 4.

23. Although, the figures are contested.

24. Quoted by Cormac Ó'Gráda, *Black '47 and Beyond: The Great Irish Famine in History, Economy and Memory* (Princeton, NJ: Princeton University Press, 2000), p. 3.

This statistical fact, that so many actually died, haunts Irish culture and arguably complicates the perception of eating within it. However, Irish culture may also be haunted by the non-statistical fact that the majority culture on the island also died as a result of the famine, due to widespread emigration, loss of the Irish language from all but a few pockets, and different uses of land and relationships to it—familial as well as economic and legal. As I hope to show, the sheer scale of the resultant losses, and the fact that their cause was famine, leaves food, drink and the lack of them freighted with particular importance (and fear) in Irish life.

It also took a very long time for the famine to be talked about in Ireland, something that has been much remarked upon recently, particularly in literary studies.[25] Since talk about the famine became more widespread, especially in the years since the 150-year commemoration and the British apology,[26] there has been almost as much discussion about how to represent it as there has been research into its history. A significant lobby describes the attitudes of the English to the Irish leading up to the famine as racist, their practices as akin to slavery and the famine itself as genocide.[27] At the same time, a smaller lobby denies that even 500,000 people died and insists their deaths were due to little more than the unfortunate failure of successive potato crops: a small, local, natural disaster.[28]

25. See, for example, Terry Eagleton, *Heathcliff and the Great Hunger: Studies in Irish Culture* (London: Verso, 1995), pp. 12–15. In this essay he famously speculates that authors seem to have been 'traumatized ... into muteness' (p. 13).

26. Issued by the British Prime Minister Tony Blair, the apology was welcomed by the Irish *Taioseach* John Bruton, but more widely received with ambivalence or disbelief, perhaps because of its mode of delivery (a letter from Blair read by the actor Gabriel Byrne at a pop concert in Cork on 30 May 1997) and because of the fact it used neither the word 'apologize' nor 'sorry'.

27. The most recent (and very visible) row over such a claim was in January 2005, in response to President Mary McAleese's comparison of the treatment of Irish Catholics with the holocaust; she subsequently apologized. Such remarks also exist in the academic arena; for a succinct survey of treatments of the famine as 'holocaust', see Melissa Fegan, *Literature and the Irish Famine, 1845–1919* (Oxford: Oxford University Press, 2002), p. 32.

28. See, for example, John Plowright, *The Routledge Dictionary of Modern British History* (New York: Routledge, 2006), p. 130—although he does note that there is debate over whether the British were guilty of neglect in how they managed the situation.

In between is a great range of opinion,[29] and a limited array of sources that, no matter what one's opinion, point to astounding arrogance and neglect on the part of many British officials over many years, extraordinary suffering on the part of a huge proportion of the population, major changes in land ownership and use, horrific conditions in the workhouses, widespread death from typhus brought on by starvation, high rates of blindness in survivors, and mass emigration under desperate conditions and with relatively low rates of success; the sum total of which is not yet a story that can be told in a single voice.[30]

When one considers the famine today, therefore, there are two problems: first, the ongoing effects of the famine itself and, second, this problem of how it is remembered and the emotive, political purposes to which such memory is so often pressed.[31] Could it be that both these problems are at play in Roman Catholic churches' ways of celebrating the Eucharist in today's Ireland? The abstention from, or non-offering of, communion wine needs to be investigated not only as a subliminal reaction to the fact of the famine (how can we eat and drink when so many were lost through starvation?), but also to the contested ways it is represented: that is, something is unresolved in society at large, and something remains unresolved in every meal in church.

In popular Irish discourse, the entity that is most often blamed for the famine is 'the British'; but as several recent studies have shown, it was the Catholic middle class that benefited most from

29. See, for example, Mary Daly, 'Revisionism and Irish History: The Great Famine' in D. George Boyce and Alan O' Day, *The Making of Modern Irish History: Revisionism and the Revisionist Controversy* (New York: Routledge, 1996), pp. 71–89. Daly's work denies the genocide argument without adopting the famine-denying position; she tends toward Peter Solar's summary, that the Irish were, simply, 'profoundly unlucky' (p. 71).

30. A short survey of which literature is presented in: Toibín, *The Irish Famine.*

31. Or, as Seamus Deane puts it, the problem is 'what the famine meant': 'historical debate [in Ireland] about nationalism and colonialism, which is also a debate about the relationship between modernity and atrocity, of which the contemporary version known as revisionism is a reprise, begins with the Famine. It is a debate generated by the question of what the Famine meant.' Seamus Deane, 'Dumbness and Eloquence: A Note on English as We Write it In Ireland,' in Clare Carroll and Patricia King (eds), *Ireland and Postcolonial Theory* (Cork: Cork University Press, 2003), pp. 109–21; 110.

the famine and, with it, the Irish Roman Catholic Church.[32] To understand this, one has to remember that only very recently was diocesan ordination an option for a man from a poor Irish family. For most of its history, the Roman Catholic Church in Ireland was staffed by vocations predominantly from the middle classes, as is reflected in the historical price of admission to the seminary at Maynooth.[33] Those children of the peasantry who became the 'Irish priests' of international consciousness, whom we hear about in *Dancing at Lughnasa*, or stories from missions throughout the worldwide church, joined Orders rather than the diocesan structure and were almost always sent abroad. The priests who served the ordinary parishes of Ireland were nearly always from the elite of Catholic society, the majority of whose families survived the famine, and many of their churches thrived in its immediate aftermath due to the radical increase in middle-class fortunes through and following the famine.

It is therefore possible to speculate that when, in the 1970s, talk of receiving communion under both kinds started to circulate, at a time in Ireland in which hardly anyone yet talked about the famine and its history was still barely even taught in school, the built-up class resentment associated with the clergy — often the sole representatives of this minority Irish middle class in a village or small town — began to be played out in church. The failure of the Irish church, unlike its counterparts around the world, to develop a means whereby the laity consumes the element of wine may have been due to a lack of interest on the part of the laity in drinking blood offered by those who were latently perceived to have had

32. See, Daly, *Social and Economic History*: 'Catholic society in Ireland in the 1840s was graded and complex ... An entire class of Irish Catholics survived the Famine; many, indeed, improved their prospects as a result of it (6) ... "ordinary Catholic traders ... and the stronger farmers speculated in food and made profits"' (p. 7).

33. Maynooth College, *The Case of Maynooth College Considered* (Dublin: Milliken and Son, 1838). 'The annual grants from Parliament provide for the [staff plus] 270 of the students. Foundations or burses have been established by private individuals for the maintenance of 20 students. The remaining number, 110, pay for their board; the full charge for which is 20 guineas per annum' (p. 24). Each student also paid 8 guineas as an entrance fee. 28 guineas (or 20 in later years) was affordable to only a tiny minority of Irish residents in 1836, and only 20 out of 400 student places (5 percent) were subsidized, thus guaranteeing an elite majority student population.

blood on their hands (priests perhaps having lingered in the imagination as emblems of the middle class profiteers from the famine).

However, so little attention has yet been given to social histories of this period that this can remain only speculation, and the lack of wine-distribution may instead have been caused, more simply, by the people's reluctance to drink with those with whom they would not normally drink in a culture in which whom you drink with, or refuse to drink with, is its own form of social bonding or distancing. The priests were doubly outsiders: middle class on the one hand and, supposedly, exemplars of temperance on the other — people who were being held to an extraordinarily high and separated standard as the flip-side of the power they were accorded in society, and these standards were displayed at their most visible through the taking or not taking of drink. As will be further explored below, drink functions as a peculiar currency in the economics of Irish social relations, and would not escape these economics when circulated in church.

Whether 1,000 or 5 million people were lost,[34] the fact that there was a famine at all, and within the bounds of the world's greatest contemporary empire, and only a few hundred miles from that empire's capital and centre of wealth, and in recent times, in modernity, has inevitable resonances in numerous aspects of private and public life in Ireland today. Its effects can perhaps be seen in things like the fact that the Irish are the world's greatest contributors, per capita, apart from Scandinavia, to government-aid overseas relief[35] — and they were the highest-level contributors of private donations as a percentage of GDP just as much before the Celtic Tiger (when they were one of the poorest countries in the Western world) as after it.[36] Furthermore, Ireland is reputed to train and send more overseas development and aid workers than any other country in the world and has done so for decades, including through

34. Joel Mokyr's analysis seems probable: 1 million deaths, 400,000 'averted births', 2.5 million emigrants. From a census count of 8.2m in 1841, the figure was 4.7m in 1891. *Why Ireland Starved: A Quantitative and Analytical History of the Irish Economy 1800–1850* (London: Allen and Unwin, 1983).

35. See the Department of Foreign Affairs report, 7 April 2008, www. reliefweb.int/rw/RWB.NSF/db900SID/PANA-7DGG6G?OpenDocument

36. See the report of the Senate debate of 3 March 1993: www.historical-debates.oireachtas.ie/S/0135/S.0135.199303030010.html

its own under-developed years. At the same time, Ireland has the highest rate of heart disease in Europe and many point to its poor dietary habits as reason for this.[37] It also has one of the highest per capita rates of eating disorders in all of the world.[38] There exists, then, both an acute awareness of the need to ameliorate the hunger of others and a deep insecurity about being able to feed themselves. It seems more than coincidental that the most generous famine relievers and the people with the poorest eating habits should also be the people in the only modern state to experience wide-scale famine in recent history. And the only people to not drink at the Eucharistic meal.

Given this context, it is not surprising that eating and drinking in church should display unique patterns in Ireland. Especially when one also considers the problem of alcoholism.

Alcoholism

Ireland has a special relationship with alcohol. Its convivial pub culture is remarked upon in travelogues and attempted reproductions all over the world, and its drinks (e.g., Guinness, Baileys and Jamesons Irish Whiskey) are international brand leaders. Very little happens in the public aspects of social life in contemporary Ireland without an alcoholic drink. The sharing of a drink signifies a very great range of human bonds. Deals are made over it, sales sealed by it, dating rarely happens without it, dancing—once fuelled mostly by tea—now happens largely with drink, difficult conversations are had over it, life events are marked by it (and have developed their own idiom: baby's heads are wetted, young couples are toasted, corpses are waked, sorrows are drowned, the hair of the dog is administered)—and all through drink. Playwright, Conor McPherson, recently observed of his native country: 'Drinking is everywhere, it's like nothing happens without it. Courtships, weddings, funerals, going to the theatre, everything: it's always alcohol, alcohol, alcohol.'[39]

37. See the 2006 report of the Irish Heart Foundation (and note that *death rate* from heart disease halved in the 15 years prior to the report, probably due to medication developments). www.irishheart.ie/iopen24/pub/positionstatements/heart_for_pdf.pdf

38. See the resources published by the Irish Mental Health Coalition (2006), for example: www.imhc.ie/publicInformation/publicInfoItem.php?id=9

39. Conor McPherson quoted in *The Guardian*, 13 September 2006.

Ireland is an exceptionally social culture in the modern world. People meet their friends in the pub weekly (if not more often);[40] people go into the pub alone and talk to whomever is there; across social classes, people drop into one another's homes just to say hello for a while (i.e., without reason); and at every point, drink is usually offered. In homes and among women, it is most often a cup of tea (although increasingly it is a glass of wine); but in public or among men, it is almost always an alcoholic drink that is offered. Many teetotalers even keep a bottle in the house to offer a drink to those who would come calling, such is the strength of convention about offering, and taking, a drink. 'Will you take a drink with me?' or 'Will we have a drink?' is not a question to which the response 'No, thanks' should be given lightly, because it indicates a refusal of relationship (or of growth in intimacy within a relationship) rather than the simple 'I'm not thirsty' or 'I don't fancy it' that the foreigner might intend. There are many people who do not drink alcohol, or do not drink much alcohol, but it is important to note that they have specific conventions of speech for turning down a drink in such a way as to not give offense. As Michael Browne, Bishop of Galway, commented of Irish drinking habits in 1959, 'The traffic in drink is not like the fish and chip business where a man stops when he has enough. In this country drinking does not mean the satisfaction of a natural thirst.'[41]

What drinking does 'mean' in Ireland and Northern Ireland, far from being related to the slaking of physical thirst, is a complicated matrix of social, religious, moral, political, economic, familial and personal indicators. Furthermore, it is commonly afforded a sort of spiritual quality, not simply because of the ritualistic trappings of its consumption (deciding which pub to meet in, meeting, buying rounds for one another, waiting for one another to be served, raising the glass and saying '*slainté*' / '*slainté maith*' in the South or the Catholic North, or 'cheers!' for the more British-aligned, taking the drink,

40. Although it should be noted that the current gender equity in this regard is a recent development; pubs were principally the domain of men until the 1980s. A man going into a pub alone was normal; a woman doing the same was the object of suspicion. A man drinking several pints was normal; a woman was expected to take only one or two small drinks — a glass of a draft or a 'woman's drink' such as a Babycham.

41. Quoted in Diarmuid Ferriter, *A Nation of Extremes: The Pioneers in Twentieth Century Ireland* (Dublin: Irish Academic Press, 2005), p. 166.

having the *craic*, getting tipsy but not getting 'maggoty', leave-taking), but also because of the theological self-understanding of the people who are meeting and drinking which might be described as an Irish existentialism which can be temporarily (but regularly) overcome through the strong bond created by meeting to drink. As the writer John Waters has rather bleakly put it:

> Drinking in Ireland is not simply a convivial pastime, it is a ritualistic alternative to real life, a spiritual placebo, a fumble for eternity, a longing for heaven, a thirst for return to the embrace of the Almighty. People drink more because they like living less than they think they ought to, and the more overwhelming the evidence of the irrefutability of life's attractiveness grates with their own experience, the more the nagging unhappiness makes alcohol the only way of filling in that shortfall, which is in essence an absence of beliefs ... In the end there is nothing but pain.[42]

Alongside these strong social conventions about the offering and taking of a drink, Irish people have a reputation as being prone to alcoholism, and from a variety of different perspectives: from scientists who claim that there is a gene that makes Irish people more susceptible to alcoholism;[43] to social commentators who believe that the Irish, like Native Americans, have succumbed to alcoholism in response to being stripped of their culture, land and language by an imperial power;[44] to the reputation of the Irish literary and artistic caste, provided by the very public excesses of a long line of popular characters up to Shane McGowan.

But these characters and their excesses are as vilified as they are beatified in Irish culture. There is a long and strong brand of rhetoric that meets the myth of the glorious soak square-on, and refuses the elision of the concepts 'Irish' and 'alcoholic'. Such resistance has a serious pedigree in Ireland also in the form of temperance movements, perhaps most notably the Pioneer Association. This Roman Catholic social movement started in the mid-nineteenth century, but reached its heyday in the 1940s, bequeathing Ireland the now iconic photographs of thousands processing through Dublin

42. John Waters, *An Intelligent Person's Guide to Modern Ireland*, 1997, quoted in Ferriter, *A Nation of Extremes*, p. 1.

43. See, for example, Joan Matthews Larson, *Seven Weeks to Sobriety* (New York: Fawcette Columbine, 1997), p. 61.

44. See, for example, Matthew Fox, *The Coming of the Cosmic Christ* (Melbourne: Collins Dove, 1989).

to Phoenix Park for Benediction: a rising cake of nation-hood, gender essentialism, moral control and Roman Catholicism. The Pioneer Association was based on 'the pledge': a life-long pledge to abstain from alcohol and, instead, to devote one's life to the Sacred Heart. Adherents wore a pin, to show they had taken the pledge and they were supported in their total abstinence from alcohol by weekly articles in *The Irish Catholic* about the perils of drinking and the spiritual privileges of life-long devotion to the Sacred Heart.

The fervent activities of and play between legislators, church officials and social workers striving to increase the number of Irish who had taken the pledge gives a good picture of the cocktail of spiritual-political codependence that characterized the infancy of the State. Such a play helps to explain why a temperance movement based on total abstinence on the one hand, and utter subservience to the power of the Church on the other, both redoubled through strict delineation of sexual and reproductive 'norms', simply could not hold up against the realities of women's liberation, church-state separation and entry into the European Union.

However, the significant levels of adherence to the pledge in even recent history, and the rhetorics that the Pioneer movement created in the public sphere (i.e.: not merely among pledge-takers, but in the general media) also helps to explain the strong traces of alcohol-etiquette visible in Irish ecclesial life today. Priests were expected to take the pledge, and many did. Whether they stuck to it in private is another matter, but in public, for most of the twentieth century, it was considered unusual, if not disreputable, for a man in a collar to be seen taking a drink in a pub. And when the priest came calling to the house, it was expected that it would be tea he would be drinking; but it was never quite that simple. There arose a whole network of charades to do with drinking between the laity and the clergy. There was never a right answer to the question, 'Will you have a drink, Father?' To say no was to be correct, holy, and a model in society — but also aloof from the person offering it; to say yes was to be a convivial, human, of-the-people, but also not worthy of the respect afforded to those scape-goated to be living lives of perfection: celibate, temperate, and with all these bodily urges under perfect control, close to God. People frowned on one another for their public actions, but behaved just the same themselves in private: social conventions regarding drink had become a thick network of hypocrisies masquerading as social niceties. Alcohol was the substance and the symbol through which the social relations between laity and clergy were thus mediated; through which clergy were, with one hand, given respect and reverence and admiration; and, with the other, taken out of ordinary human relationship, simultaneously pedestalized and demonized.

Alcoholism is undoubtedly a problem in Irish civic life, as the well-documented social costs of excessive drinking make clear. But it is also a phantom. Recent research has shown that levels of alcohol consumption in Ireland are no worse than anywhere else; indeed, they are considerably smaller than many other countries in Europe[45] and, moreover, have been so since records began.[46] So while alcohol-abuse creates problems, they are not necessarily any worse or more prevalent in Ireland than in any other European country. Yet Irish people remain haunted by the threat of imminent alcoholic collapse: it seems to have ruined so many, and they seem so peculiarly vulnerable to its power. This may be simply because, being such a social society, people under the influence of alcohol are that much more visible. In other European countries, most drinking occurs within the home, with family or friends, and over a meal; in Ireland most drinking occurs in the pub, with friends and strangers; thus, drunkenness is more public.

However, the specter of alcoholism may have another cause: it may be yet another example of the self-inscription of prejudice. As several social critics have made plain in cultural studies, Irish self-perception and thus identity-formation has been greatly influenced by centuries of external interference, particularly the barrage of damning and dehumanizing words about themselves that issued from British officials and print media. If the stereotype that 'Paddys are thick' could be resisted and pride taken in intelligence despite the prevalence of the stereotype, then the Irish might yet resist this

45. See, Donald Goodwin, *Alcoholism, The Facts* (Oxford: Oxford University Press, 2000). He reports that Ireland has a low reported rate of liver disease relative to the rest of Europe and significantly lower rates of cirrhosis than the UK or the USA. Also, 'Ireland, contrary to its popular image, has a lower consumption rate than the UK' (p. 51).

46. See, Denis Conniffe and Daniel McCoy, *Alcohol Use in Ireland: Some Economic and Social Implications* (Dublin: Economic and Social Research Institute, 1993; Denver, CO: Academic Books, 2000). 'By European standards, Irish alcohol consumption on a per capita basis is among the lowest in Europe, being less than half of that of France or Spain', p. xii.

other stereotype and accept that they are no more prone to alcoholism that anyone else. Such an awakening to 'the curious and pervasive Irish relationship with alcohol'[47] would require a radical excavation of the landscape of 'Irishness', a key constituent factor of which for so long has been said to be a propensity for drink. Is it any wonder then, that people do not want to drink in church, no matter how many 'Years of the Eucharist' are mandated?

The disciplining of the body through over- or under-indulgence in food and drink is not simply a cultural production, wherein the latent after-effects of a people's history are negotiated (or repressed) at a grassroots level. It is also matter of nation-state politics. As William Cavanaugh shows in his study of torture in Chile under Pinochet (which he describes as a 'social strategy'), the relation between a single individual's body and a state's political power is both direct and potentially devastating. But he shows how it is also, perversely, creative: it *creates* bodies. He argues the effect of the state's use of torture was, 'to discipline the citizenry into a complex performance, scripted by the state. That performance atomizes the citizenry through fear, thereby dismantling other *social* bodies [such as the church] which would rival the state's authority over *individual* bodies. I describe this not as the violation of individual rights but as the very creation of individuals.'[48] What Cavanaugh brings to light is the symbiotic relationship between individual and nation-state and the power of violence in creating both, and I suggest that in an Irish context, food-provision rather than torture is the instrument of this relationship.

During colonial rule in the nineteenth century, the state related to the people through lack of provision of food (famine), and then emergency food aid (in the form of workhouses) that proved both hopelessly inadequate as techniques for food-provision as well as torturous, and often deadly, as a mode of life. Additionally, there was an explicitly sectarian component to this in the major population centres, where several of the Protestant relief societies would offer food in return for religious instruction.[49] Those Catholics who converted (to a Protestant denomination) in order to 'take the soup'

47. Ferriter, *A Nation of Extremes*, p. 5.
48. William T. Cavanaugh, *Torture and Eucharist: Theology, Politics, and the Body of Christ* (Oxford: Blackwells, 1998), p. 2. Parentheses mine.
49. See, Desmond Bowen, *Souperism: Myth or Reality?* (Cork: Mercier Press, 1970).

were known as 'soupers' and were subject to a stigma that lasted well into the 1870s.[50] Thus 'real food' (the sort that keeps you alive when you might otherwise starve) became associated in the popular imagination with what Protestants own and control, furthering the Catholic Irish population from both any sense in which their Eucharist is functionally food and drink. If food and drink was a Protestant currency (of life and death), then all the more reason to preserve the utterly transcendent quality of Catholic communion as a currency of salvation only.[51] Then, during the early days of 'independent' Ireland, in the mid-twentieth century, the great majority of people were governed principally through the mechanism of mandatory weekly attendance at a common civic meal, the Eucharist. The 'duty' to do so, not merely as a panacea against the threat of hell and damnation, but largely as a legitimator of social belonging, as a mark of active and acceptable citizenship, and a baseline of 'respectability', remains a significant part of the culture in the Republic to this day.[52]

50. See, Irene Whelan, 'The Stigma of Souperism' in Cathal Poirtear (ed.), *The Great Irish Famine* (Cork: Cork University Press, 1995), pp. 135–54.

51. Again, the contrast with other Catholic cultures is salient. See, for example, Caroline Walker Bynum: *Holy Feast, Holy Fast: The Religious Significance of Food to Medieval Women* (Berkeley, CA: University of California Press, 1990). While Catholic mystics have argued that the Eucharist was all the food and drink they needed to survive, Irish Catholics do not seem even to have conceived of it as food and drink.

52. For an overview of the emphasis on Mass attendance through the second half of the nineteenth and through the twentieth century, see, D. Hempton, *Religion and Political Culture in Britain and Ireland* (Cambridge: Cambridge University Press, 1996). But, as I noticed in fieldwork, while Mass attendance still matters (albeit to a diminished extent), what men *do* in Mass matters less. On St. Patrick's Day, 2007, in a large Roman Catholic church in the west of Ireland, two men stood with their backs leaning on the back wall of the church and talked the entire way through the Eucharistic Prayer. They were discussing the American presidential primaries, with a full spectrum of speech. After communion, they slipped out. One was a TD (Member of Parliament), the other a powerful local merchant. No one could say they were not there. 'He goes to Mass each Sunday' still means: he is a decent and upstanding member of Irish society. Women, it should be noted, would not get away with talking the entire way through Mass; or at all. They are expected to attend, pray, not turn around, and if they were to talk through the consecration, swearing as they went, as these men had, their behaviour would be the subject of gossip rather than praise, a mark on their character rather than a confirmation of their good character. This 'norm' is, therefore, gendered.

Furthermore, the pressure to take, and keep, 'the pledge' to the Sacred Heart in the mid-twentieth century simultaneously conditioned one's relationship to both the church and to the long-standing image of 'the Irish' (i.e., oneself) as drunkards. So, for the past 200 years of Irish history, the state has controlled the people through the provision/restriction of food and drink, with the ever-present threat that the state can and will withhold it; furthermore, due to the fierce church-state alliance, the non-conforming citizen is threatened not only with hunger or thirst (the preserve of the state), not only with being outcast from their community (church and state), but also with separation from God, with their soul's eternity in Hell (church).

However, the relation between state and individual body is not a one-way flow from state to individual only. Individual bodies can erupt against the state, and may, with hindsight, be seen to have fashioned the state — perhaps especially, when most rigidly ruled by state control, even if, as frequently happens, they die in the process. In twentieth-century Ireland we had numerous examples of famous alcoholic and/or Mass-abstaining artists, who were vilified in their own lifetimes but who are now held up as exemplars of Irish culture in the new nostalgic, pseudo-secular marketplace (such as James Joyce and Brendan Behan, to name but two). But perhaps the most striking clash of individual and state bodies in recent times was the action of the hunger strikers in Northern Ireland. The possibility therefore needs to be considered that along with famine and alcoholism, hunger striking is a further significant factor in the current Roman Catholic Eucharistic practice of congregational abstention from the element of wine.

Hunger Striking

Starting in March of 1981, ten Republican prisoners in the high-security British prison in Northern Ireland (Long Kesh/the Maze), starved themselves to death as part of a hunger strike undertaken because all other negotiations to have them viewed as political prisoners instead of criminals had failed or been refused.[53] (Others

53. In March 1976, Britain changed the law in Northern Ireland, recasting prisoners once held under political categories as ordinary criminals. By criminalizing agitators, they could transform them into 'terrorists' and subject them to trial without jury and imprison them in criminal prisons. (Bobby

also starved themselves as part of the hunger strike but did not die due to their family's medical intervention when they entered a coma.) A hunger strike in late 1980 had been called off after the British government appeared to countenance some of the prisoners' demands. However, when it became apparent that the government were in fact not making the expected changes, the hunger strike began again in earnest, with one or two new prisoners joining the strike each week so that their deaths, when they came, were staggered and thus kept the issues in the public domain. All the men who died in 1981 were in their mid- to late-twenties, intelligent, politically motivated, part of the elite in terms of roles within the IRA command structure within the prison, and in prison for a slate of offenses ranging from firearms violations to murder. To this day, the images of the hunger strikers who died have an iconic value and can still be seen in murals and posters; moreover, Bobby Sands' face is, like a latter-day Che Guevara, now widely found on T-shirts on young people's chests.

The 1981 hunger strikes attracted a massive amount of attention from the media at home and abroad, as well as from international governments and human rights groups.[54] As Ruane and Todd

---

Sands, for example, was serving a long sentence for being found in possession of one quarter of a gun.) The hunger strikes happened after five years of other protests had achieved little except deepening the brutality of their punishment (no visits, no paper, confined to their cells). Demanding that they be treated as prisoners of war and not common criminals, they had refused to wear prison uniforms, covering themselves with prison blankets — hence the name for the protesters: 'Blanketmen'. They had undertaken the 'dirty protest' (excrement smeared across their cells due to a battle with warders over its disposal). They had smashed their cell windows to get rid of the disinfectant fumes, and thus froze through the winter. They had shot some warders after others treated them with brutality (repeated anal searches, forced scalding baths, and other physical attacks). Some of those who went on strike had had no contact with the outside world for five years, having been denied all 'privileges' (like visits, or reading matter) and subjected to solitary confinement on account of their protests. See, for example, Paul Bew, *Ireland: The Politics of Enmity 1789–2006* (Oxford: Oxford University Press, 2007), Padraig O'Malley, *Biting at the Grave: The Irish Hunger Strikes and the Politics of Despair* (New York: Beacon Press, 1991) and Alan Feldman, *Formations of Violence: The Narrative of the Body and Political Terror in Northern Ireland* (Chicago, IL: University of Chicago Press, 1991).

54. For a comprehensive sample of reaction, see O'Malley, *Biting at the Grave*, p. 4.

comment, 'The 1981 hunger strikes were a public drama of great symbolic power and emotional intensity which gained world-wide attention. The struggle between prisoners and warders, republicans and the British state, was symbolically fought out on the prisoners' emaciated bodies.'[55] The situation was astounding enough to the international audience, but made even more so due to Bobby Sands being elected as a member of the British parliament during the time of his fast. As the *Hindustan Times* remarked upon his death, Mrs. Thatcher 'has allowed a member of the House of Commons, a colleague in fact, to die of starvation.'[56] In these eight months in 1981 immense damage was done to the British version of both historic and contemporary events in Northern Ireland. According to Ruane and Todd, 'The hunger strikes had symbolically reversed the opposition between criminality and political principle, portraying the civilizing modernity of the British state — with which unionists so identified — as barbarism.'[57] But it is also widely understood to have given the republican movement an inkling that a deliberately symbolic, political campaign, rather than just a campaign of violence, might now be a feasible means of achieving their goals.

Fundamentally, all hunger strikes are symbolic. However, in Ireland they symbolize not one but several emotionally-charged historical and political issues, simultaneously: to name but a few, they tap mythic sensibilities about pre-colonial norms (the Brehon Laws) in Ireland which included the tradition of 'fasting against' an oppressor to get justice;[58] they recall Republican fasts in the early twentieth century as part of the struggle for independence (such as that of the Lord Mayor of Cork, Terrence Mac Swiney, who died on hunger strike against British rule in 1920); and they connote Christian beliefs in the sanctity of martyrdom on the one hand and the efficacy of a sacrificial offering as redemptive on the

55. Ruane and Todd, *Dynamics of Conflict*, pp. 111.
56. O'Malley, *Biting at the Grave*, p. 4.
57. O'Malley, *Biting at the Grave*, p. 113.
58. The Brehon laws were the ancient oral-tradition laws (written down in, it is thought, the fifth century) governing social norms for the majority of people on the island. They included provision for 'fasting against' a persecutor (such as a landlord enacting an unfair rent or eviction) to compel them to do justice. See the facsimile from the oldest known fragment (held in Trinity College Library, Dublin): *Senchas Már: Ancient Laws of Ireland with a Descriptive Introduction by R.I. Best and Rudolph Thurneysen* (Dublin: Stationery Office of Saorstat Éireann, 1931).

other.[59] In the 1981 case, however, it is possible that the strike had a peculiar symbolic resonance because of what Robert Elias has called a 'political economy of helplessness'. As was described in Chapter Two, this economy is founded on a pervasive sense of victimhood (across the whole island), whether in the face of the British crown or perceived Popery.[60] Consequently, the fact that the hunger strikers were *prisoners* possibly ratcheted up the emotional content of their symbolic valence. According to Padraig O'Malley, 'The hunger strikes are a metaphor for the entrapment of the larger society' and it is important to note that it was not just the Catholic side that felt it was held captive, against its will, and permanently threatened with extinction by a captor's threat. Furthermore, as we saw in Chapter Two, mythologies of victimhood in Ireland may be colonial in origin, but they rely heavily on Christological language and the mythos of the Babylonic exile for their reproduction, and so this acutely *vicarious* understanding of the prisoners' suffering could result in the individual strikers being seen to stand for a people's endemic situation.

Hunger strikes themselves, however, are not a uniquely Irish nor even Christian phenomenon. For instance, Mahatma Ghandi went on such a strike 17 times in the cause of independence from British colonial rule in India. As Michael Biggs has noted, hunger striking is used as a deliberate act of civil war or civic resistance across many different cultures, designed as it is to elicit very similar responses to other grassroots tactics aimed at forcing a governmental response: 'Physical suffering—possibly even death—is inflicted on oneself, rather than on the opponent. The technique can be conceived as a paradoxical inversion of hostage-taking or kidnapping...'[61] It might also be compared to self-ignition in Tibet and other Asian cultures, or to suicide-bombing in the Arab world insofar as such acts are a political tactic, a mechanism whereby young people kill

59. They also were a Bardic method of gaining justice, and a famous legend from the Bardic tradition circulated widely in early twentieth century Ireland due to W.B. Yeats' play 'The King's Threshold'. In it the chief poet of Erin, Seanchan, fasts against the King to get justice. See A. Norman Jeffares and A.S. Knowland, *A Commentary on the Collected Plays of W.B. Yeats* (Stanford, CA: Stanford University Press, 1975).

60. See O' Malley, *Biting at the Grave*, pp. 8–9.

61. Michael Biggs, 'Hunger Strikes by Irish Republicans, 1916–1923'. Paper presented at The Workshop on Techniques of Violence in Civil War, Centre for the Study of Civil War, Oslo (August 2004), p. 1.

themselves as a means of protest or agitation (although with the obvious difference that the Irish strikers killed only themselves). However, the Irish hunger strikes were not merely a method of political leverage, as in hostage-taking or kidnapping; crucially, they were also understood within a theological worldview of ultimate victory in a moral battle through sacrificial-offering, and the *self-sacrifice* of the striker was seen as a vital, and extremely powerful, part of the protest.[62] It is salient, then, to note the differences between 'hunger strikes' and self-immolation or self-explosion. First, starving the body is a very slow process, meaning that it can be called off if the striker's demands are met; it can therefore function as political leverage in the lifetime of the striker because, theoretically at least, they do not have to die for their point to be made. And second, that hunger is chosen as a method (and not, say, self-immolation or self-explosion) suggests that hunger has a particular symbolic power due to its wider symbolic currency in the culture.

However, while hunger might have a symbolic power in the culture as a whole, its specific resonances seem to have differed significantly along lines of differentiation in Protestant and Catholic theology. In the case of the hunger strikers, Protestants, by seeing this particular abuse of hunger as suicide, decried it as against the fifth commandment. Irish Catholics, however, by seeing this use of hunger as self-sacrifice, portrayed it as a model act of Christian discipleship, the ultimate act of faithfulness, obeying Jesus's commandment to 'lay down one's life for one's friends',[63] and

62. Although, as Feldman insists, the 'theological' components of the crisis were the product of their reception outside the prison rather than the self-perception of the prisoners; he argues that the inmates saw the strike only as a military tactic. 'The Blanketmen viewed the 1981 Hunger Strike as a military campaign and organized it as such. For them it was a modality of insurrectionary violence in which they deployed their bodies as weapons.' (*Formations of Violence*, p. 220). The hunger strikers were in prison, convicted of violent crime, they were not, he argues, setting themselves up as spokespeople for an entire liberation movement, nor were they interested in pacifism. This was war, and this tactic was a weapon. Objecting to those who see an equivalence between this and other hunger strikes, he argues hard that unlike Ghandi or Martin Luther King, the 1981 Hunger Strike was 'not a pacifist or religious action'. Rather, 'It was to be a prelude to violence' (p. 220).

63. Jn 15. 12–14: 'My command is this: Love each other as I have loved you. Greater love has no one than this, that he lay down his life for his friends. You are my friends if you do what I command.'

mimicking in life what every Eucharist symbolically re-presents in the Host. It is vital to note that Rome, and even the English Catholic establishment (with a significant base of Irish immigrants) did not agree: they, too, perceived it as suicide and argued that the hunger strikers should be denied communion while on strike[64] and, if they died, not buried on sacred ground. This points to the peculiarly native *Irish* Catholic link (between self-sacrifice, food and drink, and politics) that was at stake here.

It was not a new link. Irish nationalist politics were greatly influenced by the politician Padraig Pearse's eloquent brand of revolutionary mysticism, which fused doctrines of Christ's sacrifice with mandates for national sacrifice. This, for example, was his 'oath prayer':

> In the name of God
> By Christ His only Son
> By Mary His gentle Mother
> By Patrick the apostle of the Irish
> By the loyalty of Colm Cille,
> By the glory of our race
> By the blood of our ancestors,
> By the murder of Red Hugh,
> By the sad death of Hugh O'Neill,
> By the tragic death of Owen Roe,
> By the dying wish of Sarsfield,
> By the anguished sigh of Fitzgerald,
> By the bloody wounds of Tone,
> By the noble blood of Emmet,
> By the Famine corpses
> By the tears of Irish exiles,
> We swear the oaths our ancestors swore,
> That we will free our race from bondage,
> Or that we will fall fighting hand to hand.
> Amen.[65]

It is not just the framing of the Republican political cause as equivalent to Christ's sacrifice as we know it from doctrines of substitutionary atonement that is striking: it is its *liturgical* form. The 'oath prayer' may not, technically, be a 'prayer' (it does not ask for anything, it is not addressed to God), but it mimics the preface to the Eucharistic

64. It was widely reported at the time that many of the hunger strikers received the Eucharistic host while on strike (it was the only matter they ingested during their strikes).

65. Quoted in Ruth Dudley Edwards, *Patrick Pearse: The Triumph of Failure* (London: Gallancz, 1977), pp. 161-62.

Prayer (which Pearse, being a scholar and knowing Latin, would have understood): the offering of the blood poured out, the noting of the wounded flesh, and most of all the calling upon the communion of saints for solidarity in an action about to be undertaken: he might as well be saying, 'and now with the angels and saints and the whole company of heaven...'. The prayer is also liturgical in its form: it is a non-responsive litany, that ends with 'Amen'.

The use of liturgical forms (especially those connected with the commemoration of Christ in food and drink at the Eucharist) to express political beliefs is also evident in the writings of Terence MacSwiney (to whom reference was made above). He wrote about the earlier martyrs for Irish nationalism, such as those who died in the Easter Risings in 1916, thus:

> it is because they were our best and bravest that they had to die. No lesser sacrifice would save us. Because of it our struggle is holy — our battle is sanctified by their blood, and our victory is assured by their martyrdom. We, taking up the work they left incomplete, confident in God, offer in turn sacrifice from ourselves. It is not we who take innocent blood, but we offer it, sustained by the example of our immortal dead and that Divine example which inspires us all — for the redemption of our country.[66]

Saturated with both the cadences of liturgical speech, particularly creedal formulations, as well as the phrasing and vocabulary of English hymnody of the time,[67] Mac Swiney's eulogy like Pearse's oath makes clear the centrality of the Christic self-sacrificial core of the Irish understanding of the hunger strike. This is not what Ghandi, or the American civil rights campaigner Martin Luther King, had in mind; it is not what gave their hunger strikes their symbolic power. Hunger striking in an Irish context cannot, therefore, be seen simply as a military tactic. The Blanketmen may have understood the strikes as merely a 'prelude to violence', as Feldman has it, but their very understanding of violence was theological. Evidence of this came in the eruption of church people as spokespeople on either side of the Troubles in the media and politics, such as had not been seen in either Northern Ireland or the Republic before. As O'Malley remarks:

66. Quoted in P.S. O' Hegarty, *A Short Memoir of Terence MacSwiney* (Dublin: Talbot Press, 1922), pp. 78–79.
67. For example, 'Soul of My Saviour' and 'Sweet Heart of Jesus'.

> For the first time since the conflict erupted anew in the late 1960s, the churches emerged as the surrogate spokesparties for their respective constituencies ... They became the mouthpieces for the political importunings of their constituencies rather than exemplars of the Christian ethos they professed ... they were unable to put the hunger strikes in a moral context that would illuminate rather than divide.[68]

And divide they did. Some argue that the hunger strikes were what finally forced the British to enter into dialogue with Republicans. Others argue that the hunger strikes set the cause of Republicanism back, committing nationalists to a process that eventually led to the rescinding of the Republican claim over the six counties of Northern Ireland. Yet others have remarked that the hunger strikers caused England terrible consequences, and blame everything from the Queen's 'annus horribilis' to the bombing of Canary Wharf on the curse England brought upon itself by letting the prisoners starve to death while striking in protest against it. Extreme and unverifiable as such a claim is, it is nevertheless popular. In truth, the effects of the hunger strikes are still almost impossible to account, at least from a political point of view. What can be stated from an ecclesiological point of view is that through the hunger strikes, the borders around the churches, their loyalties 'when the chips were down', their theologies, and the ease with which they can be set in the service of violence, and their Eucharistic practices, were made visible in all their seemingly absolute division and irreconcilable difference.

The main currency in this theological economy is precisely the same as that upon which Feldman's brilliant political study is founded: the body. And it is this fact that provides grounds for now considering the specifically Catholic characteristic of not eating *and* drinking (i.e., not sharing the fullness of the meal that is the 'body' of Christ) in Ireland. In the context of the Northern Irish hunger strikes of the 1980s, not only was a dead body a 'politically encoded corpse', as Feldman puts it, it was also a theologically encoded corpse, invested with the power of the arch-symbol of Christ himself, the politically encoded corpse *par excellence* whom, legend has it, the Catholic strikers ingested as communion during their strike (again suggesting that, like other Irish Catholics, they did not see it as food). As Louis Marie Chauvet has insisted, the

---

68. O'Malley, *Beyond the Grave*, p. 7.

body of Christ would be just a corpse were it not for the resurrection, because that event renders his body living, not dead.[69]

One might argue that the bodies of the hunger strikers were therefore just corpses, but that would be to underestimate radically the Irish Catholic theological worldview in which the strikers were in fact using the same method as Christ (self-sacrificial protest at an occupying state which did, but did not have to, result in death) *and* drawing on his actual body (literally in the Eucharist, as well as through the 'self-sacrificing body as redemptive' signification of their strike) for power. The hunger strikers and their supporters saw their sacrifice as 'redemptive' of an oppressive political situation and, moreover, they knew their dead bodies would have currency (i.e., would serve as *living* symbols) in the struggle long beyond their deaths. As Feldman put it,

> Starvation of the flesh in the hunger strike was the inverting and bitter interiorization of the power of the state. Hunger striking to the death used the body of the prisoner to recodify and to transfer state power from one topos to another. The corpse of the hunger striker was also the artifact of the contaminated Other. The act of self-directed violence interiorized the Other, neutralized its potency, enclosed its defiling power, and stored it in the corpse of the hunger striker for use by his support community. The subsequent sacralization of the dead hunger striker completed the process of purification and commemorated the subverting transfer of power from the state to the insurgent community with elaborate funeral processions and mortuary displays ... From his dead and purified body, new cycles of violence were expected to flow [*and, moreover, with a new legitimacy, a sacralized legitimacy*] ... The Hunger Strike was a rite of differentiation that directly addressed the cultural construction of violence.[70]

Proof, if it were needed, of the success of this strategy, is those T-shirts on young people. Or the poster given to Feldman (a secular New York Jew), years later during a visit to Northern Ireland, with photographs of all ten hunger strikers who died, accompanied by

69. Louis Marie Chauvet, *Symbol and Sacrament: A Sacramental Reinterpretation of Christian Existence* (Collegeville, MN: Liturgical Press, 1995). For example, 'it is precisely in the act of respecting his radical absence or otherness that the Risen One can be recognized symbolically. ... *Those who kill this sense of the absence of Christ make Christ a corpse again.*' And, completing his distinction between a (living) body and a corpse, he goes on to conclude that the church is 'the symbolic body of the word of the Risen One' (p. 178).

70. Feldman, *Formations of Violence*, p. 237.

Republican slogans keeping the atoning rhetoric of their sacrifice alive—and all printed in Libya.[71]

Something, surely, has gone wrong here theologically? When your notion of redemption is as much, if not more, bound up in your struggle for national political independence as it is in the salvation of your soul and your participation in the eschatological body of Christ in the church, then your corpse indeed has a great deal of value.[72] The confusion of the cause of national independence with basic ecclesial formation and belonging is a mistake any Roman Catholic Irish person in the twentieth century can be forgiven for having made because, as noted in the opening chapter, the very foundations of the State were negotiated on Catholic terms.

It is because of this history that there is no understanding of sectarian violence in Ireland that can or has escaped theology. The construction of violence in Northern Ireland *is* theological. It therefore behooves us to look to the other point highlighted by Cavanaugh: the quality of your ecclesiology determines whether or not the Body of Christ is just one more body created by the state in its own image for its own purposes. It seems to me that this might be the very struggle that is being played out on Sunday mornings in Roman Catholic churches in the Republic and Northern Ireland. But no one talks about the hunger strikers in Mass, and in conversations on the bus or over dinner, they are remembered in extremely complicated and diverse ways: while some think they were heroes, others think they were, at best, idiots. We cannot therefore make the argument of the hunger strikers, as Cavanuagh can of self-sacrifice in Chile, that the Eucharist's power resides in the bodies of subversives.

One could perhaps venture the argument that in Ireland, 'power is realized in self-sacrifice' in the sense that Catholics have not demanded that their clergy introduce the international practice of drinking of Christ's blood at Mass. Catholics in Ireland have agitated for all sorts of other measures which were introduced elsewhere in the world and only later in Ireland and with the suggestions of the laity playing a major role in their introduction—such as Eucharistic

71. Feldman, *Formations of Violence*, p. 237.
72. The diary of Bobby Sands (written with a pin on cigarette papers in minute writing) would seem to support this. Bobby Sands, *Writings from Prison* (Boulder, CO: R. Rinehart Publications, 1997). Sands smuggled out a diary for the first 17 days of his hunger strike.

Ministers and girl altar-servers. Counter-intuitive though it may be for a theologian to admit, trained as we are to recognize certain practices as 'orthodox', some sort of power may be being realized in this deference regarding the wine when understood in the frames of 'resistance'. What is being resisted in the blood may be: the church-state alliance itself, or the church as the symbol of complicity in famine guilt, or the state as an unreliable food-provider, or the church as a hypocritical influence on alcohol in Irish life, or simply the notion of blood as redemptive in a society that has learned the hard way that it is often not so. Furthermore, in all this (latent) resistance there may be found a certain sort of power. But it may not be a healthy sort of power.

Eating and drinking in church for Catholics in Ireland seems to be confused. What one can observe in the non-drinking of the cup is not so much a coherent argument, not so much a position, not even a statement of desire. There is no single, linear hypothesis suggested by remembering these particular histories of famine, alcoholism or hunger strike. What one encounters in the non-drinking of the cup seems to be inertia brought on by confusion.[73] However, this inertia (or paralysis), this very density of meaning, is not a blank space; it is communicating *something*, and what it is communicating has strongly sectarian tones. As a habit, being 'just the way we do things here', the fact cannot be avoided that congregational non-reception of the cup is a uniquely Irish and a Catholic practice (English people are not doing it, Protestants are not doing it). So when it is done, it points to that Irishness and that Catholicness, and the histories composing the symbiosis between them, not as a pre-meditated conscious sort of resistance, but as an instinctive acting-out of social location.

It may not be possible to articulate precisely *how* this constitutes a specifically sectarian problem but it seems reasonable to suggest that it does, given the specifically Protestant–Catholic/British–Irish

73. As I have suggested elsewhere, it might best be compared to an eating disorder, wherein behaviours that seem life-giving to the patient are in fact diseased. What one sees performed in Roman Catholic churches in Ireland is a neurosis, expressed as disordered eating; and, as with so many of our young women, it is the product of multiple social causes and a (distorted) will to self-create, not any single, idiosyncratic cause or the conscious will to self-destruct. 'The Abjection of Religion: Irish Ritual Anorexia', Launch of the MA in Ritual Song, Irish Centre for World Music and Dance, Limerick University (16 February 2000).

dialectic that characterizes the three issues examined in this chapter. If the famine had affected the British as well as the Irish, if alcoholism had been seen historically as a British problem as well as an Irish one (or if it had not been exploited by the British as part of its racist stereotyping of Irish people), or if the hunger strike had not been undertaken by Irish Catholic republicans protesting against the terms of their imprisonment by the British, then we would have a different set of resonances on our hands. But the resonances of these episodes in recent Irish history are characteristically sectarian, and, I would like to suggest, therefore, the non-reception of the cup is also. The basic proof of this is that it is a peculiarly Irish, Catholic habit.

What is a theologian to suggest as a way forward? (If somehow, for a real peace, this situation has to change, what then is the process that will bring this peace?) Remembering the famine, reputed alcoholism, and the hunger strikes all invite interrogation of the absence of drinking at meals in Irish churches in the context of the peculiar histories of Ireland's recent past. They also strongly suggest the relation between state (politics) and liturgical practices (religion) at every turn. The non-drinking of the wine, the blood of Christ, connotes so much: resistance, guilt, military tactic, shame, confusion and not knowing who one is. Each is a profoundly sectarian-implicated (and possibly colonial-related) response. Given the distortions (from supposedly normative Eucharistic theology) represented in the above account, and given the complicating factor of the rhetorics of 'bodies broken' and 'blood spilled' the media create in Ireland and Northern Ireland, what would it take to celebrate the Eucharist in a non-distorted fashion there? What would it take for Irish people to drink from the cup, safely? Or to borrow Nathan Mitchell's accurate phrasing of the question: 'what are the conditions of possibility of celebrating the Eucharist in Ireland and Northern Ireland's communities?'[74]

I find it helpful to imagine the following two possible ways of finding out what these conditions of possibility might be in the midst of such utter messiness. The first is to admit the need for varied, non-streamlined, context-dependant theologies of the Eucharist. Given the above discussions of famine, alcoholic reputation and hunger striking and the place of the core symbols of the church in each case, one is led to doubt whether there can be

74. Conversation with Nathan D. Mitchell, Tuesday 16 October 2007.

such a thing as a useful appeal to a/the supposedly universal theology of Eucharistic practice in this case. The same theology that can lead to community growth and wholeness in, say, France, can lead to wide-scale non-participation in the Eucharist in Ireland. Just as in Chapter Two we had to discern a context-based version of reconciliation that could nonetheless supply an ideologically strong-enough counter to sectarianism, so Irish churches may have to discern in Eucharistic practices mechanisms of liturgical theologizing that strive to create a locally-relevant version of classic Eucharistic claims.

In a similar way that the Anglican church in Papua New Guinea uses the image of the pig to convey the representation of Christ's sacrifice in the Eucharist, where their western European counterparts pray to the lamb,[75] and thus fulfills the conditions of possibility of celebrating the Eucharist in Papua New Guinea, perhaps also in Ireland we may need to discover whether an alternative choice of metaphor would allow people to drink Christ's blood as the *redemptive* offering it is designed to be (and not have it lead people to think that their own violent death for the sake of a cause will have an associatedly-redemptive sign-value). Methodist communities in North America use grape juice (unfermented) for the sacramental meal, due to their historic commitment to temperance (alcohol abstention),[76] and so perhaps in Ireland we could engage in an exercise of imagining using a fluid that would convey all that the Last Supper intended while avoiding the painful place of alcohol in the culture. For example, in a similar way that some Asian Christians have come to use rice instead of bread[77] in order to realize the symbolic valence of the Christian Eucharist in

75. Due to the fact that the pig is the corresponding sacrificial animal in that culture and the lamb would not convey the fullness of this theological metaphor. See Charles E. Farhadian, *Christian Worship Worldwide: Expanding Horizons, Deepening Practices* (Grand Rapids, MI: Eerdmans, 2007), p. 14.

76. See, Edward J. Foley, *From Age to Age: How Christians Have Celebrated the Eucharist* (Chicago, IL: Liturgy Training Publications, 1991), p. 281. This practice is controversial from an ecumenical point of view, because of the Anglican and Roman Catholic insistence that it be *fermented* grape juice that is distributed among the assembly.

77. But as Foley remarks, while such substitutions may be widespread due to the cost and/or the cultural inappropriateness of bread, they 'continue to be forbidden by the Roman Catholic Church.' Foley, *From Age to Age*, p. 342. See pp. 342–44 for a discussion of the history and issues involved.

their contexts, so in this country which has seen (and in some quarters prized) so much actual human blood poured out through (sacrificially-understood) violence, and over so many years, it might help us restore the Eucharist to non-sectarian meanings by celebrating it with alternative substances to wine, such as water or milk.

Or, the necessary difference might arise not in the substance itself but how it is used. It may not be a change in material but a nuance in practice that permits the restitution of orthodox theological meaning and association in Ireland. For example: distributing the cup one to another and not via the priest or Eucharistic Minister,[78] or introducing a new prayer to clarify the cup's meaning in this context. Another possibility might be to share plentiful amounts of bread (rather than tiny wafers—the 'economic' symbol), at least for a period, in order to separate the lingering and complicated fears and self-beliefs about famine. By changing the way the bread is seen, felt and understood, there might arise a change in how the cup is also perceived; and both might aid the development of an adequate understanding of the mystical/sacrificial offering of the Eucharist *as a meal*. There are many other possible changes in symbolic choice, use, interaction, language and catechetical/ritual explanation, many more than any single author could, or should, brainstorm about: it has to be a community conversation. But I have come to the conclusion that it has to happen, even if we end up only using or imagining using an alternative substance or practice for a short time; and especially even if we end up using bread and wine— we would at least be consuming bread *and* wine, which we are not doing at the moment.

Alternatively, addressing the issues raised in this chapter might require something more radical, and this brings me to a second scenario to prompt imagination of that which might produce knowledge of the conditions of possibility of people receiving the cup. Given the too-thin understanding of the difference between the bodies broken and blood spilt on the altar and the bodies broken and blood spilt on the streets in their recent history, perhaps Irish Catholics should fast from the Eucharist for a while. Fasts are the

---

78. Which suggestion, to be clear, would not be permissible under a strict interpretation of current Catholic regulations for the distribution of communion (Code of Canon Law, Book IV, Part I, Title III, Chapter I, Article I, Can. 910).

traditional spiritual discipline in Catholicism for purification, repentance and reorientation: an individual prays and fasts (often at a time when other members of one's community are fasting, such as Lent), knowing that the body, by abstaining from particular food and drink, and by God's grace, will do a work of re-adjustment that usually leads to either insight or a beneficial change of a habit, or both, particularly when combined with prayer, which is usual. And so, particularly due to the fact that the non-reception of the cup in Ireland is a meal-problem, fasting seems like a potentially insight-providing and or habit-changing exercise, particularly if it were performed across the whole country at the same time and accompanied in all places with a profound movement of prayer and self-examination of its effects. It would of course have to be framed in such a way that distinguished it from the mediaeval norms of non-communication of the laity (and it would be a good opportunity to educate about the problems of that pre-reformation period, the legacy of which still sometimes haunts Catholic understandings of Protestantism). But, through a national-fast-day (or other time period) the body that is the Church in Ireland would be mimicking the spiritual discipline of an individual body: fasting, praying, and examining the results of those disciplines until the desired effect of a change of heart, habit or understanding came about.

Given the complications around food in Ireland, especially those possibly related to the legacy of the Great Famine, it may be that temporarily and corporately 'fasting' could have a significant power. It could be empowering to take control of a distorted food use. For such a positive outcome, however, it would be important for everyone involved to shed false associations with fasting as a feature of cultural life. Christian fasting is not starving (as in hunger striking, or in anorexia) and fasting is not being deprived of food by another (as in a famine caused by administrative neglect); nor is fasting abstaining from something to which one is addicted (that is, ideally, recovery—and the substance cannot be readmitted, at least not in the same usage patterns). Fasting is voluntarily refraining from or minimizing intake of some substance for a limited period: it should not cause physical suffering and it should be temporary. What it should cause is a controlled and safe level of hunger (literal or figurative). It is out of this moderate, temporary hunger that insight has historically often arisen in spiritually-disciplined persons.[79] These points are crucial: without them, or misunderstood, fasting runs the risk of further distorting the eating habits and the body image of the body of Christ in the church in the Republic and Northern Ireland, rather than leading to a new awareness of what the conditions of possibility of its full and healthy consummation might be.

In actuality, having Roman Catholics abstain from celebrating the Eucharist is almost certainly not going happen. The Eucharist is at the very centre of Roman Catholic theology and observance, and so not to celebrate it would effectively mean that the church would not be being church. However, by *imagining* what it would mean to refrain from celebrating the Eucharist, either by mentally picturing it in meditation and discussion, or even by replacing one Sunday Mass with morning prayer (or something else) for one week, congregations might be led in an exercise that could lead to greater awareness of what is, and is not, at stake for them in their habitual Eucharistic practices (and specifically their habitual non-reception of the cup). The hope is that such an exercise, by interrupting contemporary 'norms' and reorienting the body through temporary withdrawal/dislocation, would lead to people viewing drinking from the cup differently when it was then introduced. The shock of absence or difference in habitual patterns of ritualization could perhaps ultimately allow people to participate fully in the meal that Jesus bequeathed to his followers by, first, drawing their attention to the problem and, second, creating a space within which it might be addressed. The fact that distribution of the cup among the congregation is the practice at which one must eventually arrive is beyond debate, as the conclusions of the report for the Year of the Eucharist make clear; the urgent question is what needs to be done to make that possible.

Ultimately, the conditions of possibility for Catholics to celebrate the Eucharist in a non-sectarian-implicated way in Ireland will involve constitutional change by the nation states concerned, because only that can supply at a meta-level what O'Malley called the 'moral context' strong enough to prevent sectarianism. At a minimum, and fundamentally, even though it may seem heretical to some, the Irish

79. For a historical and contemporary overview, see Anselm Grün, 'Fasting' in Erwin Fahlbusch, Geoffrey W. Bromiley, David B. Barrett and Lukas Vischer (eds), *The Encyclopedia of Christianity Vol. 2* (Grand Rapids, MI and Leiden: Eerdmans-Brill, 2000), pp. 295–96.

constitution needs to be rid of its specifically Catholic ethos; and the British constitution needs to be rid of anti-Catholic prejudice (such as forbidding the monarch to be married to a Catholic). By doing so, church and state in the UK, Northern Ireland and the Republic of Ireland will complete their separation. Until they do so, people can still point to significant legal tenets of civic society itself and say, 'See: sectarian prejudice is inscribed in the very foundations of this state, and this is why we need to keep our backs to the wall'. So long as there remain prejudicial tones or statutes on the state's books, the perceived threat of abuse, and the consequent production of mythologies of victimhood, is not 'irrational'.

Yet moral context is not solely a matter of nation-state changes, no matter how necessary these are; it is also, and fundamentally, the web of myriad daily measures by ordinary people that constitute moving beyond sectarianism — the sorts of thoughts that Chapter One laid bare. Moral context is created over a long time and through subtle measures. It is not created through sudden argument or impassioned pleas when a crisis hits: in such crisis times, leaders need to be able to appeal to norms that have been in circulation in ordinary time. For example, the 1995 divorce referendum makes an illuminating contrast with the hunger strikes. The sermons of Roman Catholic clergy in the Republic were widely reported to have had a powerful influence on the 'no' result in the 1995 divorce referendum. If this were true, why could the sermons of Roman Catholic clergy not have similarly affected the majority popular opinion of the hunger strikers? Because with the divorce referendum, the clergy were preaching into a moral context (a particular understanding of sexual ethics) that was entirely consistent with (and indeed largely created by) what people perceived the church to have represented in the past. With the hunger strikes, however, because of the hold sectarianism had on people's basic categories, and because of the church's implication in that worldview in the popular imagination, no matter how much any individual priest preached[80] that self-starvation was suicide and

---

80. The fact that liturgies in general and sermons in particular suddenly became the place where British and Irish media looked for comment and judgment is itself interesting. Sermons were preached in ordinary churches throughout the country, with extracts from those preached by the leaders of the churches (notably Cardinal O' Fiaich and Archbishop Robert Eames) often making the national newspapers. See O' Malley, *Biting at the Grave,*

thus a mortal sin, and that the IRA was an organization condemned by the Catholic church, people nonetheless largely supported the strikes, at least at an emotional level. Moreover, they expected the church to align with that emotional knowledge because it was, after all, a sort of performance of historic Irish/Roman Catholic claims in the face of British/Protestant oppression: a sectarian play, in which nationalism itself was the thing to which they owed their loyalty and they were still waiting for the church to fulfill its long-expected role as an agent of it. [81]

The Protestant/Ulster–British response to the hunger strikes likewise revealed how foundational mythologies of colonial victimhood and the resentment they cause obfuscates official teaching or stances. For example, on the day of Bobby Sands' death, the head of the Church of Ireland preached at the funeral of a Protestant policeman who had been shot dead, and as part of his sermon he said: 'Today we have the right to recognize the real agony of Northern Ireland. We have the right to ask the world to make a fair judgment: where does the real agony lie? Is it with those who use the threat of the choice of death, or with those who

pp. 178–84. That Catholic priests condemned violence and taught that hunger striking was suicide was noted; that 60 priests attended the funeral of the hunger striker Raymond McCreesh was also noted, and the tension between those pieces of information is in large part the subject of this book: what one does with one's body, liturgically, is far more complicated than what one pronounces when asked for a sentence of opinion on a topic.

81. Note that nationalism, in this instance, comes first. In the divorce referendum, it did not. In this case, nationalism leads and the people look to — but do not necessarily trust — the church to speak up for what they want it to say, and do not heed it for what it is saying. There is a long history of the church not doing so, and so people's first loyalties are, in this case, to the nationalist cause. 'the Church has historically balanced on a tightrope between indigenous nationalist groups and the British establishment. Although it had been persecuted, by the early nineteenth century, Catholicism in Ulster was remarkable in its loyalty to the British crown and constitution, having supported the Act of Union (between Ireland and Britain) in 1800 (Rafferty, 1994: p. 127).' Naturally conservative, it has often been reluctant to assume an anti-state position. As such, the institutional Church has always tended to distrust radical political movements, and has consistently opposed armed republicanism. The Catholic Church has continually denounced the modern IRA, banning membership in 1935 and making frequent references to the sinfulness of the organization (Gallagher and Worrall, 1982: p. 198).' Claire Mitchell, 'Catholicism in Northern Ireland and the Politics of Conflict', *IBIS Working Papers* No. 33 (2003), pp. 7–8.

have no choice?'[82] Although the question was about moral context
and the archbishop was, technically, arguing for the nature of
victimhood as the only truly Christian position, to preach this
message on this day, contrasting the plight of a policeman[83] with
that of a hunger striker and claiming only one as 'victim', was a far
cry from the official stance of his church at the time, which sought
to take a non-partisan, cross-community, peace-promoting position.
For there to have been a moral context capable of aiding this
situation would have required a generation of anti-sectarian
analysis, thought, action and ritual practice *prior to* 1981. You cannot
move beyond sectarianism overnight, as Liechty and Clegg make
clear, and the alternative of slow, difficult, letting-go and forging
has still not been done, despite the peace process, and so will not
be available when the next crisis hits.

How Roman Catholics in the Republic and Northern Ireland arrive
at congregational reception of the cup will be profoundly affected
by whether and how they create a moral context that is itself moving
beyond sectarianism in the coming years. But I would like to suggest
that distributing the cup could actually aid, influence and advance
the creation of such a context, not least because it would mean
Catholics entering into solidarity (of action if not interpretation)
with their Protestant siblings, doing something they long refrained
from because it was considered 'a Protestant practice'. Distributing
the cup throughout Catholic parishes in Ireland and Northern
Ireland will be a multi-faceted process, necessitating wide scale re-
education of both clergy and laity, as well as strong practical help
for the introduction of a new practice.

82. O'Malley, *Biting at the Grave*, p. 182.
83. It is important to note that 'police' in Northern Ireland at this time
were not police in the modern sense, but rather members of the Royal Ulster
Constabulary, a security force with an almost 100 percent Protestant membership, whose part as agents in the Troubles had been already repeatedly
called into question by 1981. Systematic collusion between the RUC and
loyalist paramilitaries has now been proven beyond doubt. Therefore, it
could be argued, to join the police-force was, in fact, also a very particular
'choice' in the conflict: see, for example, Jonathan Tonge, *Northern Ireland*
(Cambridge: Polity Press, 2006). Although, as Linda Moore and Mary O'Rawe
have pointed out, officers have rarely been held accountable for their actions: see, 'A New Beginning for Policing in Northern Ireland?' in Colin J.
Harvey, *Human Rights, Equality, and Democratic Renewal in Northern Ireland*
(Oxford: Hart, 2001), pp. 181–215.

Part of that re-education must, surely, be the possibility of discussing the associations people have accrued regarding the Eucharist. The issues relating to the famine, alcoholism/temperance and the Troubles would all come up, given time, safe talking space and a good host for such a conversation. But if they do not, it might well be worth prompting a discussion of them, if only to make sure that the popular theologies they have influenced are set in their proper context. This will be a very big, and not quick, conversation. What is at stake is the symbolic valence of flesh and blood, the meaning of food and drink, the relation of church and state, the legacy of colonial rule, the very creation of bodies, and the meaning of life. All of which are currently distorted by subtly sectarian interpretations. I could not possibly end by prescribing a singular theology that would help. Theologies in the aftermath of violence need to be worked out at a local level, through a substantial and inclusive process that includes identifying what the conditions of possibility of celebrating the Eucharist in each location are. What I can say is that current ritual practices are amiss by even the lowest standards of orthodox theology and, therefore, if the practices are interrogated and changed by the community, the theology will follow.

Chapter Six

MUSIC

Irish church music is in a pretty paltry state, but, as this chapter will suggest, this may signal health rather than decay. Among the churches that form the basis for reflection in this book, relatively few had a working organ and even fewer had a choir.[1] Those that had an organ often did not have an organist—indeed, only seven congregations had a musician playing the organ on the days that I visited. In Roman Catholic churches, there were remnants of volunteer 'folk Mass' instrumental ensembles dotted across the island, although only in one case, in Northern Ireland, did they provide the music for the whole service, most others supplementing them with a CD- or record-player to accompany the congregation in singing some of the hymns. This same method was used as the only source of musical leadership or accompaniment in several churches (particularly Church of Ireland ones) that used to have organ-led singing. It was referred to at coffee hour in one such Anglican parish in the South East, with an equal mixture of fondness and shame, as 'the karaoke'.

There was considerable variety in the songs offered in worship. Traditional Protestant and Anglican churches sang largely from the classic storehouse of nineteenth century hymnody, heavy on the Wesleys ('Love Divine, All Loves Excelling') and the rousing ('Take My Life and Let it Be', 'Praise My Soul, the King of Heaven'), with occasional touches of twentieth-century 'new' hymnody ('Be Still for the Presence of the Lord', 'God is Here! As We His People' and 'I am the Bread of Life'). Within this pattern, however, lay some significant patterns and distinctions: Presbyterians and Methodists, despite their different roots,[2] favoured themes of the cross ('When

---

1. Three out of 26 had a choir, all of them in the Republic.
2. The former in Calvinism (and who were classed as 'Dissenters'); the latter in Anglicanism.

I Survey the Wondrous Cross') and triumph/victory ('He Who Would Valiant Be'), while Anglicans favoured more Romantic texts and/or tunes; Church of Ireland parishes in all four provinces had in common the singing of the hymns, 'Dear Lord and Father of Mankind', 'O Love That Wilt Not Let Me Go', and 'Praise to the Holiest in the Height'.

In the Protestant contemporary worship venues, almost nothing of this repertoire was used, the only exceptions being 'Amazing Grace' and 'Come Thou Fount of Every Blessing', both led with guitars and a ¾ beat. Instead, contemporary Christian praise and worship music was used almost exclusively: 'Better is One Day' was sung in every contemporary service I attended, and another Matt Redman composition, 'The Father's Song', was also popular, as was Chris Tomlin's 'Glorious'. Congregants knew these songs by heart, and used no visual prompts to sing them. For other songs, many of which were performed with dozens of refrain repetitions to very simple tunes, the words were broadcast on the screen (with no author credits). These were, at times, theologically confused, although they were sung with great enthusiasm, suggesting the possibility that a member of the church had composed them for this community (e.g., 'Jesus you are Holy, holy, holy/Yes you alone are Holy, holy, Lord/Jesus, truly holy, Breathe on us now.').

The songs in the Catholic churches were mostly written by Americans, many of them originating in the St. Louis Jesuit and related post-Vatican II hymnody movements. Interestingly, they were far from confined to Catholic sources and Marty Haugen's work was used in a full 75 percent of the sample, as were Taizé chants (albeit a slim selection thereof). However, apart from Haugen and Taizé, the canon of repeated songs is relatively very small. Many of the Roman Catholic churches I visited had a hymn sheet: a laminated page with 20 or so hymns (words only) printed on each side, and used throughout the year (i.e., not seasonally changing). There was remarkable congruence among the hymns reprinted on such sheets between Roman Catholic churches across all four provinces, with 'I Watch The Sunrise' appearing on all but one, and being used in one third of the liturgies I attended. '*Fáilte Romhat*' was popular on the hymn sheets, too, as was 'Soul of My Saviour' and 'Sweet Heart of Jesus', although I never heard any of these actually sung. 'In Bread We Bring You, Lord' was on the hymn sheets in three churches, but I heard it led in only one of them. Nor did any of the Catholic churches I visited sing the parts of the Mass (*kyrie, gloria, sanctus*, etc); three did include a sung 'Alleluia' (most often O'Carroll and Walker's 'Celtic Alleluia' – but only the refrain, not the verses).[3] In one church in the west of Ireland, a CD of Liam Lawton's music for the Mass was played at various points (although not, perhaps, at the points he had intended, such as a *kyrie* as a reflection after communion), and while people seemed to enjoy it (slight smiles, relaxed body language), no one was actually singing along.

As for the quality of congregational singing, I think it is fair to say that singing in Protestant churches is generally not what the Wesleys would have wanted; these churches are, however, singing somewhat, which is more than can be said for most Catholic congregations. In the Protestant contemporary worship venues, the guitar or electric keyboard playing was competent and the people were singing along, albeit generally without much gusto. All of the older-style Protestant and Church of Ireland congregations were making an effort at singing, with most people at least looking like they were singing (opening hymn books or looking at service sheets, moving mouths, breathing as if singing) – even if you could not hear much sound actually coming out of them. This was in stark contrast to most Roman Catholic churches where the vast majority of congregants in the vast majority of parishes were not even moving their mouths when the time for singing came.

This is in Ireland, a country with a reputation for nearly every Protestant child learning to sing heartily in school and nearly every Catholic schoolchild learning to play at least something on the tin whistle; a country where traditional musics have passed through generations within varied communities for centuries; where tourists flood each year to revel in a culture in which there is singing and music-making in the pub most nights and busking on the street most days; where Orange Orders have no diminution in recruitment of young people to their drum and flute bands and which has seemingly produced more composers, singers and musicians *per capita* than any country in the world, certainly exerting a strong

3. Later in this chapter, the use of 'Irish' music in worship will be discussed. It is notable, then, that this setting of the Alleluia was the only music used in Roman Catholic Churches based on a peculiarly Irish melodic structure.

influence on Western popular music in the past 20 years.[4] Something seems awry for there to be so little music in church in such a music-saturated culture.

There is scant tradition of congregational song in Irish Roman Catholic churches and no sign of such a tradition emerging any time soon. The fact that Irish Roman Catholic congregations do not sing is taken as a 'given' in most quarters, and the cause for this situation is commonly believed to be the stunted development theory, that is: unlike Western countries, Ireland was under colonial rule during the periods of great hymnody, and therefore never developed either the habit or the repertoire for congregational hymn singing. Marie McCarthy's account is representative of the standard wisdom:

> The musical life of the peasantry developed in a subculture that was radically different to that of colonial Dublin and its network of strongholds throughout the island. Severe penal laws (1690–1795) forbade native people to practise their religion or to participate in any form of education. Communal acts of worship were not allowed and, as a consequence, liturgical music did not develop in a way similar to other countries, leaving Ireland with no vernacular hymnology.[5]

What is perhaps of greatest interest, then, is not that Catholic congregations are not singing (because they never have) but that congregational song is so much weaker in Protestant and Anglican congregations than it has historically been. To a certain extent, this diminishing of congregational singing in Northern Irish and Irish churches is probably due to the same two factors that have denuded congregational singing in their sister-churches in Britain and North America. The first factor is simply lower attendance rates. Churches

---

4. Or at least claimed a substantial proportion of the market share: U2 has won more Grammy's than any other group, ever, and sales of recordings by artists such as Van Morrison and Enya are among the highest of all performers, ever. However, other bands, from The Chieftains through The Cranberries and Sinéad O'Conor to The Frames, are also widely credited with having exerted a strong influence on contemporary popular music.

5. Marie McCarthy, *Passing It On: The Transmission of Music in Irish Culture* (Cork: Cork University Press, 1999), p. 36. This theory has been built upon and extended by those looking at what happened when Irish Catholics emigrated; most famously including in the American context, Thomas Day, *Why Catholics Can't Sing: The Culture of Catholicism and the Triumph of Bad Taste* (New York: Crossroad, 1990).

that were built to house hundreds in densely-packed pews often now host only dozens. One of the Presbyterian churches I attended in Belfast, which the pastor claimed was fairly typical of that denomination's congregations in Northern Ireland, had about 300 families as members and attendance of up to 90 on a Sunday morning. That maximum of 90 people spread themselves out through the whole church building. Consequently, they just didn't have the numbers, or the proximity to other worshippers,[6] to make the sort of sound that would have been made in the days when the church had over 200 people at worship on a Sunday morning.

The second factor is the impact of the popular music industry, including particularly the highly profitable Contemporary Christian and Country-Christian music markets. One of the churches I visited in Northern Ireland posted a weekly worship song on its website. I clicked on the link expecting a hymn, probably a contemporary praise and worship song, because the style of Sunday morning worship at this church led me to expect something that a family might sing at home or that an individual might hum through the working week. Instead, the link took me to a snippet of a famous performer on You-Tube. Over a couple of years returning to check this link, it was nearly always Faith Hill's major concert performances that were selected.[7] The weekly worship song was something to listen to, to marvel at, and not something that one would sing out loud oneself. It has been widely-noted that Christian congregations across denominations are increasingly using market-driven spiritual songs which are made for consumption and not communal performance as an act of worship.[8] It represents a significant departure from Protestant traditions of singing in church because it results in congregational listening (listening to

6. John Bell states that people do not sing if they are farther than 3 ft away from another singer in the congregation. See, John Bell, *The Singing Thing, Too* (Glasgow: Wild Goose, 2007), p. 22.

7. Although I couldn't help but wonder how the Presbyterian elders felt about delivering their membership into the hands of those who advertise alongside the Faith Hill clip: on a screen which occupies almost as large a space as the music video screen, one encounters the greeting cards company whose cartoon buxom blonde woman is repeatedly starting an upper-body strip-tease under the caption: 'HAVE I GOT A SURPRISE FOR YOU?!'

8. See, for example, Bryan Gerlach, 'The Role of Music in Worship: An Evaluation of Two Twentieth Century Developments' in *Logia: A Journal of Lutheran Theology* Vol. XIV no. 3 (2005), pp. 52–58.

the experts) not congregational singing (lifting one's voice in praise to God).[9]

However, in addition to these two factors, it is necessary to ask: is there anything peculiarly Irish/Northern Irish at play here? Certainly regarding the second issue mentioned above, Britain and North America have seen a reduction in singing in the general culture, and not just in churches, as a result of music consumption patterns in recent years.[10] Yet in the Republic and Northern Ireland, by contrast, there does not seem to have been an associated reduction in singing in other public venues. Singing at football matches, in pubs, and in schools (the three main places where singing among the general public regularly takes place), has not diminished in anything like the ways that singing in church has in the past generation. One might ask, then, whether there is something else at play, a reluctance, perhaps, to sing when singing *in church* or the songs that are sung *in church* have come to represent something about which one is no longer at all certain. To be clear, it is not that Protestants have stopped singing, it is that they no longer sing lustily. The volume is low. The feeling is lukewarm. It is not the loud, committed, transformational performance of only two decades ago. What is going on seems to be more an ambivalence about singing than a 'refusal' or any other such thought-through position.

If memory of the penal laws and their immediate aftermath condition theories about lack of liturgical music in Catholic churches, they may also condition sensibilities about what was being sung by those protected by the same laws: the Anglicans.[11] If silenced Catholics were scuttling to Mass rocks to celebrate the liturgy under

9. A point made in various studies. For a recent account see, Patrick Evans, 'Musical Formation in Seminary Worship Chapel' in Siobhán Garrigan and Todd Johnson (eds), *Common Worship in Theological Education* (Eugene, OR: Wipf and Stock, 2009), pp. 62–80.

10. In 2007, the UK government announced a £10m scheme to combat the decline in singing in the general population by creating a '21st Century Songbook' for schools. (See, Steven Manning, 'Fine Tuning' in *Times Educational Supplement Magazine*, 2 February 2007, p. 42). Members of the public were invited to submit suggestions and Howard Goodall was appointed to chair the compilation. Controversy arose when Tom Robinson's 1976 anthem '(Sing if You're) Glad to Be Gay' made it into the top 30, but its inclusion was defended by the then Secretary of State for Education, Alan Johnson.

11. Note, not all 'Protestants': Dissenters as well as Roman Catholics were restricted by some aspects of the penal laws, such as non-state recognition for Presbyterian marriages.

penalty of death, members of the Established Church were free to walk or drive (in a trap) to church and sing out to their hearts' content. That, too, has its legacies, and not just in the fact that there remains a difference in the canon of hymns in Anglican and Presbyterian hymnbooks (although there is also overlap). The hymns of that era are part of what is now claimed to compose the 'cultural heritage' of all Protestants (meaning Anglican, Presbyterian, Methodist, Congregationalist and other Christian churches) and these hymns comprise a significant part of the repertoire of the music played during Orange Marches in the North each year.[12] The *sound* of them speaks at once of both an era of safety (and, for some, supremacism) and of a lost time; a time which, by being sonically remembered, points to the community's current sense of vulnerability. The eschatological overtones of many of these hymns—longing as they do for a new Jerusalem—also cannot help but echo (to the observer at least) desire for restoration to ownership, control, or, at a minimum, uncomplicated dwelling in one's land—themes to which we will return shortly.

While the level of congregational singing in Roman Catholic churches might not have seemed remarkable, given its lack of a tradition, it does nevertheless also indicate a certain ambivalence. There may have been no tradition of congregational song in Roman Catholic churches in Ireland, but there are many other aspects of cultural life wherein the things once stunted in development due to penal measures have gone on to thrive in the modern era, education being a particularly compelling case in point. If Ireland could have 'pulled itself up by its bootstraps' in so many other arenas (arts, culture, politics, technology, industry, government, etc.), it seems strange that it should be routinely excused from having done so in the area of liturgical music. When one additionally considers the importance of singing in the culture at large, in both contemporary and historic cultural expressions, its lack of development in church life becomes a rather compelling conundrum. When one then additionally considers the sheer volume of efforts to promote congregational song in Ireland since the disestablishment of the Church of Ireland, it becomes unconvincing to blame its lack solely on the aftermath of penal laws.

12. While including hymn tunes, the repertoire is also far, far broader. See, Gary Hastings, *With Fife and Drum: Music, Memories and Customs of an Irish Tradition* (Belfast: Blackstaff, 2003).

Concerted efforts were in fact made at various points since the repeal of the penal laws to develop Irish Roman Catholic liturgical music in general and congregational song in particular. The Cecilian Society worked from the 1870s onwards to create music capable of enacting Cardinal Cullen's ambitious devotional reforms. From the 1880s onwards, the Roman Catholic Church encouraged a great range of competitions in an attempt to increase both the musical literacy of their flock and the profile of music in the liturgy. The Gregorian Chant movement had support from the Irish Church at the highest level and produced texts in a form designed for ease of use in churches from late-nineteenth century onwards, and avidly so after *Moto proprio* (1903). And if all this can be said to be for the benefit of the song of choirs and not of congregations, then let us not forget that the early years of the twentieth century also saw the concerted promotion of authorship or adoption by Irish clergy of devotional hymns in the now-dominant vernacular (English), with those English-language hymns associated with Marian processions and devotions to the Sacred Heart proving particularly popular. There were also smaller, but nonetheless deliberate attempts to write hymns in the Irish language (the pre-famine vernacular of many) and to draw on the idioms of Irish song, such as the collections of hymns *Dia Linn Lá Gus Oídhche* (1917) and *Raint Amhrán* (1917).[13] As a list of attempted liturgical developments, this is all seemingly impressive and the question of why it should have failed to produce a mainstream of singing Catholic congregations appears perplexing.[14]

But upon closer inspection, the list reveals the prevalence of certain constituencies of power (and the suppression of other

13. The impetus for which must be due to the successful revival of the Irish language thanks to the efforts of the Gaelic League (established in 1892). Interestingly, the League was set up as a non-sectarian and non-partisan organization, but in 1915 Douglas Hyde (its founder and president since its foundation) resigned his presidency because he could no longer prevent it from being a Nationalist (Republican) organization. (The Rising happened the following Easter).

14. It is also remarkable that Edward Martyn's grand project for Celtic Church arts, which made Irish churches world-leaders in certain liturgical arts, such as the use of contemporary stained glass, should have stopped short of traditional music (especially as he also endowed the Palestrina choir to sing at Sunday morning Mass at the Pro-Cathedral in Dublin). See Thomas MacGreevy, 'An Irish Catholic Eccentric' in *The Father Matthew Record* (Dublin, April, 1942), p. 2.

constituencies) that, as we will see, were using liturgical music to advance their interests: a higher class; an all-male clergy; an overly clericalized ministry; and a homogenizing nationalist ideology may all be counted amongst these. The initiatives recounted in the paragraph above represent a tight weave of class, gender, ethnic, clericalist, nationalist, and denominational strands. Furthermore, it was never the case that the Irish Catholic Church promoted traditional music for use in liturgy (even though so many of its practitioners were Catholic): the Catholic clergy, being largely of higher-class than the majority of the population, favoured European art-music and other middle-class aesthetic forms.[15] Thus, for example, when it came to the revival of chant in the Mass, it was its Gregorian and not its Irish forms (from the monastic era) that were 'rediscovered'.

In its first phase of development, the art-music phase, the movement to create Irish Church music sought to impose a notion of 'proper' church music whose properness resided in its European-ness. 'Europe' accorded Catholic liturgy and its music several things in one stroke: social status through higher class pursuits and ambitions (art-music, of which there was minimal history in Ireland); authority by closeness to the Rome (and thus apparent confirmation of the power of the clergy); and, crucially, a by-passing of any and all Anglo-influences, thus strengthening the notion of Ireland in its Catholic mode as a pure, uncontaminated, moral jewel which, while half the world was answering to Empire (Britain), was itself alone aligned in spirit and in practice to Catholic Europe and the city at its heart, Rome. Through this first phase, the church could show by its promotion of particular music that when it came to England it was 'beyond all that'. Moreover, through its second phase, its Irish-idiom phase, it could create the impression that it had always been thus, promoting the idea that Ireland's roots had ever been in a pure, unadulteratedly Catholic community.

Writing about the first phase, the highly influential post-famine period when 'the terms "Irish" and "Catholic" became synonymous in the minds of many nationalists',[16] Harry White argues that,

15. See, for example, the essays in Gerard Gillen and Harry White (eds), *Irish Musical Studies 2: Music and the Church* (Dublin: Irish Academic Press, 1993); particularly Nóirín Ní Riain, 'The Nature and Classification of Traditional Religious Songs in Irish' (pp. 190–253).

16. Harry White, *The Keeper's Recital: Music and Cultural History in Ireland, 1770–1970* (Cork: Cork University Press, 1998), p. 74.

The Synod of Thurles, which effectively comprised Cullen's fist step toward the imposition of a regularized clerical and liturgical practice upon the church in Ireland, included two decrees on music which thereafter signified the Irish hierarchy's commitment to the Roman ideal of a Latinised sacred music. The question of an indigenous mode of liturgical expression was not to be seriously countenanced. Instead, these decrees ratified the means by which church music in Ireland would develop as an expression of aesthetic ideals formulated elsewhere.[17]

If it seems that such a move was born of a suspicion about Irish language and other proletarian norms, then it becomes important to consider what happened in the second phase. Even when aesthetic ideals which were formulated at home began to be countenanced for liturgical expression, they were still set in the service of the church's overarching political commitments. Analysing the effectiveness of attempts to create Irish language hymnody in the early twentieth century, McCarthy comments that: 'The provision of hymns in the Irish language in these decades was aimed at wedding Catholicism and nationalism and, in the process, developing homogenous Irish characteristics in the next generation.'[18] The dominant concern then, even as it included class and clerical power and gender, was to create and promote as normative a notion of Irish life that was not just religious, not just Catholic, but also, and very specifically, not-English and not-Protestant.[19]

17. White, *The Keeper's Recital*, p. 75.
18. McCarthy, *Passing It On*, p. 89.
19. The history of the Gaelic League in this period is salient. Mary Stakelum argues that the initial ideals of many Leaguers to spread and enhance the performance of music all over Ireland were whittled away as the League became increasingly focused on a single nationalist agenda: '[George] O'Neill's plea to "make the average Irish man a better musician" was not taken up by the new government [i.e. the Irish Free State], which appeared to be more intent on making the Irish man a better nationalist. Eoin MacNeill, a founding member of the Gaelic League [and the man who took over the presidency after Hyde], strengthened this resolve when he asserted that, "the chief function of Irish educational policy is to conserve and develop Irish nationality."' Thus, learning music in schools became a medium for learning the Irish language. Mary Stakelum, 'A Song to Sweeten Ireland's Wrong: Music Education and the Celtic Revival', in Betsey Taylor FitzSimon and James H. Murphy (eds), *The Irish Revival Reappraised* (Dublin: Four Courts Press, 2004), pp. 71–82; 81.

The people, however, never really got behind Irish-idiom liturgical music. When ethnomusicologists of religion travel the world, such as I-to Loh in Asia or Mary Oyer in Africa,[20] they find indigenous music played in churches and they record hymns and songs of praise played in the local musical idioms.[21] Such scholars, were they to come to Ireland, would have to travel far and listen hard to find anything comparable in Irish congregations, even though Christianity arrived there hundreds of years before reaching other colonized places and has had a long period, therefore, to develop. Why is Irish music not heard in Irish churches? When scholars of Christian mission praise Celtic Christianity for the ways it integrated local pre-Christian practices (i.e., practices that last until this day, such as the iconography of the high crosses, the blessing of healing wells or the rituals in graveyards), they neglect to remark that Irish music is rarely, if ever, found inside Irish churches.

It is important to note that while there have been moves by individual Irish composers in recent times to write liturgical music that uses traditional Irish musical and linguistic forms and idioms,[22] there has not been a widespread church-sponsored move to create a corpus of such work (that is, there has been no movement regarding traditional music like the ones named above for European art-music). However, this lack of 'native' music in Irish churches may not be due solely to the lack of efforts by the clergy to introduce it; it may have more to do with negative attitudes about Irish music in the general population, and it is this that I now want to examine.

Graham Linehan, comedy writer and creator of the hugely successful television shows *Father Ted* and *The IT Crowd* was recently interviewed on North American radio. Asked about criticism levied at some of his shows for stereotyping, he said that

20. For a good account of the work of these two scholars, and their impact on church life, see C. Michael Hawn, *Gather into One: Praying and Singing Globally* (Grand Rapids, MI: Eerdmans, 2002).

21. See, for example, I-to Loh, *Sound the Bamboo,* and Mary Oyer's extraordinary contributions to the Mennonite *Hymnal: A Worship Book* (Elgin, IL: Brethren Press, 1992).

22. Notably Séan Ó Ríada, Nóirín Ní Riain and Liam Lawton, although they each differ from one another in very significant ways, such that it does not work to speak of them as a group of 'Irish Liturgical Music Composers', even as each can individually warrant that description.

in *Father Ted* he was, in fact, very careful to avoid Irish stereotypes and, as his only illustration of this, he talked about how 'we really kept the amount of Irish traditional music down to a minimum, because I hate Irish traditional music: to me it's the sound of madness.' By doing so, he argued, the writers made sure the series 'didn't descend into Paddywhackery.'[23]

'Irish traditional music' has 'sounded' a house being built on the sands of sectarianism, because it has been repeatedly co-opted as the sound of a peculiar constellation of post-colonial desire and religious-political nationalism. As a result of this, as Harry White remarks, 'The metaphorical status of Irish music almost always eclipses the condition of the music itself. This metaphorical status … imposes on the music itself, and above all on the corpus of ethnic melody, an irreducibly nationalist aesthetic.'[24] Traditional music has thus been claimed as the language that was not lost, the literature that escaped appropriation by the Ascendancy, the pure remnant of true and real Irishness which, like the DNA of Irish identity itself, is the thing that links the Irish to their pre-Anglo, pre-Protestant ancestors. It has been said to resonate with the uncontaminated spirituality and benevolent wildness of the Celt, to communicate the intelligence and civilization of the Gael, and, like a latterday Babel, to enable the communication of authentic Irishness to any who would care to look, or listen, no matter who they are or where they are from.[25] Madness indeed.

From the beginning of the nineteenth century onwards, in tandem with increasingly polarized conceptions of national identity, music in Ireland functioned as shorthand for the two main camps of Nationalism and Unionism, such that White describes it as operating

---

23. Interview with Graham Linehan, 'The Sound of Young America', *National Public Radio* (3 November 2008, found at podcast time point: 19: 17: 00).

24. Harry White and Michael Murphy (eds), *Musical Constructions of Nationalism: Essays on the History and Ideology of European Musical Culture, 1800–1940* (Cork: Cork University Press, 2001), p. 258.

25. See, for example, McCarthy: 'In the various phases of nationalism from the late eighteenth to the mid-twentieth century, Ireland's musical heritage was drawn upon consistently as a means of revitalizing and legitimizing an authentic, Gaelic culture. In the process, myths and images about the origins and development of music were reinvented, and they became part of the cultural canon that was transmitted to succeeding generations.' *Passing It On,* p. 29.

as 'an intelligencer of cultural separatism,'[26] which resulted from 'the ethnic-colonial division of musical culture.'[27] Consequently, as the campaign for independence evolved, music (as a cultural symbol) became ever more implicated in the argument. It is no coincidence that the first major collection and transcription of traditional Irish tunes (a previously essentially oral phenomenon) was made in Chicago (by its police chief), nor that it was first printed in 1913, nor that it became one of the key totems of Irish identity in the twentieth century: it was hyper-reality[28] before its time, but in the service of nation-state assertion rather than economic development. As Philip Bohlman puts it in his survey of music's place in the creation of European nationalism:

> O'Neill's collections appeared — and were exported to Ireland — during the period of Ireland's greatest and eventually successful struggle for independence from the British Empire. As the Irish nation itself took leave of the empire that had encumbered its ethno-nationalism, it could and did embrace Francis O'Neill's volumes of Irish music, which today are one of Ireland's national icons.[29]

There have been various points at which hope emerged for the development of an art-music tradition in Ireland, especially through broader cultural commerce with Europe, 'but so vulnerable was this tradition to the claims and counterclaims of nationalism and colonialism, respectively, that it collapsed inwards under the weight of ideological pressures from both sides.'[30] Thus the influential contemporary composer and performer Mícheál O Súilleabháin can report that from the foundation of the Irish Free State until very late in the twentieth century, 'composers in Ireland have had to

26. White, *Musical Constructions*, p. 264.
27. White, *Musical Constructions*, p. 268.
28. References to hyper-reality are to the stream of continental philosophy typified in the work of Jean Baudrillard (and not to the artistic technique). The concept basically points to the phenomenon whereby people in a media-driven world only become conscious of themselves when their identity affects are commodified and represented to them, usually by a mechanism related to (capitalist) markets. See, for example, Jean Baudrillard, 'Simulcra and Simulations', in Mark Poster (ed.), *Selected Writings* (Stanford, CA: Stanford University Press, 1988).
29. Philip Bohlman, *The Music of European Nationalism: Cultural Identity and Modern History* (Oxford: ABC–CLIO, 2004), p. 62.
30. White, *Musical Constructions*, p. 259.

cope with the belief that European art-music produced in Ireland should either be based on Irish folk tunes or else should involve a setting of an Irish language text. Fruitless efforts were made to force a wedding between Irish language and the European art-music tradition in the interest of "de-anglicanisation".'[31] The production of hymnody in this period seems to have suffered a similar fate, and for similar reasons.

Furthermore, 'Irish traditional music' when placed alongside its 'European art-music' counterpart also became increasingly associated with sectarian frameworks of Irish Nationalism and British Colonial Rule ('the Crown') respectively, with the reductive result that for much of the twentieth century, Irish traditional music became emblematic of an Irishness that was essentially Catholic and intrinsically nationalist. *Comhaltas Ceoltóirí Éireann*, the national body for Irish music, did nothing to help counter this when it cancelled the annual *fleadh cheoil*[32] in 1971 in protest at the introduction of internment in Northern Ireland. Despite its membership having included Protestants since its foundation in 1951, and despite its rhetorical insistence that it was a cultural organization with no partisanship regarding religion or politics, they stated that by 'postponing' the fleadh, 'We wish to demonstrate our solidarity with our fellow Irishmen in the North at this decisive hour ... Traditional music, song and dance are marks of nationhood and we view them in this context.'[33] Thus, Irish churches exist in (and have helped to create) a culture in which Irish traditional music is seen as the music of the (Catholic) people, and European art music is seen as the music of the (Protestant) governing body, except where it is Latinized sacred music or a setting of Irish language texts and then (with the support of the clerical hierarchy) it might be possible to see it as Catholic; but, in truth, it has never been widely accepted as such by the laity.

This mapping of native music as Catholic is not just a Catholic perspective. The loyalist paramilitary group who planted a bomb in the Newtownards bar where a traditional music session was in

31. Mícheál Ó Súilleabháin, 'Irish Music Defined', *The Crane Bag* 5.2 (1981), p. 85.
32. A large gathering of musicians for competition (to win the prize of 'All-Ireland' Champion in various categories), talks and musical sessions.
33. Fintan Vallely, *Tuned Out: Traditional Music and Identity in Northern Ireland* (Cork: Cork University Press, 2008), p. 88.

progress in 1993 followed it up with a decree that anyone playing Irish traditional music was a legitimate paramilitary target, such music being seen not merely as Catholic but as 'Fenian' (Republican). Although they withdrew the threat after realizing that the majority of musicians in that bar that night were Protestant and after receiving education from loyalist politicians about the fact that Protestants played — and owned — this music too, their initial perception is a commonplace one across the whole island. A Protestant fiddler is seen as an anomaly by Irish Protestants, just as she or he is by Irish Catholics. This perspective is relatively new. Up until the 1970s, Protestant players of traditional music, while never constituting anything approaching a majority of practitioners, were nevertheless plentiful at home and in the diaspora as well. So, while it is true that nationalism corralled traditional music for its purposes up through the nineteenth century and particularly around the time of the foundation of the State, it is a mistake to think that nationalism's strongest claims on music rests there.[34] In the past generation, the division has not only grown, but grown along ever more bitterly sectarian lines.

Irish traditional music is enormously varied and the presentation of it as a predominantly Catholic concern is itself a product of colonial myth making, part of what David Lloyd terms 'the organizing concerns of official history.'[35] Irish traditional music is in fact as thorough a hybrid as almost every other feature of Irish life. For example, because of the co-mingling of cultural life over several centuries, the exact same 'traditional' tune appears as an Orange march, a Scottish ballad and a traditional Irish dance tune.[36] Furthermore, *sean-nos* songs in English are often older than those in Irish, and Lambeg drums are played by Catholics as well as Orangemen. Each of these myth-debunking facts reflects the reality of commerce between parties that has composed life on the island

34. 'It is important to remember that the apparently strict separation between the cultural traditions in Ireland today cannot be projected backwards in time. ... [Before the twentieth century,] [d]ance music belonged to everyone and would not have been seen as "Irish" in any political or culturally definitive sense within the country.' Hastings, *With Fife and Drum*, p. 55.

35. David Lloyd, *Ireland after History* (Notre Dame, IN: University of Notre Dame Press, 1999), p. 37.

36. Vallely, *Tuned Out*, pp. 98–99.

for centuries, and each confounds the artifice of music and song as the birthright of one or other culture.[37]

Indeed, Irish traditional music embodies such a diversity of histories and performance practices that little can be said of it as a genre *in toto*. A reasonable summary seems to be:

> It is best understood as a broad-based system which accommodates a complex process of musical convergence, coalescence and innovation over time. It involves different types of singing, dancing and instrumental music developed by Irish people at home and abroad over the course of several centuries. [It is] essentially oral in character, and is transmitted from one generation to the next through performance ... Within the bounds of the established tradition, experienced performers use improvisation in their interpretation of tunes, songs and dances.

But that is about it: to say any more requires significant nuancing, and while Seán Ó Ríada is to be lauded for both his attempts to gain for Irish traditional music the respect it deserves and his art-music arrangements of the Irish idiom, his influential preaching of the music as part of '*An Naisiún Gaelach*' belies a perspective on the idiom fuelled more by nationalist rhetoric than fact.[38] Irish music was the music of the lower classes, for sure, and the lower classes formed the great majority of the people; however, they included Protestants and Travelers and many others who were not normatively Irish and Catholic (and the impetus for its revival/preservation in the nineteenth century had come largely from Protestants). For reasons like these, White can conclude that: 'In Ireland, it is music which tends to stimulate political thought, rather than the other way around ... The association between nationalism and music is so strong that it can become an obstructive *donné* in almost any consideration of the history and development of musical thought.'[39] The association between nationalism and music is so

37. 'What is at stake in the current claims for the purity of tradition is, as in earlier centuries, an insistence on national integrity in the face of denationalizing influences.' Leith Davis, *Music, Postcolonialism, and Gender: The Construction of Irish National Identity, 1724–1874* (Notre Dame, IN: University of Notre Dame Press, 2006), p. 224.

38. His biographer reports that, 'Ruth [his wife] had difficulty restraining him in 1969 when the Northern troubles broke out in earnest, as he very much wanted to take his gun and fight for his own Gaelic nation on the barricades of Belfast.' Tomás Ó Canainn, *Sean Ó Ríada: His Life and Work* (Cork: The Collins Press, 2003).

39. White, *Musical Constructions*, p. 258.

strong in Ireland and Northern Ireland that it is also, evidently, an obstructive donné in any attempt to improve the music of worship in the various churches on this island.

Perhaps part of the reason for 'traditional' music being absent from liturgy and 'hated' by many of Ireland's most celebrated contemporary artists and insightful cultural critics (and Linehan undoubtedly is both) is that it subtly conveys the desperate and pathetic struggle to form identity in the face of multiple distortions: first, the colonial one (including the outlawing of music in successive and sometimes lengthy periods of violent imposition of repressive penal law); next, the religious ones (attempts to enforce homogenous 'family' life-worlds created by and, in turn, contributing to essentially nationalist ideologies); and finally, the supposedly post-colonial ones (a period in which Irish music becomes the cultural product *par excellence* by which the Irish sell themselves to others in order to buy themselves back in a form they can finally value: a hyper-realist mash of self-commodification, all in the hope of finally possessing a sense of identity and belonging, albeit in global capitalism). At each stage we are dealing with a clash of modernities.

For many Irish people, Irish dance music was the sound of resistance to the notion of modernity itself and, given the poverty (and loss through emigration) from which so many suffered, from the time of the famine up until the early 1990s, modernity was desperately wanted. It therefore must be highlighted that, contrary to popular media representation, for much of the past century traditional music has been a minority interest among most Irish people (and it must correspondingly be noted, also contrary to current popular perception of it as a minority interest, that an extremely high proportion of the Ulster Protestant population play Orange music).[40] Only with the 'folk music' revival of the late 1950s did Irish traditional music regain any sort of popular appeal, and even then it was still very small relative to the interests of the population as a whole. Irish traditional music has, thus, become the

40. Hastings estimates that 'the number of musicians participating throughout Ulster at any Twelfth day could be as high as 12,000' which, as he says, 'is more musicians than in most other musical traditions in the British Isles perhaps, and certainly in Ireland.' *With Fife and Drum*, p. 10. And he comments: 'That the tradition is so strong is a sign of the cultural and political significance of what is going on in Northern Ireland-this is not just music' (p. 11).

metaphor not only for 'nationalism' but also, on the flipside, for Irish identity never actually being given the breathing space it needed to become; a metaphor of frustrated nationalism, if you like. It sounds both the imposition and the preservation of supposed identity claims in each of these different phases, and it also sounds the resultant paralysis. It is the constant symbol across each thwarted attempt at identity-definition, proving the point, for the Irish case at least, that 'music ... is not an act of self-expression but of externally imposed identity.'[41] This struggle is still going on and Irish music still supposedly says something about culture, about what it 'means' to be Irish.

It is salient to remark, however, that while so many people in post-war Ireland rejected Irish traditional music and opted for British and North American rock and pop instead, others listening to Irish rock and pop music discern an unmistakably 'Irish' sound, a sound which, to the listener's ear, has a great deal in common with Irish traditional music. Thus U2 claim that traditional music had little influence on them while people throughout the world can be heard claiming that U2 sound distinctively Irish. Perhaps it is the way Bono sounds his 'r's, or perhaps it is the band's passion, or some 'lilt' in the music itself, or else something technical, like specific chord progressions—no one seems to know; what is asserted is simply that it *feels* Irish. Irish traditional music is, then, it would seem, not optional as the sound of the culture, even when it is being most refused; what is optional is how it is interpreted. It might 'sound' Irish, even in its most rocked-out traces, but does that have to mean it is Catholic/Fenian or Protestant/Unionist?

Now, my father playing old tunes on his accordion in a cousin's kitchen in Connemara on a Saturday night while people dance or listen or sing, and then playing similar tunes to accompany the congregation's prayer at Mass on Sunday morning, seems just about as far removed from a sectarian event as you can possibly imagine. The tunes, the socializing that is the context for them, the stories they tell and the emotions they tend are undertaken as both self-expression and communal ministry. But when the music of the kitchens of the *gaeltacht* is claimed as a whole people's unique, peculiar, authentic and oppressed heritage, then, like language, it becomes a political football. The politics then infects its performance

41. Richard Leppert, *Music and Image* (Cambridge: Cambridge University Press, 1988), p. 159.

practices at almost every level (including, in fact, the domestic), but especially in church.

As with the raising of flags in schools in Chapter One, when we interrogate the absence of Irish music in church, we are returned to the question of the line between honouring cultural heritage and contributing to sectarian expression, because while that honouring is vital, so is a certain hermeneutic of suspicion about every claim that something is or is not part of one's (whose?) cultural heritage. This is because a lot of what constitutes 'cultural heritage'-speak in post-GFA Ireland is just sectarianism in a new guise, an instrument for ossifying mechanisms of division and separation. As Gary Hasting comments of music in particular, 'There are certainly unique facets of culture attached to Protestant unionism in Ulster, but these are the result of intermingling and development and growth, and did not fall like grace from the saddlebags of King William's horse.'[42] It is the long-practiced association (in rhetoric and then in performance practice) between the kitchen and the horse that has produced the madness in the sound. It is also, as we will now note, a madness nursed by the apparatus of empire.

When we assume that Ireland is a marvelously musical culture, and when ethnomusicologists are flummoxed by the absence of music in churches given the saturation of music in the culture, we are forgetting to ask: is it, in fact, an especially musical culture? And, if so, why? Once challenged, the assumptions yield unexpected results. Music is hardly ever taught in elementary schools, and instrumental music is rarely taught in high schools;[43] traditional music is not in fact being passed on except in all but the most minoritized communities; and among educational researchers and musical advocates alike, the earnest campaigns of the 1970s to promote widespread engagement with music have faded into a bitter resignation—the result of multiple political failures and emphatic lack of financial or moral support for such projects at either state or local level. As McCarthy remarks:

> A deeper look at the status of music in the culture at large exposes
> the weak economic base that has been associated with musical

42. Hastings, *With Fife and Drum*, p. 78.
43. 'Political and economic conditions in Ireland did not support the development of instrumental music in formal education, and this absence marks a major difference between music education in Ireland and other Western countries to this day.' McCarthy, *Passing It On*, p. 91.

development over the past two centuries ... Consider the legacy of music education—the absence of music specialists in primary and some secondary schools, the lack of instruments and instrumental music in primary schools, the dearth of home-produced teaching materials and media, the amount of bonuses granted to secondary schools for establishing and maintaining ensembles, and the minimal government resources devoted to school music supervision and the professional development of music educators.[44]

Moreover, music is only Ireland's 'most important cultural medium' to those on the outside looking in, probably buying (or marketing) Irish products.[45] Ireland's most important cultural medium for those living on the island, the one which launched the Republic and has occupied a dominant role in both the construction of Irish and Northern Irish ideologies ever since, as well as their critiques, is literature.[46]

Why, then, is Irish music perceived by outsiders as the pride of its people? Because, it would seem, it was the only thing that Irish people were praised for by their colonizers. Giraldus Cambrensis was the first to do so, in his report to King John of England around 1187: amid his otherwise scathing description of the natives and his resultant and multiple justifications for English occupation, he says that, 'It is only in the case of musical instruments that I find any commendable diligence in the people. They seem to me to be incomparably more skilled than any other people that I have seen.'[47]

44. McCarthy, *Passing It On*, p. 181.

45. Leith Davis argues in *Music, Postcolonialism and Gender* that nowadays, 'the operative other against which the Irish self is defined is not British colonial authority dominating a British market but the global market for culture' (p. 223) and thus Irish music offers its non-Irish players and consumers 'a connection to a rooted community' (p. 225). 'For members of the "global Irish community", as for those musicians who choose to play Irish music, the appeal of Irish music is its offer of a rooted identity in a rootless world.' (p. 225) What is at stake is still, in a sense, authenticity (and a yearning for pre-modern notions of such). See Leith Davis, *Music, Postcolonialism, and Gender: The Construction of Irish National Identity, 1724–1874* (Notre Dame, IN: Notre Dame Press, 2006).

46. This is the central argument of Harry White, *The Keeper's Recital: Music and Cultural History in Ireland, 1770–1970* (Cork: Cork University Press, 1998).

47. Giraldus Cambrensis, *Topographia Hiberniae* (c.1187), trans. John J. O'Meara; and reproduced in Seamus Deane (ed.), *The Field Day Anthology of Irish Writing Vol. 3* (Derry: Lawrence Hill/Field Day Publications, 1991), p. 239.

Many others followed, grudgingly and perplexedly acknowledging the quality of both the music and the musicianship of an otherwise barbaric (and, therefore, seemingly ownable) race.[48] Consequently, the 'identification of Ireland as a musical nation was produced within the colonial dynamic between Ireland and Britain.'[49]

Moreover, it lives on as such, with America's power to sell the stuff thrown in for extra imperial measure, as has been seen on, literally, a world stage with the *Riverdance* phenomenon. That same world stage is claimed by some to undo sectarianism. For example, Bill Whelan said of his creation, *Riverdance*, 'In Belfast, both Protestants and Catholics identified with it; it transcends nationalism.'[50] However, to others it signals more a displacement of colonial relationship than a resolution of it. In today's arena, as Davis puts it: 'the operative other against which the Irish self is defined is not British colonial authority dominating a British market but the global market for culture'[51] and, as such, it redoubles the political investment in music's place in society. It also redoubles the complication of whether and what to sing in church.

As with the last chapter's discussion of Catholic Eucharistic practices, so with music: it would seem that liturgical life is held hostage to sectarian norms in the wider culture, albeit, in this case, in quite different ways, and across denominations. However, here we can see a significant difference and, perhaps, a glimmer of hope. By *not* singing in church (Roman Catholics), or singing noticeably more weakly in church (Protestants), Irish congregations have opted out of combining sectarianism and liturgical life/theology: they have de-coupled national and ecclesial integrity. Moreover, they have done so with the cultural symbol that has the metaphorical power to do so (because it has *sounded* nationalism). While I have been able to argue in previous chapters that the churches inadvertently participate in the sub-conscious structures of sectarianism and that we can change these by becoming conscious of them, when it comes to this activity (music, song) which politics has necessarily already rendered to a higher point in public consciousness, the churches seem to have fudged things for constructive ends.

48. Davis, *Music, Postcolonialism, and Gender*.
49. Davis, *Music, Postcolonialism, and Gender*, p. 1.
50. Sam Smyth, *Riverdance: The Story* (London: Andre Deutsch, 1996), p. 87.
51. Davis, *Music, Postcolonialism, and Gender*, p. 223.

I say 'fudged things' because it was not my finding that people refuse music or intentionally dissent from it. They did not—and this is the crucial distinction—they just did not sing in church like they sang outside of church. In pubs and clubs, Catholics still sing their hearts out, and in Orange Halls Wesley would have no problem with the audibility or passion of the participation in the musical components.[52] If Irish and Northern Irish people's deep dependence upon church is expressed in their persistent attendance rates, perhaps their deep ambivalence toward church (particularly insofar as it has become an emblem of their relation to colonialist/ nationalist frameworks of power and identity) is expressed in the fact they do not currently sing out. It represents, arguably, an instance of resistance.

People ask why Liam Lawton's music is not more popular and why Ó Ríada's Masses are not more widely used in Roman Catholic churches. It is probably true that there has not been the necessary investment in gaining musicians or cantors of sufficient expertise to lead them. However, it seems possible that congregations recognize in these delicious and defiantly 'Irish' refrains a strong and unmistakable comment about the supposed allegiances of those singing them. Whereas such things as chair arrangement, cross-revering, naming of 'our' or 'the opposite' communities are all subtle, unconscious ways in which we enact sectarian worldviews (and which, once remarked, most people would wish to address), the accrued nationalistic meanings of music is something about which people are generally already *conscious*, even if they may not regularly articulate their consciousness in exactly those terms.

People recognize musical sounds as a cultural symbol that has long been presented as 'belonging' to one community or another, as 'sounding' particular moments in recent ecclesial and political history, and, therefore, as something that has been used to make statements of a more explicitly sectarian nature; and so they demur from singing them as it was imagined they might by the liturgists who promoted the composition of such pieces. 'Let the people sing indigenous song!'—but the people know that indigenous song has been profoundly implicated in the projects of colonialism and

52. (Although the connections between church and Orange Order do raise a question mark; but one that is beyond the remit of this study, theirs not being Sunday morning worship).

nationalism and in their sectarian productions, and they hesitate, therefore, to sing it in church. The hope in this is that there is some real sense in which 'church' stands against sectarianism in the people's minds, even as it is also—in another part of their minds, the part conditioned to think sectarianly—the very thing they wish to 'defend'.[53]

Likewise the reticence of Protestants to sing with gusto the old hymns of church and chapel: the continuing resonance of these hymns as a battle cry in an era in which the great majority of Protestants want an end to all violence is just too easy to hear, as are the outmoded syntheses between lyrics expressing their hoped-for and God-promised occupation of the promised land and their believed-to-be hard-won and God-ordained right to govern the land they dwell within. It all cuts too close to the bone. While they can be challenged to reconsider their prayers about the 'opposite religion' or the 'resting victorious in the triumph of the cross' because of their inadvertent overtones with a sectarian world-view, they are already challenging their singing. Not claiming too much. Not associating. Disassociating, in fact.

If, following O'Malley, we could in the last chapter criticize the churches because when the chips were down (with the hunger strike crisis) they abandoned their stated purpose as non-partisan harbingers of peace, jumped in on either side and participated in some unfortunate sectarian name-calling (a failure of moral context, as O'Malley had it); then in this chapter we must remark that when it comes to what congregations have done over many years rather than just in that single moment of crisis, their reticence to sing is salient. If music in Ireland is intrinsically nationalist, and nationalism in Ireland is composed of inherently colonial mythologies, and those colonial mythologies give rise to sectarianism, then music in the public realm is inevitably jingoistic. Therefore, to demur from it altogether in church, or to demur from getting too much involved in it in church, is to make a significant statement about what 'church' is holding out for: a non-sectarian view of life.

So what is to be done about singing in church in the Republic and Northern Ireland? People sing as part of worship all over the world and it is widely seen as an essential component of praise, which is what worship is about. Is there is a way of doing it in Ireland that

53. See, Liechty and Clegg, *Moving Beyond Sectarianism*, e.g., pp. 31–62, 316–17.

can avoid jingoism and that does not fall prey to sectarianism? By attempting to answer this question we realize, as no preceding chapter has been able to fully expose, that sectarianism was not invented by anyone currently living in Ireland or Northern Ireland, and that any and all who would take responsibility for their part in maintaining it are rowing on the surface of an ocean that goes down fathoms beneath them.

By considering music we realize how terribly, utterly and deeply the entire culture has been saturated by the ethic of sectarianism, and not just since the 26 counties garnered their independent status, in everything from hard material effects (the commodities of printed and recorded matter) to soft symbolic suggestions (the metaphorical nature of Irish music or song language). By considering *the idea of music*, tracing its hybrid history, discovering its co-optation for colonial/nationalist ends and thereby de-bunking the myths associated with its popular perception, we can see how sectarianism could, theoretically at least, be challenged or perhaps moved-beyond. But by considering the *practicalities of introducing new music in Irish worship* we come face to face with what an incredibly difficult task is ahead of us when we commit to moving beyond sectarianism. What would we sing? How would it sound relative to the rest of the culture?

Thinking about how music works (or fails to work) in church, the enormity, complexity and opacity of the work of imagining a form that dismantles (or otherwise moves beyond) sectarianism is brought into sobering relief. Do we start by 'Bringing it all Back Home' — but to church — as the famous 1990s TV series on Irish music had it; or do we continue to embrace the global market and sing American; or do we give up on singing altogether, at least for a while, as many Roman Catholic parishes have pretty much already done; or do we mount a programme of intensive re-education about the *shared* roots and ideologies of our music, creating a new sonic moral context?

Imagining *Bringing it All Back Home,* but to church, would consist of a decidedly post-modern method for the composition of hymnody, in which a cornucopia of instruments, voices, sounds and influences ('Irish Plus', perhaps) would connote something that sounded like it was of Ireland but, through its melding of various influences, would also circumvent all the old politics of the music. In the TV series *Bringing it All Back Home,* and its sequel, *A River of*

Sound, Irish musicians played with American[54] and Scottish musicians to create a narrative that went like this: look how much influence Irish music has had on other people's music through emigration, and look what happens when we reincorporate that music: isn't it a wonderful musical fusion, and, really, isn't fusion what it has always been about? Many agreed and were delighted to see the 'fused' character of Irish music not only acknowledged, at last, but also seemingly de-religionized and celebrated. Many more were happy just to see a really positive, modern and non-insular presentation of Irish music on television. And many players were thrilled to see publicly-represented what they recognize as deeply true to their own practices: the excitement and joy of sharing music with others who are different to yourself but with whom you find a way to play, thus enriching both your own practice and theirs and, often, creating something new and delightful in the process. It is this that, one imagines, might be built upon for church.

However, these projects also attracted considerable (and at times vitriolic) criticism, and thus ignited a debate of equal relevance to the question of liturgical composition. To begin with, the programmes were seen as too America-oriented and the notion of the Irish gaining their legitimacy primarily by winning American approval was suspect to some (although, there is a risk of hypocrisy here, given that America has frequently been claimed as Ireland's salvation ideologically, financially, and politically—that is, in a lot more than music). Then, the almost complete lack of song was seen as a major mis-understanding of and mis-representation of the tradition. Related to this (because the sort of song that is in question is that usually performed by an individual singer), and constituting perhaps the most serious complaint was the charge that the series completely overlooked the contribution of the solo performer[55] (a

54. Meaning, from the USA. It is unfortunate that 'American', which technically refers to what belongs to the continents of North and South America, should be used to refer to merely the USA. It unjustly adds to the imperial force the USA has in the globalized markets of which we are speaking. However, it is also how Irish people refer to the USA, and how inhabitants of the USA refer to themselves. So I reluctantly keep it for the purposes of this chapter, so as not to be at odds with those I am quoting.

55. Indeed, Breandán Breathnach, in his influential study, defines Irish music as essentially the art of solo performance. See, Breandán Breathnach, *Folk Music and Dances of Ireland: A Comprehensive Study* (Cork: Ossian/Mercer Press, 1996).

significant charge, given the honoured place of the solo performer in the tradition).[56]

Considering the music that might be developed for use in worship in Ireland, therefore, the telling word is 'authentic', because in the culture at large, both the neurosis and the supposed criteria for curing it are lodged in an assessment of what is and is not 'real'. As Kieran Keohane points out, this is a profoundly ambivalent fascination: 'what we fear about the processes of globalisation — loss of coherence of place and time, homelessness — we simultaneously desire.'[57] How we articulate and manage this desire sees all roads leading back to a need for authenticity: 'There is a desire for post-national, cosmopolitan identification, to escape from the bonds of tradition to a free, but fearfully lonely, existential condition of rootlessness and, at the same time, a desire to return to, to re-collect and re-live in the tradition(s) of "real" (that is to say imagined) Ireland(s).'[58] The question that the *Bringing it All Back Home* experience therefore prompts when thinking ecclesially is not so much that of solo versus group performance practice (because we in liturgical theology are long used to dealing with that issue as it affects every other), but of what is being claimed as 'real', theologically, and ecclesiologically, and by whom, and why?

Perhaps instead, 'home grown' sounds, newly understood as both hybridly-originated and culturally-shared, can be used in worship in such a way that they circumvent 'the sound of madness'; but if they are to be advocated in such a way that they cause less and not more embarrassment, then the question arises of which forms can be used in worship to enable a congregation's song without inviting even more of the sense that this is 'Hiberno–Jazz

56. The Clare accordionist, Tony MacMahon, for example, asked: 'Can anybody seriously suggest that the music that this describes signals the position of Irish traditional music as it enters into its Third millennium? Where can a space be found here for the spirit of the authentic solo performer from West Cork or South Armagh, in this Hiberno–Jazz, scrubbed clean of roots, ritual and balls?' The Crossroads Conference, 1996. Quoted at: www.irishmusicreview.com/aros.htm

57. Kieran Keohane, 'Traditionalism and Homelessness in Contemporary Irish Music' in Jim MacLaughlin, *Location and Dislocation in Contemporary Irish Society: Emigration and Irish Identities* (Cork: Cork University Press, 1997), p. 274.

58. Keohane, 'Traditionalism and Homelessness' in MacLaughlin, *Location and Dislocation*, p. 302.

scrubbed clean of roots, ritual and balls' and, moreover, set in the service of God. So before this sends anyone scooting off to sanitize Ó Ríada of his romantic nationalism and thereby reclaim his music for liturgical use or, if that is still not authentic enough (which for many it can never be, with its sumptuous instrumentation and other art-music 'corruptions'), setting someone's granny up with a pot of tea and her fiddle on the dais, then let us note that the fundamental questions that give rise to this issue *already* haunt current liturgical practice in Ireland, whether it is the organist striking up to accompany the (non)singing of 'Faith of our Fathers' or the pastor posting a link to Faith Hill as the weekly worship song. What are we (entitled to be) drawing on? Whom are we accountable to? What imagination do we have of what it is we are doing when we sing in worship? One must also bear in mind that any and all 'authentic' traditions, whether African, Asian or Irish are inevitably somewhat compromised when they are used as the foundation for the composition of hymnody because hymnody is a peculiar and unique mode of communal singing (that is 'native' to almost nobody's 'tradition').

There seem to be two moves at stake here: push and pull. On the pull, there is the ongoing, addictive quest for authenticity: as Bohlman and Stokes put it, 'the search for a hitherto misapprehended "real" coupled with a (less explicit) demand for its institutional rehabilitation remain unshaken ideological components in thinking and writing about music on the Celtic fringe.'[59] Such a pull can be seen in attempts to 'rehabilitate' Ó Ríada's Masses, attempts built on a basic yearning for authenticity 'from within', pulling it up from within the tropes of one's own history. Or in Lawton's claiming of the language of 'Celtic' for his work, rather than 'Irish', in order to locate his music in a simultaneously older (pre-politics, supposedly) and newer (the global demand for Celtic consumables as cultural anchors in the face of rootlessness) world. Talking about similar moves, albeit not in liturgical music, Bohlmann and Stokes remark:

> There is a restless cultural logic at work here, which continues to separate "the real" from "fakelore" long after the nationalist moment that initially invested the process with such urgency. The institutions and agencies of cultural nationalism continually

59. Philip V. Bohlman and Martin Stokes (eds), *Celtic Modern: Music at the Global Fringe* (Lanham, MD: Scarecrow Press, 2003), pp. 1–27; 5.

fall victim to the very rhetoric that was instrumental in their coming into existence. They too are subsequently deemed to speak an elite and politically invested (i.e., "nonreal") language. They too are seen to live in a world of fabrication and artifice, cripplingly dependent upon what they define themselves against; the quest for the real must, therefore, go on.[60]

On the other hand, there is also simultaneously a 'push' outwards: a claim of greater reality, truer reality, a new and more trustworthy reality in how Irish music is seen 'from outside'. This has habitually taken one of three forms, all of them as mythic as a pure Gaelic past: Atlantis,[61] universalism,[62] or simply America. In all of them, a high degree of projection is in play, although 'America' and the American dream it is founded upon, also brings with it the promise of tangible monetary benefits and it is perhaps, therefore, no coincidence that falling 'Into the arms ... of America'[63] is currently by far the most powerful mechanism for claiming authenticity when it comes to music. Catholics hear in Marty Haugen's music not only 'safe space' (it seems 'Catholic' without being nationalistically so), but something 'familiar', something 'real'. Anglicans can sing with Thomas Dorsey about things they know to be real in their own lives (divine comfort, hopes for justice) without having to echo the sounds of their imperial past. And the Faith Hill Presbyterians have turned to America to help them become more authentic in their faith in a way that speaks for itself; by doing so, they have found a way, against significant odds, of having at least some music in their worship, some *praise* in their prayer.

One of the songs on *Bringing It All Back Home* was, 'My Love is in America'. Written in the 1980s (although it could have been from any period of great poverty at home in the past 200 years) it has two voices: first, the wife lamenting her loneliness due to her separation from her husband who had to go to America to make money to send home for the family and, later in the song, the husband, who laments his own homesickness and worries that it's not worth the separation given that the money he sends home 'is

60. Bohlman and Stokes (eds), *Celtic Modern*.

61. See Colin Graham, *Deconstructing Ireland: Identity, Theory, Culture* (Edinburgh: Edinburgh University Press, 2003).

62. See Luke Gibbons, *Transformations in Irish Culture* (South Bend, IN: Notre Dame University Press, 1996).

63. As U2 had it in their hit song, 'Bullet the Blue Sky'.

barely enough'. Sending one's heart to America, the Irish know
well, comes at a cost. This is as true for music as any other aspect of
personal or cultural discourse. Regarding music, the main cost is
the loss of cultural forms, idioms, nuances and characteristics as
the result of the homogenizing requirements of market forces (not
to be confused with the tradition versus innovation debate, which
can just as easily happen internally to a region—or a family—and
without any reference to the power exerted by the drive for profit).
Crucially, it is also the loss of the creation of artistic forms (including
liturgical forms) in specific communities, with all the testing and
honing that brings. America is so mighty in this vein not simply for
ideological reasons (melting pot, religious freedom, church-state
separation, any one can get ahead, etc.) but because its music
industry dominates the whole world's music industry. This means
that for Irish hymn writers and liturgists, as for any other artist or
consumer, a certain peace may come through adopting American
forms, but the challenge to do so while retaining the distinctive or
authentic aspects of their musical and linguistic heritage is
considerable.

Moreover, given this chapter's discussion of the relation of music
and nationalism, to resist homogenizing forces while yet not
resorting to 'unique' norms is especially difficult. As McCarthy
remarks, 'Given the homogenizing pressures of a global market,
the stakes are high for Irish music to articulate a nation whose
citizens, like those of other nations, are engaged in a struggle to
articulate multiple identities, identities based not on essential purity
but on hybridity.'[64] This brings us full circle, because by taking
refuge in America, and thus participating in the neo-colonial project
of global capitalism (something the Republic and Northern Ireland
also do through their participation in the European Union, although
more through its directly economic benefits and less as a cultural-
turn for music, art and ideology), musicians in Ireland are thrown
back on their 'own' music only to find it carries certain unpleasant
associations whether they want it to or not. Commenting on the
spanner this throws into the works of any theoretically anti-sectarian
approach to music, Gary Hastings, who is an accomplished traditional
Irish musician (flute player), a Church of Ireland rector, and a key
member of the team who compiled the new Church of Ireland

64. Davis, *Music, Postcolonialism and Gender*, p. 231.

Hymnbook (2000) makes the vital point that, as far as supposedly Protestant/Unionist versus Catholic/Republican music in Ireland is concerned,

> there is no clear divide between one kind of music and another. They have fed off each other and off influences from many other directions. *But, I am not naïve enough to forget that if people say they are different, and believe they are different, then they are at one level truly different.* We are talking about perceptions here. The important job is to help people realize this for themselves ... Which customs and traditions go to build up inclusive, supportive, peaceful and healthy community, and which go to destroy, divide and define?[65]

This, I suggest, is exactly what is ultimately needed to move liturgical music beyond sectarianism and allow singing to become part of worship in the Republic and Northern Ireland. Re-educating about the shared roots of our traditional musics needs to happen, and churches can play a very significant part in this. Use of American idioms is inevitable, but if Irish congregations are to recover their singing voice it also needs to be kept from taking over entirely if at all possible. The effort must be made to sing, even if it seems impossible. But it can only happen at a local level.

How this is done must, at the end of the day, be figured out one deanery, one session, one diocese at time. It must work with local and denominational nuances in symbol structure so that, as Chapter Two suggested, it can tailor the reconciling practice that singing potentially holds to meet the needs of the particular community. The basic resources required for this project are already there: in the various denomination's hymn books, in the liturgical materials published by the ecumenical communities of Iona, Taizé and others, and in the creativity, talents, faith and desire for peace of ordinary church members and parishioners. The question is how to use them, and it would be well worth setting up teams around the country to work out not only what should be sung, but how to get it sung in the churches. Catholics are used to not singing; Protestants have become used to not singing in church like they used to; and too little leadership is being offered by the Irish church bodies regarding attention to the ministry of music.

Several churches in Northern Ireland and Dublin have employed John Bell of the Iona Community to give workshops on empowering

---

65. Hastings, *With Fife and Drum*, pp. 78–79. Italics mine.

congregational song, and some have taken up his methods to reportedly great effect. What Bell offers is musical theological education/catechesis for our times.[66] Moreover, running such workshops is itself a potential ecumenical event in a district, because a group of churches can join together across denominational lines and be led in singing (and learning what and how to sing), for an evening or a series of evenings. Such cantoring agents-provocateurs[67] are vital to introducing non-sectarian singing into the Irish churches. It will be a sign that we have a real peace when we can sing about it; until then, we can trust that by learning to sing we are taking steps to help create that peace; we are, in effect, singing it into being.

66. See, John Bell, *The Singing Thing: A Case for Congregational Song* (Chicago, IL: GIA, 2000) and *The Singing Thing, Too: Enabling Congregations To Sing* (Glasgow: Wild Goose Publications, 2007), in addition to the many musical resources co-authored by him and published by Wild Goose Publications.

67. Or 'Animateurs', as C. Michael Hawn calls them — See, *Gather into One*. Although in footnote no. 6 on p. 243, he notes the difficulties of this word for his North American audiences and suggests the need for an alternative to either 'cantor' or 'animateur' for these contexts.

Chapter Seven

CONCLUSION

"If, as we argue, the conflict is the product of a system of relationship which constitutes two communities with radically conflicting interests, aspirations and identities, then the solution lies in dismantling that system."[1]

"so long as the churches see challenging the sectarian divide as a marginal responsibility, or no responsibility at all, or a responsibility we will address when everything else has been settled, the sectarian system will go on employing well-intentioned, positive, community-building activities as sustenance for itself."[2]

"The church cannot rely on the state to do justice. The church must take itself seriously as a kind of public body, the body of Christ, that creates spaces of justice and peace in the world. It often must do so in resistance to the nation-state."[3]

'The Church' in Ireland is not the homogenous body it might seem or once have claimed to be in Irish society. While much is made of the two or three Roman Catholic priests who supported the IRA, the work of those hundreds of priests and pastors who supported grass-roots peace-making initiatives tends to be

1. Joseph Ruane and Jennifer Todd, *Dynamics of Conflict in Northern Ireland: Power, Conflict and Emancipation* (Cambridge: Cambridge University Press, 1996), p. 14.

2. Joseph Liechty and Cecilia Clegg, *Moving Beyond Sectarianism: Religion, Conflict and Reconciliation in Northern Ireland* (Dublin: Columba Press, 2001), p. 14.

3. William T. Cavanaugh, interviewed in the *Christian Century*, 13 December 2005. He continues: 'In Chile, some bishops excommunicated those responsible for torture, and the grassroots church aided victims of the regime and carried out acts of civil disobedience. Change did not come quietly, as it usually doesn't.'

overlooked.[4] However, also overlooked are the thousands of clergy and laypeople alike who have buried their heads in the sand: as the *Moving Beyond Sectarianism* project repeatedly found, by far the most widespread response by the church to sectarianism is inertia.[5] My hope is that by paying attention to ritualizing (beginning with space, symbols, bodies, language, songs, meals and music), church people can begin to imagine a way out of that inertia, a way out—*via* ritualization—that the more conventional method of dialogue is not alone able to achieve. This critical liturgical theology seems realistic because when we are confronted with embodiedness, we react differently than we do to textual analysis or verbal debates. Christian worship, being a matrix of bodily acts, is, then, a potentially privileged location for the next steps in the peace process because, as the place where subjectivities are liturgically created, it offers the opportunity for the Church to own its responsibility *vis-a-vis* sectarianism.

The churches in the Republic and Northern Ireland do not bear sole responsibility for sectarianism in these countries, but they do bear some of the responsibility for dismantling the system of relationship that constitutes habitual sectarian hatred on the island. Or, to put it another way, the churches in Ireland and Northern Ireland currently have an excellent opportunity, and one that no other institution shares, to help society move from a cold peace to a real peace by, on the one hand, making some relatively simple

4. See, for example, Claire Mitchell, *Religion, Identity and Politics in Northern Ireland: Boundaries of Belonging and Belief* (Abingdon: Ashgate, 2006), pp. 42–45. She provides numerous examples of the Catholic Church consistently decrying sectarian violence of every sort, as well as specifically condemning the IRA. But she also notes how years of official teaching was regularly undercut by but one evening's TV coverage of *liturgy*, showing a church hosting a paramilitary funeral, and thus creating the illusion of unity of purpose between 'the Church' and 'the struggle' (p. 44).

5. 'Sectarianism induces a sense of powerlessness, overwhelming people with the immensity of the problem and making them feel isolated and insignificant in the face of it. When people start to address sectarianism, however, even the first small steps, especially when they are taken alongside others, begin to lift that aura of powerlessness and isolation' (Liechty and Clegg, *Moving Beyond Sectarianism*, pp. 19–20). While sympathetic to the fact that this sort of apathy is 'inspired by hopelessness,' they nonetheless insist that it must be routed, because: 'The silence and inaction of the majority can be, and has been, taken as a mandate by the tiny minority who espouse violence' (p. 109).

changes to their Sunday worship, and, on the other, by engaging in longer-term reflection on more complicated aspects of their worship. Under the first category, this book has proposed several starting points for considering such changes: from greeting practices, to how crosses are talked about, through which words are chosen to refer to our siblings in faith, to how Irish events are named and commemorated; and it has suggested several specific possibilities, such as that common anniversaries be made more of and that flags be made less of. Under the second category, this book has suggested starting-points for talking about some important things that need to change (such as congregational singing being so weak and Catholics not distributing the wine at communion).

However, there are yet more things that the churches can and perhaps must do if they are to contribute to actually dismantling the system of relationship that endlessly constitutes two opposing communities, and thus to move beyond sectarianism in Ireland, North and South. These will be the subject of this conclusion, starting with a query about the nature of worship, moving through further practical suggestions for Sunday morning worship, and ending with a note about the nature of theology itself in a sectarian context.

One of the most challenging aspects of this study for me was that it ended up suggesting that trusted and beloved forms of worship might fail. Like many, I was brought up to believe that God gave us worship and our job was simply to fulfill it by faithfully following its forms. Obviously, that belief became more complicated through studies in theology, liturgy and ritual studies (particularly as they have been informed by analyses of race, class, gender and colonization), all of which teach that the human element in worship is not just inevitable but also vital to its success. But nothing had prepared me to witness a worship service where my first instinct was to think, 'There is absolutely nothing remarkable about any of this', only to visit many others, read back over my notes from them and start to realize the sorts of things this book has described, simultaneously noticing their connections to the wider culture, and finally admitting that the worship might be conveying something that is at least askew and quite possibly not right.

One cannot be naïve about the fact that worship is constructed: it is the work of human beings, even as it is also in a sense God's work, 'the work of people-with-God', as Matt Boulton has termed it after considering whether God in fact had anything to do with it, or even wanted it.[6] Or, similarly, as Bryan Spinks has carefully framed it: 'liturgy, even if divinely mandated, is also a human activity, and as such, is influenced by the culture in which it is celebrated and developed.'[7] As every mainstream church's liturgical guidelines maintain, the key to ensuring that worship retains its God-given aspects is the creation of a balance between faithfulness to tradition and faithfulness in contemporary performance, which means resisting changing worship just for fun, or without reference to the authorities of scripture and lineage of practices, or in ways that lose awareness of God as other.[8] However, if a rite is thus faithfully performed, can it yet do harm? By remarking that some aspects of worship in Ireland mirrored, mimicked or perhaps even fed sectarian norms in the wider culture while seeming to be operating well within liturgical rules, we are challenged to revise the view that adequately performed worship is inevitably or even probably benign. Perhaps faithfulness to something additional—such as an ability to critically engage its terms—is also required.

The issue at stake, as Spinks notes, is that of the connection between worship (or theology) and culture. That worship (and theology) are the products of cultures and only make sense within the terms of each particular host culture is now well-established thanks to both the histories of missionary fields and some recent groundbreaking theological formulation.[9] But in this place from

6. Matthew Myer Boulton, *God Against Religion: Rethinking Christian Theology Through Worship* (Grand Rapids, MI: Eerdmans, 2008), p. 10. He also suggests: 'a collective work of God-with-us' as an antidote to the translation of *leitourgia* as 'work of the people' (p. 10).

7. Bryan D. Spinks, 'Liturgical Theology and Criticism—Things of Heaven and Things of the Earth; Some Reflections on Worship, World Christianity, and Culture' in Charles E. Farhadian, *Christian Worship Worldwide: Expanding Horizons, Deepening Practices* (Grand Rapids, MI: Eerdmans, 2007), pp. 230-52, 231.

8. See, for example, Spinks's assessment that, 'St. Aldate's Church in Oxford has been recently re-ordered as a brave attempt to adapt a medieval parish church for modern English evangelical worship. But the south nave stage for the band and worship leaders, the vast audio centre and the hanging monitors convey little sense of transcendence or the other, but only intermittent entertainment at a small-town airport.' See Spinks, 'Liturgical Theology and Criticism' in Farhadian, *Christian Worship Worldwide*, p. 252.

9. See, for example, Graham Ward, *Cultural Transformation and Religious Practice* (Cambridge: Cambridge University Press, 2005).

which so many missionaries originated, we have worship that is patently failing, and needs to be, perhaps, anti-culturated rather than in-culturated. If the norms of Irish culture(s) are being reflected in Sunday worship, and those norms are sectarian, then worship is not just infected with, but also set in the service of, something it ought to be working against. Enough has been said about the connections between worship and Irish–British sectarian culture in the body of this book, at least for a preliminary study of the subject; what I want to turn to here is not so much the issue of the 'culture at large' as the specific cultures of being Church of Ireland or Presbyterian or Methodist or Roman Catholic in Ireland and Northern Ireland, that is, *denominational* enculturation. In practice, as described in Chapter One, the Church of Ireland, Presbyterian and Methodist confessions are merged into the single *de facto* denomination of Protestantism, and the Roman Catholics are denominated simply as 'Catholics'.

One of the most complicated aspects of writing about Ireland and Northern Ireland from the point of view of religious practices, is that liturgical/ritual practices are strongly identified as religious *via* their denominational location and character. This is because 'what happens in church' happens in *either* a Protestant church *or* a Catholic church. The formation of liturgical subjectivity through even the most basic ritualizing acts is happening in distinctively denominational frames. Thus, one does not have an umbrella view of Christianity but, rather, one *feels* Protestant things, Catholics things, etc. What is complicated about this for a study that hopes to contribute to the movement beyond sectarianism is that one ends up never able to move beyond denominationalism. Now, despite the unfortunate accidents of etymology (denomi-nationalism) for this society in which nationalism (along with other factors such as religion and colonialism) has co-produced sectarianism, denominationalism and sectarianism are not necessarily the same thing. Yet in Ireland, due to the events and interpretations of history, the rhetorics of politics, the passions of religious identification, the consequences of socio-economic discrimination, the aftermath of state and paramilitary violence, and the peculiar ethno-nationalist self-understandings of the people, denominations are indeed implicated in the problem of sectarianism.

This basic problem is expressed in the common shorthand description of the British-Irish conflict as being between 'Protestants and Catholics'. It is also expressed in the numerous practices by which people participate in denominational events (primarily worship), events which are rendered potentially sectarian merely by virtue of their being denominationally housed in a context in which denominationality is one of the prime indicators of identity. Given this context (in which the vocabulary of denominations and the division between denominations has given the basic names to the conflict), is it sectarian to celebrate a Catholic Mass in a Catholic church? Is it sectarian to preach Protestant theology in a Protestant church?

Objecting to the 'moral judgment implied in the use of the term' 'sectarianism', the theologian Alan Ford argues that:

> Whilst not denying the destructive capacity of sectarianism in Irish history, it is not *necessarily* a negative phenomenon – at one moderate extreme it shades off into pride in one's own identity ... It is possible that the blanket use of the concept as a term of abuse may import negative judgments which are not necessarily applicable to all the aspects being studied and which would be missing from a more value-neutral term such as confessionalisation.[10]

Furthermore, he argues that self-segmentation happens in a completely benign way in lots of other arenas of life and should be able to happen regarding religious identity in an Irish context as well. Personally, I have found Liechty and Clegg's view to be true: that sectarianism is in fact always a bad thing,[11] which is best handled when it is explicitly value-laden as a negative phenomenon, and when everyone who has been touched by it takes responsibility for it (i.e., when it is not considered someone else's problem).[12] Throughout this study, I have treated 'sectarianism' as a term like racism or anti-semitism (with which, Ford complains, it has been equated), in order to name something that has historically proved hard to name and, therefore, also hard to resist for those embroiled *in medias res*. What Ford suggests as being constitutive of self-

10. Alan Ford, 'Living Together, Living Apart: Sectarianism in Early Modern Ireland' in Alan Ford and John McCafferty, *The Origins of Sectarianism in Early Modern Ireland* (Cambridge: Cambridge University Press, 2002), pp. 1–23; 10–11.

11. Liechty and Clegg, *Moving Beyond Sectarianism*, (p. 38): '"Sectarianism" and "sectarian" always refer to something bad, a problem.'

12. Liechty and Clegg, *Moving Beyond Sectarianism*, pp. 17–19.

segmentation and confessionalization are not, in fact, aspects of sectarianism, but different things, with different instincts, ideologies and, more importantly, effects. That said, at root, Ford is pleading for a distinction to be made between sectarianism and confessionalism, and in doing so he offers a hint about how we might escape the denomi-nationalism knot in Ireland: by taking pride in the difference in our confessions, but not seeing them as necessarily divisive.

Worship practices can help to accomplish this in almost innumerable ways, by forming people in distinctive ways while simultaneously re-forming any associated sense that these distinctions are antagonistic. Thus Catholic Mass can be celebrated in a Catholic church but it can be done in such a way that is confessional (of what Catholics believe) and not denomi-national (bolstering a Catholic identity in oppositional mode) through preaching, through the words of the prayers and songs that surround it, and through many additional aspects of the rite (confessing the sin of sectarian thinking during contrition, praying for our siblings in faith during the prayers, passing the peace, talking about society in church, finding love for *all* people on the cross, and eating and drinking in the fullness of this meal of freedom). Likewise Protestant theology can be preached in a Protestant church, but it can be done in such a way that it is set in the service of moving beyond sectarianism, it can be used to excavate the landscape of sectarianism, to convict people of their complicity in it and help them recover from it — and not to vilify 'Popery' or endlessly contrast what 'we' do with what Catholics (supposedly) do.

Denominationality has become implicated in sectarianism and not the other way around: it is quite possible, therefore, as nearly every other modern Western country has demonstrated, to have denominations without having sectarianism. The question in our context then becomes: how can we have denominations without having sectarianism? Or, specifically regarding the goals of this book: how can we make sure that our worship is not sectarian simply by virtue of its being denominationally-housed, i.e., Protestant worship or Catholic worship? This is not as easy a question to answer as it might at first seem. As Geraldine Smyth has repeatedly and insightfully insisted, it is not simply the case that there are Nationalists and there are Unionists; rather there are webs of ontological conceptualization involved in being either Protestant or Catholic and, more to the point, a 'chasm' of complete non-understanding between the two, making communicative action between them almost impossible. She considers that the *Good Friday Agreement* 'failed to bridge the chasm of different meaning systems in the wider community. There remains an inability to envisage peace as a new experience of right relationship, rooted in new experiences of encounter—in theological terms, as a New Creation.'[13]

I would like to suggest that new experiences of encounter can be envisaged, and that they take two basic forms: working in inter-denominational ways, yes, but also, and mostly, working in intra-denominational worship. Alongside the terrible grief and violence of the past 30 years, there have been many new and constructive encounters between Protestants and Catholics in Ireland and Northern Ireland at community and neighbourhood levels (and Smyth holds up as examples many ecumenical and women's grass-roots organizations in particular); but there seems at this time to be an urgent need for new experiences of *intra*-denominational, *intra*-community encounter.[14]

Reaching out to those who are different from ourselves from the same old bedrock of (perhaps unwittingly) sectarianized self-understanding can only go so far; the sectarianized self-understanding can (and needs to be) broken down not only *via* encounter with the other who is of the 'opposite religion', but also through encounter with God and trusted-neighbour, and this is where denominational worship holds a particularly powerful potential as an agent in moving beyond sectarianism. Worship, done within a denominational context and done well, can provide new experiences of encounter with God and with members of one's own tradition. Indeed, I would like to suggest, it is only when single-confessional worship is supplying the context within which God can be encountered in a new way and seen to be ever making all

13. Geraldine Smyth, 'Envisaging a New Identity and a Common Home: Seeking Peace on our Borders', *Milltown Studies* 46 (Winter 2000), pp. 58–84.

14. Although they must be activities that do not lead to self-absorption, that is, to the risk that people engage in them for their own sake and use them as a mechanism to become negligent of the wider community. This is phenomenon (of church folks doing 'worthy' things, like worship, as a means of avoiding inter-church engagement) is more fully described by Liechty and Clegg, *Moving Beyond Sectarianism*, pp. 316–17.

things new, and praiseworthy for being so, that it can justify itself as merely confessional-denominational and not at all sectarian-denominational. Before considering what Christians might do with inter-denominational worship, therefore, I will suggest two further practical methods for fostering new encounters in intra-denominational worship because, I contend, ecumenism begins at home.

One very simple technique for moving beyond sectarianism that every Christian can do when they plan, lead or just participate in worship, is to imagine what it would be like if a person from a different tradition to their own were present. Such acts of imagination have been shown to prevent the hardening of sectarian arteries as well as steering worship away from of sectarian-producing effects. What this entails is that if you are Protestant, imagine a Catholic whom you respect sitting there within your field of vision in the nave or on the dais, and, if you are Catholic, imagine the same about a Protestant. What this visualization does is to lessen the chance of you saying or doing something sectarian in that service or else having a mechanism to challenge yourself when you do. The thought of someone you respect or admire sitting there feeling hurt by your words or actions personalizes the issue in exactly the way that sectarianism needs to be personalized if it is to be dismantled.

Of course, many Irish people do not know enough people of the 'opposite religion' well enough to be able to have a fully-rounded, realistic imagination of even one of them. Until I left home, I had encountered only two Protestant families in real-life (our next-door neighbours), and I knew only one of them well enough to be able to feel empathy with them. At university, I met other Catholics who had never even spoken to a Protestant first-hand, and *vice versa*. This was in England, in 1987, and I understand this radical lack of 'mixing' was even more exaggerated in Ireland at the same time, in both the Republic and Northern Ireland. For people who are from a background like mine, or a more pronounced one than mine, it will probably not be possible to imagine an actual 'friend' from another community sitting in the worship space; these people can perhaps imagine instead someone whom they have encountered on radio or television, or whom they have read about in the papers. For example, it might be someone who has behaved constructively in community relations or it might be someone who was a survivor of sectarian violence whose courage they admire; the point is that they should be someone from the other community by whose story one has been touched.

Mary Boys, an expert on interfaith relations in general and Jewish–Christian dialogue in particular, has pointed to the value of the imagination of 'the other' in the process of planning and leading worship. She relates accounts of Christian worship leaders who were expecting to proclaim a text that spoke negatively of Jewish people, but who changed how they did so when they realized that Jewish people were present in the midst of the congregation. In one such story, a rabbi had been invited to offer the homily on a certain day at a Catholic church and when he looked up the lectionary to see what texts he would be teaching from, he found that the Gospel was from John 20 and included the phrase, 'the doors were being shut for fear of the Jews'. However, when the day came and the priest read the text, he changed it at the last minute to: 'for fear of the authorities.' Reflecting on this experience, the rabbi asked, 'If the physical presence of a "Jewish Rabbi" (as if there were any other kind!) on the dais could prompt such an editing, then what does that tell us, especially if you realise that there is a Jew and a Rabbi on the altar every week in the representation of Jesus.'[15] There is no Protestant present on a Catholic altar each week in any literal sense, nor *vice versa*, but the rabbi's main point pertains to our own situation: if the physical presence of 'the other' could have such an instant and dramatic effect on the theology performed in the midst of the community, then 'what does that tell you?' Perhaps what that tells us is that we human beings only find it possible to scapegoat others when we are not confronted with them as present, as full beings in interrelationship with us.

Boys comments that, 'the "presence" of Jews, whether in our midst physically or through our imagination, leads us to inquire more deeply into our texts. ... When we Christians proclaim New Testament texts in the presence of Jews, we find ourselves challenged to search more profoundly for the truth to which they draw us.'[16] Although Boys is speaking about Christian-Jewish

15. Rabbi David Whiman quoted in Mary Boys, *Has God Only One Blessing? Judaism as a Source of Christian Self-understanding* (New York and Mahwah, NJ: Paulist Press, 2000), pp. 29–30.
16. Boys, *Has God Only One Blessing?* p. 29.

relations, and particularly about Christian interpretation of texts, I am suggesting that her prescription works analogously for Protestant-Catholic relations, and particularly for the full range of worship practices in both Protestant churches and the Catholic Church.

Now, the nature of Christian-Jewish conflict is very different to that of the Irish-British Catholic-Protestant conflict. Christian persecution of Jews down the centuries has been largely one-sided (Jews have not engaged in comparably widespread persecution of Christians through history), whereas Catholics and Protestants have both habituated to contempt for and violence towards one another in the post-modern expression of the Irish conflict. This means that Christians need to imagine Jews at their services because those services regularly include the reading of texts that express contempt for Jews and this has translated historically into violence against Jews, even annihilation of them; however, Jews do not need to imagine Christians among them at their services because their core texts are not frequently anti-Christian and their worship practices have not translated into systemic violence against Christians down the years. The analogy then, when applied to our situation, only works if it runs both ways, and not just one way: Catholics need to imagine Protestants among them in Mass, and Protestants need to imagine Catholics among them in Sunday morning worship.

Furthermore, I am proposing that this manner of thinking needs to be part of the planning and leading of worship for every Sunday, and not just for occasional Sundays, nor just for ecumenical gatherings, 'mixed' marriages or funerals. If such an imaginative act is performed in every worship service, then it becomes a habit, and not just a 'special' concession. Over a relatively short amount of time, it could become normative. Once it becomes normative, it will have begun the work of undoing sectarianism, because it will have reoriented people's thinking away from oppositional patterns of thought, and toward joint-consideration about one another. (That is without even beginning to assess the ways in which any actual changes made might also contribute to a reordering of the sectarian landscape.)

Developing her suggestion of the imagination of the presence of a Jewish person in Christian worship, Boys notes that: 'Of course, sensitivity to Jewish reaction is important but we should not modify our reading of texts merely to mollify one group or another-and then carry on as usual when Jews are not present. *Rather, we must ask ourselves how our sacred texts should be read to foster faithful living of Christianity in our time.'*[17] Of the many potentially helpful lines of thinking in this quotation, there are two points in particular that I should like to distinguish in order to develop the possibilities for thinking about what should be the effects of this 'imagined presence' in Catholic and Protestant worship. First, by imagining a Protestant present in a Catholic setting, or *vice versa*, we must not make changes merely 'to mollify' the other group. This has been one of the unfortunate consequences of much naïve ecumenical interaction. Instead, Boys' model advocates imagining the presence of a person from the other group in order to make sure our *own* thinking and acting is properly aligned (for our own sakes).

Second, translating Boys' remark to the subject under investigation here, *we must ask ourselves how our worship should be performed to foster faithful living of faith tradition in our time*. Thus, we are not 'imagining a Protestant/Catholic is present' in order to do 'extra', or to 'be good', and we are not looking for admiration or applause by doing so; rather we are using it as a mechanism for our own liturgical critical theory, in the hopes of performing our worship more faithfully. Moreover, doing so will help us learn about (and perhaps love more or perhaps grow more critical of) the distinctive aspects of our own denomination. Growing out of sectarianism might mean growing deeper in love with our own confessional tradition; but it will not be a love of it because it is anti-Catholic or anti-Protestant. It will be a love of it because it suits us, has spoken to us, formed us and helped us, and others are *related* to it. When we kill our fellow Christians with sectarian attitudes and practices, we are killing our own relations: our siblings, or our spouses.

The phenomenon of Protestants marrying Catholics and Catholics marrying Protestants has both a terrible and an inspiring history in the Republic and Northern Ireland. Regarding its terrible aspects, the effects on society as a whole of the widespread stigma against intermarrying are now widely assessed to have been deleterious, exacerbating ethno-nationalist sentiment and inhibiting the development of mutual understanding. Adrian Hastings, in his study of the relation between religion and nationalism around the modern world comments that, 'I too find it hard to believe that the conflicting

---

17. Boys, *Has God Only One Blessing?* p. 29 (original emphasis).

nationalisms of modern Ireland would have remained so intense if there had been a wider practice of Catholic-Protestant marriage.'[18] The fact that there was not a wider practice of Catholic–Protestant marriage (unlike miscegenation in Sarajevo, with which Hastings contrasts it), points to the severity of the division between communities and suggests the probable severity of punishment for those who did it—historically, they were often shunned by both communities, they often had elopement as the only option for a wedding rite and emigration as the only option for a married lifestyle.

Despite the persistently high rates of endogamy in both the Republic and Northern Ireland[19] almost every family has had some experience of sorrow or broken relationship caused by the intersection of a mixed-denomination couple wanting to marry and a church not wanting to marry them. Many families do not react well to one of their members wishing to marry a person from the other 'religion'; although this has different characteristics for Protestants than it does for Catholics, and yet more differences among residents of the North versus the South.[20] Thus, for example, members of the Church of Ireland in the South might object to a family member marrying a Catholic because of a feeling that the community is facing extinction and the worry that their Anglican lineage will end with this generation (because of the requirement on Catholics in 'mixed marriages' to raise their children Catholic). Catholics in the North, on the other hand, might object to a family member marrying a Protestant out of fear for their well-being, based on some highly publicized hate-crimes against Catholics in inter-denominational couples in certain regions, historic aversion to intermarriage, or just ignorance or loathing of the other community.

Then, when it comes to the marriage liturgy itself, it still happens that some Roman Catholic priests will offer a mixed-denomination couple only a blessing in the sacristy and not any sort of service in

18. Adrian Hastings, *The Construction of Nationhood: Religion, Ethnicity and Nationalism* (Cambridge: Cambridge University Press, 1997), p. 206.

19. See, Richard O'Leary, 'Religious Intermarriage and Modernisation in Ireland' in Alistair Crockett and Richard O'Leary, *Patterns and Processes of Religious Change in Modern Industrial Societies* (Lewiston, NY: E. Mellen Press, 2004), pp. 117–38.

20. See, Ruane and Todd, *Dynamics of Conflict*, pp. 65, 248–49.

the church (although the official guideline is for a service in church if the couple go through a period of instruction and the Catholic in the couple intends to be a member of the parish), and it still happens that Protestant pastors will not even attend (never mind conduct) an inter-denominational marriage service (and for most members of the Orange Order, participation in *any* form of worship service with Roman Catholics is prohibited.)[21] In those 'lucky' situations where the ministers from both traditions are willing to perform a wedding rite together, or to attend in an official capacity a rite in one or the other's church (and these are by no means as common in Ireland as they are in the rest of the world), Mass can never be said because of the Roman Catholic prohibition on intercommunion — a prohibition which is more strictly taught now than at any time in the past half-century, due to the recent discourse of the Roman Catholic Church in the documents *One Bread, One Body*[22] and *Dominus Iesus*.[23]

Yet alongside such a history of sorrow and division is also the extraordinary Christian witness of those brave souls who have married someone from across the Protestant/Catholic divide, and I would like to suggest that in such couples the church has a profound model of life beyond sectarianism. During my research I met several mixed-denominational couples. One long-married couple (who wished to remain anonymous) told me that younger couples now come to them regularly and ask: how do you do it? The question is not meant in any sort of abstract sense, but, rather, very practically, meaning what are the skills and techniques for inter-marrying. In response, this couple tells what they have learned, for example: that 'you baptise children with the Catholics but confirm them with the Protestants'. Couples such as these have figured out an exceedingly important corpus of knowledge, but, more than that, they have found ways of navigating waters that the rest of society

21. See, Joseph Liechty, 'A Strategy for Living in Peace When Truth Claims Clash' in David R. Smock, *Interfaith Dialogue and Peacebuilding* (Washington, DC: United States Institute of Peace Press, 2002), pp. 89–100.

22. The Catholic Bishops Conferences of Ireland, Scotland, England and Wales, *One Bread, One Body: A Teaching Document on the Eucharist in the Life of the Church, and the Establishment of General Norms on Sacramental Sharing* (Dublin: Veritas, 1998).

23. Congregation for the Doctrine of the Faith, 'Declaration — *Dominus Iesus*: On the Unicity and Salvific Universality of Jesus Christ and the Church' (4 April 2001).

has yet to enter, metaphorically and in practice. John Brewer relates the story of Jim McKinley, a former Loyalist prisoner in Northern Ireland who told him that,

> Upon release from prison I met my future wife, who is a Roman Catholic from the Irish Republic. From the moment we met we knew that God had brought us together to work in reconciliation and peacemaking. This has not occurred overnight. We first had to learn in our marriage to respect each other's culture, religion, and political viewpoints. This journey has been slow and painful as both of us shed off the baggage that we carried with us from our upbringing in "the troubles". But the lesson of reconciliation we learned in our marriage is relevant, as we later came to realize, for Northern Ireland.[24]

I suggest that in this narrative of the domestic struggle to come to mutual understanding we have a model for the challenge currently facing people across the whole island. Such a model is further developed by considering the traditional Christian view of marriage as analogous to Christ's marriage to the church. Given the special place of this image – of an unlikely marriage as the model of God's love itself – in the Bible and Christian tradition, Irish couples who intermarry might help us to envision a society and a church for the twenty-first century. By seeing the inter-marrying couple not as a source of shame or disappointment for their communities, but as a model of God's incarnate love in Ireland today, we can see our worship, where we the church meet Christ as its spouse over and over again, in a new and more open light.

I am not saying that Catholics and Protestants need to worship together; but I am saying that in their respective worship they each need their attitudes and practices to be moving beyond sectarianism. That said, in addition to new encounters 'internal' to confessional worship, there also exist at this time many opportunities to create, foster and participate in new encounters with other Christians across the denominational divide. Christians in Ireland, South and North, can build a relationship with a specific community of a different denomination to their own, and may even make going to

---

24. Jim McKinley, former Loyalist prisoner, quoted by John D. Brewer, 'Northern Ireland: Peacemaking among Protestants and Catholics' in Mary Ann Cejka and Thomas Barmat (eds), *Artisans of Peace: Grassroots Peacemaking among Christian Communities* (Maryknoll, NY: Orbis Books, 2003), pp. 67–95; 68.

one another's worship a vital part of that relationship. The relationship that has been built over many years between the congregations at the Clonard Redemptorist Monastery and the Fitzroy Presbyterian Church in Belfast serves as an inspiring example. The Monastery's website describes the relationship like this:

> Since 1981 we have developed a special relationship with Fitzroy Presbyterian congregation which represents a profound change in the Church at grassroots level in Northern Ireland. We have laid to rest the polemic of the past and have come to see ourselves as Catholic and Presbyterian for one another, not against one another. The link with Fitzroy is now an essential part of Clonard; the link with Clonard is now an essential part of Fitzroy. We are now able to address together significant issues of difference between our Churches. The ability to do so in friendship is an immense contribution to the transformation of the whole society of Northern Ireland. In 1999 Pax Christi awarded its International Peace Award to the Clonard/Fitzroy Fellowship commending it for: 'exemplary work at grassroots level towards building the kingdom of the Prince of Peace'.

Forming a friendship between two specific church communities undercuts the habituated sense in which the person from the 'opposite religion' is 'out there' and replaces it with a much more immediate experience of them as real, present and inevitably in-relationship with ourselves. It also produces the realization that those whom we have been trained to encounter as other, while believing and behaving differently to us, are also like us in very many regards.

Contextualizing these discoveries from the outset in *friendship*, rather than in 'visiting' or 'being guests' or 'extending hospitality to the stranger' makes for a far more dynamic (and potentially more productive) experience because it implies an expectation of *ongoing* relationship. It sets up a greater level of commitment as well as a strong expectation of (some form of) mutuality and, importantly, it allows for paths into and out of encountering difficulty. By this I mean that if interaction is couched as, for example, 'visiting' rather than 'friendship', then when differences are experienced, there is no necessary impetus to work through them. As a visitor one expects both to encounter difference and to walk away from it; but as a friend one is expected to stay with it, work through it if possible, and, if not, live with it in an accepting way.

One of the key ways in which the Clonard and Fitzroy congregations grew in friendship was by sharing in one another's prayer and worship. Worship supports Christian friendship in ways that simply meeting for a cup of tea cannot because it allows the experience of intimacy through its invitation to a shared encounter with God. However, it is not always possible in the Irish context because of prohibitions — the aforementioned actual ones as well as various mythical ones.[25] This issue is a difficult one not just for those seeking to grow in friendship as a means of sectarian reconciliation, but also for many of the mixed-denominational families in Ireland. The complexity of the matter became the subject of intense media scrutiny and debate in 1997 when the Roman Catholic hierarchy criticized the Irish President, Mary McAleese (Roman Catholic), for receiving communion at St. Patrick's Cathedral (which is Church of Ireland). While the official teachings of the church have remained the same (and were even reinforced locally in 1998 and universally in 2001),[26] in practice there are many Protestant-Catholic families that receive communion together; and, sadly, there are also probably many families for whom this tension became one of the factors in their decision not to attend worship, or not to attend it as regularly as they used to.

At a practical level, for the most part, there seems to be a 'don't ask don't tell' policy in most Catholic churches (whereby priests, acknowledging the pastoral dimensions of the situation, simply give communion to any who come forward for it), and most Protestant churches will, likewise, welcome Catholic participants. Church of Ireland parishes in particular often end up housing mixed-denomination families because they have no official teaching

25. Actual prohibitions include the Roman Catholic interdict against non-Catholics receiving communion and the Orange Order's interdict against its members worshipping with Catholics. Imagined prohibitions include such things as folkloric beliefs that a Catholic's foot will wither if it crosses the threshold of a Protestant other church, or that holy water will burn a Protestant's skin (see, Liechty and Clegg, *Moving Beyond Sectarianism*, p. 129). For an assessment of the current situation regarding Eucharistic sharing, including the legacy of folkore, see, Jeffrey VanderWilt, *Communion with Non-Catholic Christians: Risks, Challenges, Opportunities* (Collegeville, PA: Liturgical Press, 2005).

26. See Liechty, 'A Strategy for Living in Peace' in Smock, *Interfaith Dialogue*, pp. 89–100. Also see, The Catholic Bishops Conferences, *One Bread, One Body*.

preventing them from doing so. At a theological level in Ireland, however, there have been many calls for changes in rules on shared participation in worship.[27] The Eucharist being the central act of worship for Catholics, and Catholics making up the majority of the population in the Republic, it is perhaps not surprising that this has surfaced as a topic demanding urgent attention in this context (i.e., in a way that it has not in other cultures). Additionally, some prominent commentators, frustrated at the pace of international dialogue in the face of an urgent pastoral situation at home, have called for the faithful to take the matter into their own hands. James P. Mackey, for example, was Thomas Chalmer Professor of Theology in the University of Edinburgh from 1979 until 1999. When he wrote this, he was Visiting Professor at Trinity College, Dublin.

> In the case of the eucharist in particular, the breaking and pouring and sharing of the bread and wine between Christian communities and to all who will take part in it, is so crucial to the Christian presence in the world that it must not be delayed until theologians of the different churches have agreed about foundation myths and about the account to be given of their related elements such as real presence. In actual fact much inter-church theological agreement on these and other matters is already in existence, though Roman Catholic leaders have been slow to either acknowledge it or to act upon it. Therefore, if this most serious damage is to be undone, the ordinary laity, the priestly people who in fact bring about eucharist, must take the initiative in the case of eucharist, like they did, also of right, in the case of the morality of contraception, and are now beginning to do by demanding episcopal accountability in the case of worldwide abuse by clergy and religious.[28]

Mackey's vision, while both pastorally motivated and sympatheti-cally impassioned, neglects the strength of authorities of prohibitions on this issue at a popular level, strengths that are culturally-compounded by sectarianism in ways that the debates over

27. See, for example, Mary Cullen and Enda McDonagh, *Irish Challenges to Theology: Papers of Irish Theological Association Conference* (Dublin: Dominican Publications, 1986), and Ian M. Ellis, *Vision and Reality: A Survey of Twentieth Century Irish Inter-Church Relations* (Belfast: Institute of Irish Studies Papers, 1992).

28. James P. Mackey, 'The Internal Politics and Policies of the Roman Catholic Church at the Turn of the Millennium' in James P. Mackey and Enda McDonagh (eds), *Religion and Politics in Ireland at the Turn of the Millennium* (Dublin: Columba Press, 2003), pp. 13–40; 39.

contraception or clerical abuse were not. In this context, the prohibition on sharing communion takes on the mantle of legitimating division because it symbolically represents the basic separation of Protestant from Catholic (densely containing in its symbolic self everything from the Reformation split, through debates about real presence, through the penal laws and the Troubles: all with their messages that 'your body cannot be part of my body').

The subject of intercommunion in an Irish context warrants — and would require — a book-length study all by itself, and so all that can be offered here is the following: by orienting so much more of our (sole-denomination) worship toward reconciliation with the 'other', we will be able to sift out those parts of table-separation that are due to national sectarian attitudes and those that are due to international ecclesial polity. By doing so we may hope to reach a maturity of ecclesial self-identity that we do not currently have. Yet beyond single-denominational worship, the question remains: without calling for widescale religious disobedience, are there yet ways in which Protestants and Catholics can worship together?

One success story in this regard is the 'Unity Pilgrims', which is another initiative of the Clonard Monastery with its neighbouring Protestant churches. The Clonard Community supports Roman Catholic parishioners in visiting Protestant churches and welcomes visitors in return. The emphasis is not on meeting people from other denominations and talking about faith or other aspects of life in structured discussions or workshops. Nor is it on working on a common project or campaign together. Nor yet is it on building friendships. The emphasis is simply on worship, and on occasionally going to worship in one another's church as a means of growing in one's own faith journey — hence the language of pilgrimage. Pilgrimage involves exploring new territory, heading towards a destination but knowing the journey is difficult and uncertain, and walking singly but on a path traveled by many others past and yet to come. By couching this initiative in terms of pilgrimage, both each individual's own spiritual growth and each community's slow journey towards greater understanding and relationship are expressed in a way that they would not be with metaphors of 'friendship', 'joint worship', 'intercommunion' and so forth. It allows something concrete and not tentative while being realistic about the fact that shared worship in the Irish context is a destination with a difficult path leading to it.

After the 1994 cease-fires the good-will which Cornerstone Community[29] enjoyed with the Presbyterian, Church of Ireland and Methodist churches of the nearby Shankill enabled Clonard Monastery to develop its own special relationship with these Churches. Visits by our "unity pilgrims" a few times annually to each congregation have since then transformed relationships. They have discovered what we call 'the grace of the unity pilgrimage'. That grace is a new awareness of the Holy Trinity at work in the whole Christian community, making one Church in many Churches. By going to worship with Protestant congregations on the Lord's Day our unity pilgrims are helping to end the destructive alienation of Christians from one another which has benighted Northern Ireland society for hundreds of years.[30]

At the conclusion of my research into contemporary Irish worship, I can see no reason why such a model of inter-church engagement could not be replicated all over Ireland. The language of pilgrimage may seem unpalatable to some Protestants and Catholics alike (although for different respective reasons) and so perhaps alternative metaphors will need to be found, but the basic model described above is one that any Christian who wanted to move beyond sectarianism could try, whether they call it a pilgrimage or not. By doing so, people would hopefully encounter the movement of the Holy Spirit, but through encounter with actual, concrete difference (and not, as some imagine, an experience of similarity). According to the Clonard reflection on this initiative, it is in reckoning with the realities of difference, and not in the subsuming of differences into a supposed synthesis, that 'the grace of unity' arises. People on either side of the sectarian divide in Ireland and Northern Ireland have, according to Geraldine Smyth, 'largely failed to recognise the reality of the other group as concretely different from their own. The tendency is to move *tout court* from the perspectives of one's own group to a totalising of political identity on the basis of expecting the other group to adopt one's own perspective.' By occasionally attending worship in the other group's

29. The Cornerstone Community, a multi-denominational meeting place on the west Belfast peace line, was a very important place for building inter-church and cross-community relations at a grassroots level, but also a venue in which significant leaders met for the first time with members of the 'other side'.

30. See, http://www.clonard.com/pilgrims_vision.htm

church in the mode of a unity pilgrim, such fundamental misconceptions can be broken down.

However, participants in such an initiative would probably have to commit to creating the sort of on-going follow-up conversations that the Cornerstone Community provided, not only because the reactions from such experience need to be discussed and prayed-about, but also because a great deal of misunderstanding arises when one encounters significant difference, particularly in a situation in which difference is long embedded. Speaking of the 'discourse of peace', for example, Smyth points out that between the two communities in Northern Ireland it 'is shared only in the words used. Words, like "peace", "justice" or "security" are contested. They break apart into two meaning systems, influenced by significantly different approaches to the state, to law and order, to violence, and to the dynamics of democracy.'[31] Just as in Chapter Two it became apparent from liturgical analysis that what one community understands as 'reconciliation' is different to the other's understanding of the same word, so with peace, justice, security and even community, worship and hope. However, slowly, if we refuse to conceptualize the differences between our fundamental notions as necessarily divisive, understanding can grow (even as the differences will surely remain).

Miroslav Volf, considering the relationship between divided churches, has written that:

> As the Gospel has been preached to many nations, the church has taken root in many cultures, changing them as well as being profoundly shaped by them. Yet the many churches in diverse cultures are one, just as the triune God is one, No church in a given culture may isolate itself from other churches in other cultures declaring itself sufficient to itself and its own culture, Every church must be open to all other churches.[32]

Asserting ecumenicity anywhere in the world is difficult when the Roman Catholic church does not think other Christian communities worthy of the word 'churches'; but it is especially difficult in Ireland, where not only the basic knowledge of what it means to be the 'catholic' church — the church universal — is radically limited but some

---

31. Geraldine Smyth, 'Envisaging a New Identity and a Common Home: Seeking Peace on our Borders', *Milltown Studies* 46 (Winter 2000), pp. 58–84.

32. Miroslav Volf, *Exclusion and Embrace: A Theological Exploration of Identity, Otherness and Reconciliation* (Nashville, TN: Abingdon Press, 1996), p. 51.

Protestant churches have refused even pan-Protestant ecumenical dialogue.[33] Nonetheless, Volf's insistence on the relationship between catholicity and ecumenism is an essential connection and one around which unity pilgrimages to one another's worship could be conceptualized for the wider context.

At a fundamental level, the spaces, words, gestures, symbols and sounds of worship in Irish churches are where one receives a weekly chance to assess Brian Lennon's well-rehearsed but not much-answered question: 'What is the priority for the Christian community in Northern Ireland: is it reconciliation with justice or is it the maintenance of separate communities?'[34] My proposal is that one opportunity to go from the latter to the former lies in worship practices themselves. My goal is not to propose a theology of reconciliation, or a theology beyond sectarianism. My goal is not, in fact, to propose 'a theology of' anything at all. When one writes a theology of something, one seeks to talk about a contemporary problem by setting it in the light of the biblical witness, and so it usually begins, proceeds and concludes with scriptural interpretation. In this book I have suspended appeal to scripture. This is not because I think it irrelevant to the work demanded by this book. On the contrary, it is of core relevance, and it will need to be read, preached, meditated upon and acted out: indeed, my goal is that this book will lead others to engage scripture voraciously in their moving beyond sectarianism, and to encourage them in that task. However, for me to do it in this text would be to alienate one group or another from the content and main purpose of the book, because in Ireland even how one reads the Bible is potentially sectarian because biblical hermeneutics itself is divided along Catholic–Protestant lines.[35]

The resultant theology ('a theology of …') is, therefore, inevitably perceived to be in the service of one community or another, even when it is met with fondness, respect and interest by readers on 'the other side'. Any theology I would write to speak to these

33. For example, for a full account of the Presbyterian Church in Ireland's withdrawal from the World Council of Churches and subsequent statements on 'friendship but not fellowship' with other churches, see, Maria Power, *From Ecumenism to Community Relations: Inter-Church Relationships in Northern Ireland 1980–2005* (Dublin: Irish Academic Press, 2007).

34. Brian Lennon, *After the Ceasefires: Catholics and the Future of Northern Ireland* (Dublin: Columba Press, 1995), p. 124.

liturgical-theological issues would be perceived by the majority of Protestant readers in Ireland as straight-up Catholic theology; simultaneously, it would be perceived by most Catholic readers in Ireland as theology written by someone primarily trained in, and sympathetic to, Protestant modes of scriptural interpretation. Both groups would be likely to say, therefore, that my theology was not relevant to them. Ours is not a situation in which a singular theology is going to offer much insight. Indeed, ecclesial efforts at reconciliation may well have been hampered by the supposed norm of needing to discover a common theological formulation in order to acknowledge belief in the one and the same God.

The logical corollary of contextual approaches to theology is that there can be no singular common theology, except at the most basic of levels (even the creeds are contentious in our situation) — and these are not levels that have any power to help communities move beyond sectarianism. For example, at a reductive level, we might say that only a robust theology of the cross can accomplish a version of reconciliation strong enough to speak to our need for peace. However, the content of that theology would need to contain really quite different elements for it to be comprehensible to the native speakers of Anglicanism, Protestantism, and Catholicism. The starting-point would need to be substantially different for each group because, as we have seen, the theology in circulation in those liturgical cultures — the way the cross is seen, held, used, sung about and understood — is radically different between traditions. Furthermore, such a theology would need to proceed in very different directions: for example, for a revised theology of the cross to lead to reconciliation in Protestant quarters, it will need to address an over-emphasis on triumphalism; in Catholic quarters an over-emphasis on victimhood: two very different themes in the Christian life.

In one sense, this is simply pragmatism: if you want to reach the castle from different towns, you need to come by different roads. Building a new, common road (or claiming to unearth an intact

---

35. For an exposition of the ways in which difference in confession affect difference in scriptural hermeneutics, and then how these produce differences in liturgical theology, see Melanie C. Ross, 'The Serious Drama of Worship' in Melanie C. Ross and Simon Jones (eds), *The Serious Business of Worship: Essays in Honour of Bryan D. Spinks* (New York: Continuum Books, *forthcoming* 2010).

older pre-existing one) rarely works. In another sense, it is also a product of the semiotics of our particular location in church history. Theology is and always has been cultural, in all its forms, and this sometimes plays out in the modern world in unexpected ways. The only reason that anyone (anyone who acknowledged that theology is always a product of culture) would think that a common theology of reconciliation were a potential solution in the Irish-British situation, would be if they underestimated the extent to which the cultures that co-exist in this Ireland are actually different cultures. Yes, take two people from Northern Ireland, one Protestant and one Catholic, and stick them in New York, and, as time has told over and again, they have far more in common with each other than they do with almost anybody else around them. But look at them in their native environment, within their own codes of behaviour and language games, and the differences between their cultures are remarkable and non-reducible. This conditions how the Bible can be read and, therefore, how worship can be performed and, therefore, how theology is constructed in this context.

Theology, time has also taught us, only works insofar as it is practical in its local environment. Charity begins at home because theology does. Transbustantiation made sense to millions not because they were told that it must but because it fitted the codes by which they understood all else in their lives. Likewise the notion that one is saved by grace and not works. These are not minor nuances in an otherwise streamlined theological opus: the differences in theology through the centuries have been vital to the continuation of the faith, to its being adopted by successive generations of people, and in every corner of the earth. Reconciling Protestants and Catholics does not mean they have to believe all the same things. That would be impossible (not least because there is so much disagreement between Catholics, and between Protestants), but it is also unnecessary: surely we can all claim to be Christians while simultaneously honouring the very significant differences between us.

It is to this end, then, that this book does not appeal to scripture in its making of an argument. To do so would be to speak in either a Protestant way or a Catholic way, and, besides, it is unnecessary because this book makes no claim to be writing the theology that can solve the problem of sectarianism. What it has claimed is that by looking at our practices, we can begin to re-orient ourselves to non-sectarian ways. The way we read the Bible is one such practice. By this I refer to the ways we read it at home alone or with our loved ones, as well as the ways we read it in worship with those who share our confession; but also, potentially, the ways we read it together.

My final suggestion for worshipping our way beyond sectarianism in Ireland, therefore, is a simple one, and one that many places are already trying: ecumenical Bible study. I propose this not as 'study' in the sense of debate or discussion or education, but rather as prayer. Conceptualizing the study of the Bible as an act of worship is gaining significant traction in inter-faith initiatives between adherents to the Abrahamic religions at this time. Pointing out how the 'deed' of joint scripture-study has the potential to significantly complement and advance the 'word' of inter-religious dialogue, Marc Gopin suggests that, 'The use of the word as the principal means of peacemaking is ubiquitous in Western culture, at least among those who consider themselves peacemakers and diplomats. This is fundamentally flawed as far as an accurate picture of how, in fact, human beings reconcile and make peace, when they manage to do so.'[36] While he has in mind engagement across religious traditions, and across Western and non-Western boundaries, I consider his proposal to be equally relevant to our own peculiarly Western, European, situation. Moreover, given the fact that the Bible has remained common to both Protestants and Catholics (with slight differences in canon) even as most other worship artifacts have not, and despite the depth of conflict that history and habit have bequeathed us, reading the Bible together seems a feasible first step in beginning the process of worshipping our way beyond sectarianism.

36. Marc Gopin, 'The Use of the Word and Its Limits: A Critical Evaluation of Religious Dialogue as Peacemaking' in Smock, *Interfaith Dialogue*, pp. 33–46; 33.

BIBLIOGRAPHY

Alcobia-Murphy, Shane, *Governing the Tongue: The Place of Art/The Art of Place* (Newcastle: Cambridge Scholars Press, 2005).

Amstutz, Mark R., *The Healing of Nations: The Promise and Limits of Political Forgiveness* (Lanham, MD: Rowman and Littlefield, 2005).

Anderson, E. Byron and Bruce T. Morrill, *Liturgy and the Moral Self: Humanity at Full Stretch before God: Essays in Honor of Don Saliers* (Collegeville, MN: Liturgical Press, 1998).

Anderson, E. Byron, *Worship and Christian Identity: Practicing Ourselves* (Collegeville, MN: The Liturgical Press, 2003).

Appleby, R. Scott, *The Ambivalence of the Sacred: Religion, Violence, and Reconciliation* (Oxford: Rowman and Littlefield, 2000).

Arendt, Hannah, *The Human Condition* (Chicago, IL: University of Chicago Press, 1998).

Barnes, L. Philip, 'Was the Northern Irish Conflict Religious?', *Journal of Contemporary Religion* 20.1 (January 2005), pp. 55-69.

Bell, Catherine, *Ritual Theory, Ritual Practice* (Oxford: Oxford University Press, 1992).

Bell, John, *The Singing Thing, Too* (Glasgow: Wild Goose Publications, 2007).

Bew, Paul, *Ireland: The Politics of Enmity 1789-2006* (Oxford: Oxford University Press, 2007).

Bhabha, Homi, *The Location of Culture* (New York: Routledge, 1994).

Biggar, Nigel, 'Forgiving Enemies in Ireland' in *Journal of Religious Ethics* 36.4 (2008), pp. 559-80.

Bohlman, Philip V., and Martin Stokes (eds), *Celtic Modern: Music at the Global Fringe* (Lanham, MD: Scarecrow Press, 2003).

Bohlman, Philip V., *The Music of European Nationalism: Cultural Identity and Modern History* (Oxford: ABC-CLIO, 2004).

Boulton, Matthew Myer, *God Against Religion: Rethinking Christian Theology Through Worship* (Grand Rapids, MI: Eerdmans, 2008).

Bowen, Desmond, *Souperism: Myth or Reality?* (Cork: Mercier Press, 1970).

Boyce, D. George and Alan O'Day, *The Making of Modern Irish History: Revisionism and the Revisionist Controversy* (New York: Routledge, 1996).

Boys, Mary, *Has God Only One Blessing? Judaism as a Source of Christian Self-understanding* (New York and Mahwah, NJ: Paulist Press, 2000).

Bradshaw, Paul F., *Eucharistic Origins* (Oxford: Oxford University Press, 2004).

Breathnach, Breandán, *Folk Music and Dances of Ireland: A Comprehensive Study* (Cork: Ossian/Mercer Press, 1996).

Brewer, John D., and Gareth I. Higgins, *Anti-Catholicism in Northern Ireland, 1660–1998* (London: MacMillan, 1998).

Brewer, John D., 'Northern Ireland: Peacemaking among Protestants and Catholics' in Mary Ann Cejka and Thomas Barmat (eds), *Artisans of Peace: Grassroots Peacemaking among Christian Communities* (Maryknoll, NY: Orbis Books, 2003), pp. 67–95.

Brocklehurst, Helen, 'Kids R Us? Children as Political Bodies' in Mark Evans (ed.), *Ethical Theory in the Study of International Politics* (New York: Nova, 2004).

Bryan, Dominic and Clifford Stevenson, 'Flagging Peace: Struggles over Symbolic Landscape in the New Northern Ireland' in Marc Howard Ross (ed.), *Culture and Belonging in Divided Societies: Contestation and Symbolic Landscapes* (Philadelphia, PA: University of Pennsylvania Press, 2009), pp. 68–84.

Carroll, Clare and Patricia King (eds), *Ireland and Postcolonial Theory* (Cork: Cork University Press, 2003).

Catholic Bishops Conferences of Ireland, Scotland, England and Wales, *One Bread, One Body: A Teaching Document on the Eucharist in the Life of the Church, and the Establishment of General Norms on Sacramental Sharing* (Dublin: Veritas, 1998).

Cavanaugh, William T., *Torture and Eucharist: Theology, Politics, and the Body of Christ* (Oxford: Blackwells, 1998).

Cejka, Mary Ann and Thomas Barmat (eds), *Artisans of Peace: Grassroots Peacemaking among Christian Communities* (Maryknoll, NY: Orbis Books, 2003).

Chauvet, Louis Marie, *Symbol and Sacrament: A Sacramental Reinterpretation of Christian Existence* (Collegeville, MN: Liturgical Press, 1995).

Coen, Mark, 'Religious Ethos and Employment Equality: A Comparative Irish Perspective' in *Legal Studies* 28.3 (July 2008), pp. 452–74.

Coleman, Steve, *The End of Irish History? Critical Reflections on the Celtic Tiger* (Manchester: Manchester University Press, 2003).

Condren, Mary, 'Mercy Not Sacrifice: Toward a Celtic Theology', *Feminist Theology* 5: 15 (May 1997), pp. 31–54.

Congregation for the Doctrine of the Faith, 'Declaration – *Dominus Iesus*: On the Unicity and Salvific Universality of Jesus Christ and the Church' (4 April 2001).

Conniffe, Denis and Daniel McCoy, *Alcohol Use in Ireland: Some Economic and Social Implications* (Dublin: Economic and Social Research Institute, 1993; Denver, CO: Academic Books, 2000).

Crockett, Alistair and Richard O'Leary, *Patterns and Processes of Religious Change in Modern Industrial Societies* (Lewiston, NY: E. Mellen Press, 2004).

Cronin, Michael (ed.), *Irish Tourism: Image, Culture and Identity* (Bristol: Channel View Publications, 2003).

Cullen, Mary and Enda McDonagh, *Irish Challenges to Theology: Papers of Irish Theological Association Conference* (Dublin: Dominican Publications, 1986).

Daly, Mary E., *Social and Economic History of Ireland since 1800* (Dublin: Longman, Browne and Nolan, 1981).

Darby, J., and S. Dunn, 'Segregated Schools' in R.D. Osborne, R.J. Cormack and R.L. Miller (eds), *Education and Policy in Northern Ireland* (Belfast:

Queens University and The University of Ulster, Policy Research Institute, 1987), pp. 85-98.

Davis, Leith, *Music, Postcolonialism, and Gender: The Construction of Irish National Identity, 1724–1874* (Notre Dame, IN: Notre Dame Press, 2006).

Day, Thomas, *Why Catholics Can't Sing: The Culture of Catholicism and the Triumph of Bad Taste* (New York: Crossroad, 1990).

Deane, Séamus (ed.), *The Field Day Anthology of Irish Writing Vol. 3* (Derry: Lawrence Hill/Field Day Publications, 1991).

Denard, Hugh, 'Séamus Heaney, Colonialism, and the Cure: Sophoclean Revisions', *PAJ: A Journal of Performance and Art* 22:66 (September 2000), pp. 1–18.

Derrida, Jacques, *On Cosmopolitanism and Forgiveness* (New York: Taylor & Francis, 2001).

Dews, P. (ed.), *Autonomy and Solidarity: Interviews with Jürgen Habermas* (London: Verso, 1992).

Dillon, Martin, *God and the Gun* (London: Orion, 1997).

Dorr, Donal, *Time for Change: A Fresh Look at Sexuality, Spirituality, Globalization and the Church* (Dublin: Columba Press, 2004).

Dudley Edwards, Ruth, *Patrick Pearse: The Triumph of Failure* (London: Gallancz, 1977).

Eagleton, Terry, *Heathcliff and the Great Hunger: Studies in Irish Culture* (London: Verso 1995).

Ellis, Ian M., *Vision and Reality: A Survey of Twentieth Century Irish Inter-Church Relations* (Belfast: Institute of Irish Studies Papers, 1992).

Enright, Robert and Joanna North (eds), *Exploring Forgiveness* (Madison, WI: University of Wisconsin Press, 1998).

Evans, Sara Margaret, *Journeys that Opened Up the World: Women, Student Christian Movements and Social Justice 1955–1975* (Rutgers, NJ: Rutgers University Press, 2003).

Farhadian, Charles E., *Christian Worship Worldwide: Expanding Horizons, Deepening Practices* (Grand Rapids, MI: Eerdmans, 2007).

Farrell, M., *Northern Ireland: The Orange State* (London: Pluto Press, 1976).

Farrington, Christopher (ed.), *Global Change, Civil Society and the Northern Ireland Peace Process: Implementing the Political Settlement* (Basingstoke: Palgrave Macmillan, 2008).

Fegan, Melissa, *Literature and the Irish Famine, 1845–1919* (Oxford: Oxford University Press, 2002).

Feldman, Alan, *Formations of Violence: The Narrative of the Body and Political Terror in Northern Ireland* (Chicago, IL: University of Chicago Press, 1991).

Ferrell, Karie, *Guide for Ushers and Greeters* (Chicago, IL: Liturgical Training Publications, 2008).

Ferriter, Diarmuid, *A Nation of Extremes: The Pioneers in Twentieth Century Ireland* (Dublin: Irish Academic Press, 2005).

Finlayson, James Gordon, *Habermas: A Very Short Introduction* (Oxford: Oxford University Press, 2005).

Flannery, Eoin, *Ireland and Postcolonial Studies: Theory, Discourse, Utopia* (New York: Palgrave Macmillan, 2009).

Foley, Edward J., *From Age to Age: How Christians Have Celebrated the Eucharist* (Chicago, IL: Liturgy Training Publications, 1991).

Ford, Alan and John McCafferty, *The Origins of Sectarianism in Early Modern Ireland* (Cambridge: Cambridge University Press, 2002).

Foster, Dean, *The Global Etiquette Guide to Europe* (New York: Wiley, 2000).

Foster, Roy F., *Luck and the Irish: A Brief History of Social Change c. 1970–2000* (London: Penguin, 2007).

Fox, Matthew, *The Coming of the Cosmic Christ* (Melbourne: Collins Dove, 1989).

Gallagher, T., A. Smith and A. Montgomery, *Integrated Education in Northern Ireland: Participation, Profile and Performance* (University of Ulster: UNESCO Centre, 2003).

Garrigan, Siobhán, *Beyond Ritual: Sacramental Theology after Habermas* (Abingdon: Ashgate, 2004).

Garrigan, Siobhán and Todd Johnson (eds), *Common Worship in Theological Education* (Eugene, OR: Wipf and Stock, 2009).

Gerlach, Bryan, 'The Role of Music in Worship: An Evaluation of Two Twentieth Century Developments' in *Logia: A Journal of Lutheran Theology* Vol. XIV no. 3 (2005), pp. 52–58.

Gibbons, Luke, *Transformations in Irish Culture* (South Bend, IN: Notre Dame University Press, 1996).

Gillen, Gerard and Harry White (eds), *Irish Musical Studies 2: Music and the Church* (Dublin: Irish Academic Press, 1993).

Goodwin, Donald, *Alcoholism, The Facts* (Oxford: Oxford University Press, 2000).

Graham, Colin, *Deconstructing Ireland: Identity, Theory, Culture* (Edinburgh: Edinburgh University Press, 2003).

Graham, Colin, '"Every Passer-by a Culprit?" Archive Fever, Photography and the Peace in Belfast', *Third Text* 19.5 (September 2005).

Grimes, Ronald L., *Beginnings in Ritual Studies* (Washington DC: University Press of America, 1982).

Grimes, Ronald L., *Ritual Criticism: Case Studies in Its Practice, Essays on Its Theory* (Columbia, SC: University of South Carolina Press, 1990).

Grimes, Ronald L., *Deeply into the Bone: Reinventing Rites of Passage* (Berkeley, CA: University of California Press, 2002).

Grün, Anselm, 'Fasting' in Erwin Fahlbusch and Geoffrey W. Bromiley (eds), *The Encyclopedia of Christianity Vol. 2* (Grand Rapids, MI: Eerdmans, 1999), pp. 295–96.

Halgren Kilde, Jeanne, *When Church Became Theater: The Transformation of Evangelical Architecture* (New York: Oxford University Press, 2005).

Hart, Peter, *The IRA and Its Enemies: Violence and Community in Cork, 1916–1923* (Oxford: Clarendon, 1998).

Harvey, Colin J., *Human Rights, Equality, and Democratic Renewal in Northern Ireland* (Oxford: Hart, 2001).

Hastings, Adrian, *The Construction of Nationhood: Religion, Ethnicity and Nationalism* (Cambridge: Cambridge University Press, 1997).

Hastings, Gary, *With Fife and Drum: Music, Memories and Customs of an Irish Tradition* (Belfast: Blackstaff, 2003).

Hawn, C. Michael, *Gather into One: Praying and Singing Globally* (Grand Rapids, MI: Eerdmans, 2002).

Hayes, Michael A., and Liam Gearon (eds), *Contemporary Catholic Theology: A Reader* (New York: Continuum, 1999).

Healy, Nicholas, *Church, World and the Christian Life* (Cambridge: Cambridge University Press, 2000).

Heaney, Séamus, *Collected Poems* (London: Faber & Faber, 2002).

Hempton, D., *Religion and Political Culture in Britain and Ireland* (Cambridge: Cambridge University Press, 1996).

Hickey, J., *Religion and the Northern Ireland Problem* (London: Gil and McMillan, 1984).

Hogan, Linda and Dylan Lee Lehrke (eds), *Religion and the Politics of Peace and Conflict* (Eugene, OR: Wipf and Stock, 2009).

Hogan, Patrick Colm, *Empire and Poetic Voice: Cognitive and Cultural Studies of Literary Tradition and Colonialism* (SUNY Press, 2004), pp. 1-3.

Huddart, David, *Homi K. Bhabha* (London: Taylor & Francis, 2005).

Inglis, Tom, *Moral Monopoly: The Catholic Church in Modern Irish Society* (Dublin: University College Dublin Press, 1998).

Jarman, Neil, 'No Longer a Problem: Sectarian Violence in Northern Ireland', *Institute for Conflict Research: Papers* (March 2005), pp. 1-64.

Jeffares, A. Norman and A.S. Knowland, *A Commentary on the Collected Plays of W.B. Yeats* (Stanford, CA: Stanford University Press, 1975).

Kennedy, Liam, *Colonialism, Religion and Nationalism in Ireland* (Belfast: Institute of Irish Studies, 1996).

Kirby, Peadar, 'The Death of Innocence: Whither Now? Trauma in State and Church' in *Studies: An Irish Quarterly Review* 84: 335 (Autumn, 1995), pp. 257-65.

Kirby, Peadar, Luke Gibbons and Michael Cronin (eds), *Reinventing Ireland: Culture, Society and the Global Economy* (London: Pluto Press, 2002).

Knox, Colin, 'See No Evil, Hear No Evil: Insidious Paramilitary Violence in Northern Ireland', *British Journal of Criminology* 42: 1 (2002), pp. 164-85.

Lambkin, B.K., *Opposite Religions Still? Interpreting Northern Ireland after the Conflict* (Aldershot: Avebury, 1996).

Larkin, P., *A Very British Jihad: Collusion, Conspiracy and Cover-Up in Northern Ireland* (Belfast: BTP Publications, 2004).

Lennon, Brian, *After the Ceasefires: Catholics and the Future of Northern Ireland* (Dublin: Columba Press, 1995).

Leppert, Richard, *Music and Image* (Cambridge: Cambridge University Press, 1988).

Liechty, Joseph and Cecilia Clegg, *Moving Beyond Sectarianism: Religion, Conflict and Reconciliation in Northern Ireland* (Dublin: Columba Press, 2001).

Liechty, Joseph, 'A Strategy for Living in Peace When Truth Claims Clash' in David R. Smock, *Interfaith Dialogue and Peacebuilding* (Washington, DC: United States Institute of Peace Press, 2002), pp. 89-100.

Lloyd, David, *Ireland after History* (Notre Dame, IN: University of Notre Dame Press, 1999).

Lloyd, David, 'Regarding Ireland in a Post-colonial Frame' in *Cultural Studies* 15.1 (2001), pp. 12-32.

Mackey, P., and Enda McDonagh (eds), *Religion and Politics in Ireland at the Turn of the Millennium* (Dublin: Columba Press, 2003).

MacLaughlin, Jim, *Location and Dislocation in Contemporary Irish Society: Emigration and Irish Identities* (Cork: Cork University Press, 1997).

Matthews Larson, Joan, *Seven Weeks to Sobreity* (New York: Fawcette Columbine, 1997).

McCarthy Brown, Karen, *Mama Lola: A Vodou Priestess in Brooklyn* (Berkeley, CA: University of California Press, 1991, 2001).

McCarthy, Marie, *Passing It On: The Transmission of Music in Irish Culture* (Cork: Cork University Press, 1999).

McCaughey, Terence, *Memory and Redemption: Church, Politics and Prophetic Theology in Ireland* (Dublin: Gill and Macmillan, 1993).

McClintock Fulkerson, Mary, *Places of Redemption: Theology for a Worldly World* (New York: Oxford University Press, 2007).

McDonagh, Enda, 'Church–State Relations in Independent Ireland' in J.P. Mackey and E. McDonagh (eds), *Religion and Politics in Ireland and the Turn of the Millennium* (Dublin: Columba Press, 2003), pp. 41–63.

McGarry, John, and Brendan O'Leary, *Explaining Northern Ireland: Broken Images* (Oxford: Blackwell, 1995).

Mitchell, Claire, *Religion, Identity and Politics in Northern Ireland: Boundaries of Belonging and Belief* (Abingdon: Ashgate, 2006).

Mitchell, Nathan D., *Liturgy and the Social Sciences* (Collegeville, MN: Liturgical Press, 2000).

Mokyr, Joel, *Why Ireland Starved: A Quantitative and Analytical History of the Irish Economy 1800–1850* (London: Allen and Unwin, 1983).

Moore Keish, Martha, *Do This in Remembrance of Me: A Performed Approach to Eucharistic Theology* (Grand Rapids, MI: Eerdmans, 2008).

Morris, Ewan, *Our Own Devices: National Symbols and Political Conflict in Twentieth-Century Ireland* (Dublin: Irish Academic Press, 2005).

Murray, D., *Worlds Apart: Segregated Schools in Northern Ireland* (Belfast: Appletree Press, 1985).

Ó'Canainn, Tomás, *Sean Ó Ríada: His Life and Work* (Cork: The Collins Press, 2003).

O'Hegarty, P.S., *A Short Memoir of Terence MacSwiney* (Dublin: Talbot Press, 1922).

Ó'Gráda, Cormac, *Black '47 and Beyond: The Great Irish Famine in History, Economy and Memory* (Princeton, NJ: Princeton University Press, 2000).

O'Malley, Padraig, *Biting at the Grave: The Irish Hunger Strikes and the Politics of Despair* (New York: Beacon Press, 1991).

Penn, Michael P., *Kissing Christians: Ritual and Community in the Late Ancient Church* (Philadelphia, PA: University of Pennsylvania Press, 2005).

Phillips, Edward L., *The Ritual Kiss in Early Christian Worship* (Cambridge: Grove Books, 1996).

Plowright, John, *The Routledge Dictionary of Modern British History* (New York: Routledge, 2006).

Pollak, Andy (ed.), *A Citizens' Inquiry: The Opsahl Report on Northern Ireland* (Dublin: The Lilliput Press, 1993).

Poole, Susan, *Frommers Comprehensive Travel Guide: Dublin and Ireland* (New York: Simon and Schuster, 1991).

Porter, Norman, *The Elusive Quest: Reconciliation in Northern Ireland* (Belfast: Blackstaff, 2003).

Poster, Mark (ed.), *Jean Baudrillard: Selected Writings* (Stanford, CA: Stanford University Press, 1988).

Powell, Jonathan, *Great Hatred, Little Room: Making Peace in Northern Ireland* (London: Bodley Head, 2008).

Power, Maria, '"Of Some Symbolic Importance, But Not Much Else": The Inter-Church Meeting and Ecumenical Dialogue in Northern Ireland, 1980–1999', *Journal of Ecumenical Studies* 43.1 (Winter 2008), pp. 111–23.

Power, Maria, *From Ecumenism to Community Relations: Inter-Church Relationships in Northern Ireland 1980–2005* (Dublin: Irish Academic Press, 2007).

Riggs, Marcia, *Awake, Arise, Act: A Womanist Call for Black Liberation* (Cleveland, OH: The Pilgrim Press, 1994).

Ross, Melanie C. and Simon Jones (eds), *The Serious Business of Worship: Essays in Honour of Bryan D. Spinks* (New York: Continuum, 2010).

Rotberg, Robert I., and Dennis Thompson, *Truth v. Justice: The Morality of Truth Commissions* (Princeton, NJ: Princeton University Press, 2000).

Ruane, Joseph, and Jennifer Todd, *Dynamics of Conflict in Northern Ireland: Power, Conflict and Emancipation* (Cambridge: Cambridge University Press, 1996).

Ruhs, Martin, 'Ireland: A Crash-Course on Immigration Policy', *Migration Policy Institute Papers* (Washington, DC: 2004).

Saliers, Don E., 'Afterword' in E. Byron Anderson and Bruce T. Morrill, *Liturgy and the Moral Self: Humanity at Full Stretch: Essays in Honor of Don E. Saliers* (Collegeville, MN: Liturgical Press, 1998).

Sands, Bobby, *Writings from Prison* (Boulder, CO: R. Rinehart Publications, 1997).

Scheper-Hughes, Nancy, 'Violence and the Politics of Remorse', in Joao Biehl, Byron Good, Arthur Klienman (eds), *Subjectivity: Ethnographic Investigations* (London: University of California Press, 2007), pp. 180–229.

Schimmel, Solomon, *Wounds Not Healed by Time: The Power of Repentance and Forgiveness* (New York: Oxford University Press, 2002).

Schmemann, Alexander, *Introduction to Liturgical Theology* (Princeton, NJ: St. Vladimir's Seminary Press, 1986).

Seasoltz, R. Kevin (ed.), *Living Bread, Saving Cup: Readings on the Eucharist* (Collegeville, MN: Liturgical Press, 1982).

Shirlow, Peter and Brendan Murtagh, *Belfast: Segregation, Violence and the City* (London: Pluto Press, 2006).

Shriver, Donald W., *An Ethic for Enemies – Forgiveness in Politics* (New York: Oxford University Press, 1995).

Simpson, John and Jennifer Speake, *The Concise Oxford Dictionary of Proverbs* (Oxford: Oxford University Press, 1992).

Smock, David R., *Interfaith Dialogue and Peacemaking* (Washington, DC: Institute of Peace Press, 2002).

Smyth, Geraldine, 'Envisaging a New Identity and a Common Home: Seeking Peace on our Borders', *Milltown Studies* (Winter 2000), pp. 58–84.

Smyth, Marie, *Truth, Recovery and Justice after Conflict* (New York: Routledge, 2007).

Smyth, Sam, *Riverdance: The Story* (London: Andre Deutsch, 1996).

Spice, Gerald, *Ushers and Greeters: A Worship Handbook* (Minneapolis, MN: Augsburg-Fortress Press, 2002).

Stringer, Martin, *On the Perception of Worship* (New York: Continuum, 1999).

Swinton, John, *Raging with Compassion: Pastoral Responses to the Problem of Evil* (Grand Rapids, MI: Eerdmans, 2007).

Tanner, Kathryn, *Theories of Culture: A New Agenda for Theology* (Minneapolis, MN: Fortress Press, 1997).

Taylor FitzSimon, Betsey and James H. Murphy (eds), *The Irish Revival Reappraised* (Dublin: Four Courts Press, 2004).

Taylor, Rupert, *Consociational Theory: McGarry and O'Leary and the Northern Ireland Conflict* (Abingdon: Routledge, 2009).

Toibín, Colm, *The Irish Famine* (London: Profile Books, 2001).

Tombs, David and Joseph Liechty (eds), *Explorations in Reconciliation: New Directions in Theology* (Aldershot: Ashgate, 2006).

Tonge, Jonathan, *The New Northern Irish Politics?* (New York, NY: Palgrave Macmillan, 2005).

Tonge, Jonathan, *Northern Ireland* (Cambridge: Polity Press, 2006).

Vallely, Fintan, *Tuned Out: Traditional Music and Identity in Northern Ireland* (Cork: Cork University Press, 2008).

VanderWilt, Jeffrey, *Communion with Non-Catholic Christians: Risks, Challenges, Opportunities* (Collegeville, MN: Liturgical Press, 2005).

Volf, Miroslav, *Exclusion and Embrace: A Theological Exploration of Identity, Otherness and Reconciliation* (Nashville, TN: Abingdon Press, 1996).

Vorgrimler, Herbert, *Sacramental Theology* (Collegeville, MN: Liturgical Press, 1992).

Walker Bynum, Caroline, *Holy Feast, Holy Fast: The Religious Significance of Food to Medieval Women* (Berkeley, CA: University of California Press, 1990).

Walker Bynum, Carolyn, *Wonderful Blood: Theology and Practice in Late Medieval Northern Germany and Beyond* (Philadelphia, PA: University of Philadelphia Press, 2007).

Ward, Graham, *Cultural Transformation and Religious Practice* (Cambridge: Cambridge University Press, 2005).

Weisser, Henry, *The Hippocrene Companion Guide to Ireland* (New York: Hippocrene, 1990).

Whalen, Teresa, *The Authentic Doctrine of the Eucharist* (Kansas City, KS: Sheed and Ward, 1993).

Whelan, Irene, 'The Stigma of Souperism' in Cathal Poirtear (ed.), *The Great Irish Famine* (Cork: Cork University Press, 1995).

White, Harry, *The Keeper's Recital: Music and Cultural History in Ireland, 1770–1970* (Cork: Cork University Press, 1998).

White, Harry and Michael Murphy (eds), *Musical Constructions of Nationalism: Essays on the History and Ideology of European Musical Culture, 1800–1940* (Cork: Cork University Press, 2001).

White, Robert W., 'Social and Role Identities and Political Violence: Identity as a Window on Violence in Northern Ireland' in Richard D. Ashmore, Lee Jussim and David Wilder (eds), *Social Identity, Intergroup Conflict and Conflict Resolution* (New York: Oxford University Press, 2001), pp. 133–58.

Wills, Garry, *Why I am a Catholic* (Boston, MA: Houghton Mifflin Harcourt, 2003).

Witvliet, John, 'The Opening of Worship: Trinity' in Leanne Van Dyk (ed.), *A More Profound Alleluia: Theology and Worship in Harmony* (Grand Rapids, MI: Eerdmans, 2005), pp. 1–27.

Worthington, Everett L. (ed.), *Dimensions of Forgiveness: Psychological Research and Theological Perspectives* (Philadelphia, PA: Templeton Foundation Press, 1998).

Worthington, Everrett L., 'Unforgiveness, Forgiveness and Reconciliation and Their Implications for Societal Interventions' in Raymond G. Helmick and Rodney L. Petersen (eds), *Forgiveness and Reconciliation: Religion, Public Policy and Conflict Transformation* (Conshohocken, PA: Templeton Foundation Press, 2002).

Wright, Julia M., *Ireland, India and Nationalism in the Nineteenth Century* (Cambridge: Cambridge University Press, 2009).

Young, Robert J.C., *A Very Short Introduction to Postcolonialism* (Oxford: Oxford University Press, 2003).

Index of Subjects

INDEX OF NAMES

CPSIA information can be obtained at www.ICGtesting.com
Printed in the USA
BVOW011743040612

291743BV00003B/16/P